Abolitionist Intimacies

Abolitionist Intimacies

*Queer and Trans Migrants
against the Deportation State*

EITHNE LUIBHÉID

Duke University Press   *Durham and London*   2025

Project Editor: Liz Smith
Typeset in Warnock Pro by Westchester Publishing Services

Library of Congress Cataloging-in-Publication Data
Names: Luibhéid, Eithne, author.
Title: Abolitionist intimacies : queer and trans migrants against the
deportation state / Eithne Luibhéid.
Description: Durham : Duke University Press, 2025. | Includes
bibliographical references and index.
Identifiers: LCCN 2024033058 (print)
LCCN 2024033059 (ebook)
ISBN 9781478031239 (paperback)
ISBN 9781478028024 (hardcover)
ISBN 9781478060260 (ebook)
Subjects: LCSH: Sexual minority immigrants—Political activity—
United States—History. | Immigrants—Political activity—United
States—History. | Noncitizens—Political activity—United States. |
Deportation—Government policy—United States. | Emigration and
immigration law—Social aspects—United States.
Classification: LCC JV6346.5 .L85 2025 (print) | LCC JV6346.5
(ebook) | DDC 325.73086/6—dc23/eng/20250225
LC record available at https://lccn.loc.gov/2024033058
LC ebook record available at https://lccn.loc.gov/2024033059

Cover art: Karla Rosas, *Manifest Beyond*, 2020. Courtesy of
the artist.

Contents

A Note on Terminology

Deportation

I use the term *deportation* to refer to a range of practices that states use to forcibly remove or expel noncitizens from their territory.[1] Adam Goodman explains that the US government typically relies on three main expulsion mechanisms: judicial processes leading to deportation orders; so-called voluntary departures that are usually made under conditions of coercion; and self-deportations.[2] These mechanisms are part of the modern nation-state immigration regime but have deep roots in histories and practices of expulsion through which the United States became the nation-state that it is today. As K-Sue Park shows, from the earliest days, colonists relied on both direct and indirect methods for ensuring the "mass removal of groups they viewed as outside their polity," including the people of numerous Native nations whose lands were expropriated, as well as the poor and religious dissenters.[3] After the abolition of slavery, lawmakers also explored possibilities for the mass removal of African-descended people.

Nathalie Peutz and Nicholas De Genova explain that deportation practices assert and enact the sovereignty of the US settler state and create citizenship norms through which legal citizens, migrants of various statuses, and deportees become constituted as legal, political, and social subjects.[4] Scholars theorize that deportation coproduces nation-based citizenship not just as a legal status but also in terms of who is seen as "belonging" (and that, in a racist, settler, capitalist, and cisheteronormative nation-state, one's legal status may not align with perceptions and experiences of belonging).[5] De Genova underscores that deportation produces legal statuses and (un)belonging not just through actual deportations but also through "deportability": the possibility of becoming deported. "It is deportability, and not deportation per se, that has historically rendered undocumented migrant labor a distinctly disposable commodity."[6] Deportability, which also affects those with precarious, uncertain, disputed, temporary, or transitional legal status, renders people vulnerable in all aspects of their lives. Deportability and deportation are part of cycles of displacement and dispossession that often continue long after people have been expelled.

Deportation works hand in hand with major policies and programs that try to prevent people from entering the United States in the first place. These prevention strategies include invading other countries that are experiencing instability and crisis in order to preempt mass migration; enlisting other countries to prevent migration to the United States in return for aid, trade, and other benefits; interdicting migrant boats at sea before they reach US territory; containing and confining migrants in sites like Guantánamo that are not officially part of US territory; turning back migrants who want to claim asylum or requiring them to wait outside US borders; public messaging campaigns that stress the dangers of migration and the unlikelihood of getting legal status; and Prevention Through Deterrence policies at the southern border that route migrants into dangerous terrain that greatly heightens their risks of disappearing or dying.[7] These policies and practices involve significant bilateral and multilateral agreements with nation-states and supranational bodies who take on immigration control functions on behalf of the United States in return for aid and other benefits, while deepening the rightlessness facing people in transit. I honor and grieve those who have disappeared or died in transit as a result of these practices.[8]

The expansion of deportation has been central to the growth of state power and the production of exploitable labor.[9] Deportation has "fueled xenophobia and demonized" numerous communities and groups.[10] Deportation has especially and disproportionately been directed at Mexicans, who "make up around half of the undocumented immigrant population in US history, but . . . account for nine out of every ten deportees."[11] Tanya Maria Golash-Boza highlights that young men from Central America and the Caribbean are also disproportionately targeted.[12]

Bearing in mind that innumerable people have been prevented from entering the United States in the first place, this book centers people who have lived under the shadow of deportability or faced deportation from within the United States. The scale of deportation is enormous: Goodman calculates that some fifty-seven million people were deported from the United States between 1882 and 2018—which is more people than were granted permanent residence.[13] Yet grasping the scope and impact of deportation remains challenging. By Goodman's reckoning, 85 percent of these deportations occurred through voluntary departure, a process that "enable[s] low-level officials to use administrative orders to expedite the expulsion of people charged with immigration violations and other minor infractions" without due process.[14]

Yet voluntary departures, as well as self-deportations, generally leave no records. He asks, "How does one write a history of something designed to leave no paper trail," even while its scale and impact are enormous?[15] The impact of living under the shadow of deportability is also enormous but often unrecorded.

Queer, Trans, LGBTQ

In the book, I use *queer* and *trans* as umbrella terms for people who do not adhere to dominant sexual and gender norms. This includes people who may self-identify or be identified by others as queer, gay, lesbian, bisexual, transgender, gender nonconforming, nonbinary, two spirit, *loca*, *mati*, and many related terms. These identity categories are not essential, universal, or timeless. Rather, the terms emerged through and remain implicated in histories and geographies of power. They are tied to and uphold state regimes for making populations legible and governable, involve self-attribution or attribution by others, and offer compromised but important means for making claims. People claim, inhabit, give meaning to, and continually transform these categories, navigate state and other institutional demands in relation to the categories, and transit among the categories, too.[16]

When using *queer*, *trans*, or related terms as identity categories in reference to specific individuals, I do so based on available information about how people publicly represented themselves at that time. People's self-identifications and public representations may switch over time and among possibilities. When discussing specific organizations or reports, I follow their uses of these terms while recognizing changes over time and differences in meanings. For example, differences between the US government's use of *LGBT* and critical trans or queer organizations' use of the term are evident in chapter 4.

As analytic rubrics, *trans* and *queer* may not refer to identities or identifications at all. Rather, they commonly "call[] into question the stability of any . . . categories of identity," critically historicize the material and ideological work performed by all identity categories, and direct attention to questions of power, intersectionality, normalization, dispossession, and transformation.[17] *Queer* and *trans* as analytic rubrics highlight the need to analyze how sexual and gender regimes differentially affect not just nonnormative subjects but everyone, though not in the same ways. Moreover, since whiteness, settler/colonialism, and capitalism are constitutive of sexual and gender normativity, an intersectional approach is always necessary. Many queer and trans analytic rubrics conceive political change as emerging from work that is differential, coalitional, and transformative, and rooted not in demands for shared identity or history "but in our shared marginal relationship to dominant power that normalizes, legitimizes, and privileges," beginning from the perspectives and priorities of those who are most harmed by the current system.[18]

Allies

In recent years, the construct of "allyship" has become critiqued on the grounds that it offers opportunities to pay lip service to progressive politics without showing up, engaging in action, or risking one's privileges. The term *accomplice* was seen as underscoring that lip service was not enough; action, including action that required people to put something of value on the line, was required. In recent years, *coconspirator* has emerged as a term to describe people who work alongside marginalized communities, offering meaningful support and being accountable, without co-opting others' struggles or using others' struggles to enhance their own status. The term *coliberator* recognizes that "our freedom is intertwined" and that in working toward liberation for any group, "we will all benefit."[19] In this book, I use *allies* as a general term to describe migrants and citizens who offer a variety of kinds of support, including, in some cases, acting as accomplices, coconspirators, or coliberators.

Migrant

Rather than making distinctions based on people's state-conferred legal statuses, this book generally uses the term *migrant* to refer to anyone (except tourists) who has crossed an international border. I follow this practice because legal statuses reflect not supposed types of migrants but the workings of power and knowledge that seek to differentiate among migrants, delimit rights and protections that they will have or be denied, and shape forms of surveillance, discipline, normalization, and dispossession to which they are subjected.[20] Thus, my use of the term *migrant* participates in the call by critical migration researchers to problematize scholarship that reifies and objectifies people on the move by uncritically recirculating the state's categories for apprehending and managing them.[21]

Sometimes I use the terms *asylum seeker* or *refugee*. The terms emerged after World War II and commonly refer to people who have crossed an international border and who seek protection under international human rights (rather than national immigration) law.[22] People seeking or holding these statuses make claims and navigate jeopardies that somewhat differ from (yet overlap with) those who go through nation-state immigration systems. People may also transit between the immigration, refugee, and asylum systems.[23]

Citizen and Noncitizen

Migration regimes operate around, reproduce, and normalize the distinction between citizens and noncitizens. This book treats "citizen" and "noncitizen" not as natural or ontological categories but as status distinctions that have been created and contested within histories of power involving settler colonial, capitalist, cisheteronormative, and racist nation-state formation processes (see the introduction for discussion). Immigration systems including deportation are critical loci where the practical and symbolic meanings of these status distinctions are continually contested and reconfigured. When referring to someone as a "citizen" or "noncitizen," I do not presume to know anyone's understanding of, investment in, or performance of that category; rather, my purpose is to mark that people carry and are navigating within the terms of this state-mandated status distinction. Deportation constitutes meanings of citizenship, so when—*when*—there is no more deportation, *citizenship* and *noncitizenship* will not mean what they mean now.

Acknowledgments

This book is made possible by the courage of those who came before, extraordinary activisms and theories that created building blocks, badass dreamers and fighters who inspire, and people who asked generative questions. It is fueled by uncountable acts of kindness, encouragement, and practical support from friends, family, and colleagues, as well as people who crossed my path. No words can convey how grateful I am.

A research fellowship at the Latino Research Institute (LRI) at the University of Texas at Austin provided time, resources, and congenial fellowship for drafting the book. I am especially grateful to LRI director Deborah Parra-Medina for this opportunity and making me feel welcome. I am also deeply grateful to Karma Chávez, the chair of Mexican American and Latino/a Studies, for her unflagging support, encouragement, and assistance during that time and throughout. Thanks to C. J. Alvarez for his interest and great conversations in the basement of the Gordon White Building.

A Benjamin Meaker Visiting Professorship at the University of Bristol, organized by Katharine Charsley, created opportunities for generous engagement with her and other amazing migration studies faculty at Bristol that made this book better. Anne-Marie D'Aoust at the Université du Québec à Montréal, and members of the Research Group on Managing Citizenship, Security, and Rights: Regulating Marriage Migration in Europe and North America that Anne-Marie convened, also provided invaluable feedback, comparative perspectives, and insight.

Míle buíochas to Rob Buffington, Karma Chávez, Adela Licona, and Erica Rand for careful, generous, and generative feedback about chapters (in Adela's case, the entire manuscript), constant encouragement, and practical assistance whenever needed. There would be no book without you. Huge thanks to Sylvia Organ and Reid Gómez, whose constant friendship, support, and humor kept life and the book ticking along. Huge thanks to Ronit Lentin, who deeply influenced my choice of materials and analytic strategy while always inspiring me. Warm thanks to Mengia Tschalaer, Ruben Zecena, Monisha Das Gupta, and Bridget Anderson for support and inspiration during the book's journey.

I am very grateful to many people who created generative and generous spaces for discussing ideas from the book with engaged audiences. These include Anouk de Koning, the principle investigator for the Reproducing Europe project, and students and faculty at Radboud University; a Centre for Research on Ethnic Relations and Nationalism research seminar organized by Saara Pellander at the University of Helsinki; the seminar "States of Intimacy: Gender, Sexuality, and Governance in Modern US History," organized by Nancy F. Cott and Robert O. Self at the Radcliffe Institute for Advanced Study; the symposium A Different Dream: A Symposium on Undocumented Immigration, Gender, and Sexuality, organized by Linda Greenberg at California State University, Los Angeles; the symposium Human Rights and Carceral Sovereignties, organized by Rachel A. Lewis at George Mason University; the panel "Gendering Migration," organized by Jenna Loyd for the University of Wisconsin–Madison Latin American, Caribbean and Iberian Studies Program Migration Symposium; the "LGBT Immigrant Stories" roundtable and discussion, organized by Erika Lee for the University of Minnesota's Immigration History Research Center; "Immigration, Family, and Sexuality," organized by Bill Johnson González at DePaul University; the conference Crossing Sexual Borders: Gender and Sexuality in Migration, organized by Éric Fassin and Manuela Salcedo at Université Paris 8; the conference Queer Displacements: Sexuality, Migration and Exile, organized by Tina Dixson and Renee Dixson at Australian National University; the Borderlands Institute series Responsibility and Immigration organized by Francisco Lozada at the Brite Divinity School; copresenters at the Queer Liberalisms and Marginal Mobility series, organized by Bridget Anderson, Fadi Saleh, and Mengia Tschalaer and hosted by the Barnard Digital Humanities Center; presenters at the Transforming Systemic Violence: Experiences of Female and Non-binary Identifying Queer Migrants series, organized by Mengia Tschalaer and me, moderated by Ruben Zecena, and hosted by the Barnard Digital Humanities Center; Anouk de Koning and students and faculty at Leiden University; the workshop "When Justice Migrates: How Mobility across Borders Reconfigures Rights, Equity and Belonging," organized by Sara Friedman, Jayanth Krishnan, and Irit Dekel at Indiana University; and the Queer Demography Summit organized by Kristopher Velasco at Princeton University.

The American Studies Association (ASA) enabled generative discussion spaces with wonderful copanelists and audiences. Particular thanks to presenters and audiences at the following panels: "Illegal Imaginaries" (organized by Armando Garcia for 2016), "Trafficking Theory, Migrating Method, and Cross-Disciplinary Pedagogy: Sex Trafficking and Queer Migration Scholars in Conversation" (organized by Annie Hill and Karma Chávez for 2017), "No Borders, No Prisons, No Travel Bans: Emerging from the Settler-State Deportation Regime" (organized by me for 2018), and "Caring More for One Another Than for Nation-States: Love and Solidarity against the Deportation Regime" (organized by me for 2023). A shout-out to the fantastic "Undocumented Epistemologies" panel at ASA 2022. Thanks to speakers and audiences at the panels "Indigenous Futures and Settler Coloniality: Revisioning Migration Politics" and "Trans and Queer Migrant Organizing as Transnational Feminist Praxis" that Karma and I co-organized for the National Women's Studies Association Annual Conference (2021).

Warmest thanks to those who generously made time for me to interview them for chapter 2 (their listed affiliations reflect their positions when I interviewed them in 2016): Yesenia Acosta, attorney, Law Offices of Scott Warmuth; Pamela Denzer, director of client programs, Immigration Equality; Sharita Gruberg, assistant director, LGBT Research and Communications, Center for American Progress; Jamila Hammami, executive director, Queer Detainee Empowerment Project; Jason Ortega, Equal Justice Works Fellow, Los Angeles LGBT Center; and Marco Antonio Quiroga, director of public policy, True Colors Fund.

Huge thanks to Courtney Berger, two anonymous reviewers who provided deeply helpful feedback, and the Duke University Press staff.

To Hai Ren, míle buíochas and a giant heart always.

INTRODUCTION

Against the Deportation State

On February 17, 2013, Osmani R. Alcaraz Ochoa, a queer person born in Jalisco, Mexico, who worked as an organizer with migrant families, day laborers, domestic workers, and detained LGBTQ asylum seekers in Tucson, Arizona, was bicycling to a meeting when he saw three Tucson Police Department (TPD) vehicles surrounding a car.[1] The driver, René Meza Huerta, was handcuffed and the children inside the car were crying frantically.[2] Huerta's partner, Perla López, was sobbing on the side of the road. Alcaraz Ochoa stopped, asked what was happening, and learned that the car had been pulled over after someone had called to incorrectly report that children were being abducted. After determining that no abduction was taking place, police officers asked Huerta for a driver's license, which he did not have. Suspecting that he was an undocumented migrant, they called Border Patrol.

Since childhood, Alcaraz Ochoa had witnessed this kind of scene play out countless times as family, coworkers, and community members were "pulled over by police and then handed over to Border Patrol and disappeared from their communities."[3] Enough was enough. He rolled under the wheels of the Border Patrol vehicle, wanting to prevent them from wrenching another person away from family and community for deportation. Border Patrol started taking pictures of him; he used his cell phone to reciprocate. He also messaged people to come to the scene. Border Patrol threatened to charge him with impeding the work of federal agents, which is a felony. Alcaraz Ochoa heard them discussing whether Tasering or using pepper spray to extricate him would cause the least harm to their vehicle. Eventually they pepper sprayed him, pulled him out, handcuffed him, and took him to the Border Patrol station with Huerta. A community rally the next day demanded the release of Alcaraz Ochoa and Huerta, an end to deportation, and an end to TPD's cooperation with Border Patrol. Alcaraz Ochoa was released, but Huerta was not—he was processed for deportation, leaving behind his children, whom his partner, US citizen Perla López, planned to care for, along with her children. Deportation did not end, and TPD did not stop cooperating with Border Patrol. Alcaraz Ochoa continued working for justice and dignity for everyone.

This incident captures the key concerns of the book, which centers writings by and about queer- and transgender-identified migrants of color and allies mobilizing intimacies to contest deportation, a system for forcibly removing people, while laying the groundwork for a future without deportation. As US deportations have skyrocketed, much has been written about the system. Yet little has been written about the diverse queer- and trans-identified people, many of them migrants, who participate in and often spearhead creative, critical antideportation actions.[4] The gap is surprising. The United States has the largest migrant-detention system in the world and an enormous deportation apparatus.[5] Unknown numbers of the estimated 1.3 million queer and trans migrants in the United States live in the system's shadow or within its walls, while still others have been deported.[6] Although deportation scholarship has burgeoned, analyses of US deportation practices generally focus on normative families or, occasionally, on queer, trans, and sex worker migrants framed as vulnerable victims. With few exceptions, queer and trans studies scholarship also says little about deportation, although it increasingly addresses carcerality and prison abolition.[7] This book begins to fill these gaps and builds bridges among deportation, queer, trans, and racial-/migrant-justice scholarship. It highlights new knowledge that emerges when we center the experiences and analyses of queer and trans migrants and allies who contest deportation.

Mainstream media, public discourses, and much scholarship minimize the significance of deportation by framing it as an unfortunate or deserved event that befalls individuals who have broken the law. This book, like Alcaraz Ochoa and numerous antideportation activists, organizers, scholars, and collectives, challenges these individualizing and ahistorical analyses by framing deportation logics and practices as cornerstones of the US immigration system that emerged from histories of settler colonialism, empire, slavery, capitalism, and racialized gender and sexual normativity. That immigration system reproduces and normalizes global apartheid, the denial of Indigenous sovereignty, structural inequalities among the citizenry, and transnational circuits of displacement and confinement that strip people of social legibilities and rights claims while making them available for exploitation and the production of value for others.[8]

Deportation is never just a discrete event that removes someone from their country of migration to their country of citizenship; rather, it's a long process that unfolds over time and across transnational spaces while articulating multiple forms of violence. Furthermore, deportation often returns people to the situations of unemployment, displacement, political instability, and precarity that impelled their migration in the first place, and it negatively affects families and communities in the countries they are deported from and deported to.[9] Those who had fled discrimination, violence, marginalization, and precarity based on their economic status, gender, sexuality, race/ethnicity/ Indigeneity, and other systemic inequalities end up back where they fled from. Not surprisingly, many seek to remigrate.

While migrants who are undocumented or hold precarious legal status on US soil are obvious targets of the US deportation regime, the regime also coproduces the "good migrant," the "normative citizen," and the "marginalized citizen" as categories that relationally define one another in structures of inequality.[10] This means that not just migrants but also citizens have important but varied stakes in the struggles over deportation. This includes marginalized citizens whose precarious standing is underlined by the threat or experience of having family and community members deported, or who get swept up in deportation proceedings despite being citizens; citizens who actively support deportation in order to imbue their own standing with greater meaning; citizens who resist state deportation; and many others.

Most chapters and the book as a whole center written materials by and about queer and trans migrants and allies who are organizing not just to prevent specific migrants' deportations, which is critical, but also to entirely end the deportation system and related systems of violent dispossession.[11] Efforts to abolish rather than reform deportation build on and contribute to the extraordinary activisms ignited by BIPOC feminist, queer, trans, and anticapitalist organizers.[12] A. Naomi Paik explains, "Black-led abolitionist movements and organizations, like Critical Resistance and Black Lives Matter, and immigrant justice organizations like UndocuBlack, United We

Dream and Mijente together demand the simultaneous dismantling of police, ICE, CBP, military, and other institutions of state violence, as well as the ideologies of racism, imperialism, patriarchy and capitalism that undergird them. To achieve the goal of abolishing police and creating a new society where all can thrive, we need to make these connections and fight against all fronts of policing power."[13] Scholarly fields, including queer studies and trans studies, have been deeply engaged in conversations and activisms about abolition. The introduction to a 2022 special issue of GLQ: A Journal of Lesbian and Gay Studies asserts, "Prison abolition is a project of queer liberation and queer liberation is an abolitionist project. No ifs, ands, or buts."[14] Abolition work seeks not just to end interlocking systems of violence but also to rebuild the world anew from the conditions that we face now.

Abolition work requires navigating contradictions and ambiguities that are "located . . . between necessary responses to immediate needs and collective and radical demands for structural and ultimately revolutionary change."[15] Navigating these contradictions requires "letting go of the idea that anyone can have a definitive pathway for knowing how to rid ourselves of carceral logic" and, instead, experimenting, trying out new possibilities.[16] The distinction between reformist versus nonreformist reforms—changes that reform but preserve the system versus changes that contribute to dismantling the system— offers valuable guidance for these efforts and experiments.[17]

The thought-work and actions at the center of the book, and the book itself, do not claim to offer a grand theory of how we can get rid of deportation or the migration-control system that depends on deportation to wreak multiple harms, or what life would be like without them. Instead, inspired by Ara Wilson's suggestion that infrastructure conditions but does not determine intimacies, this book frames the US migration-control system, including its deportation logics and practices, as infrastructure.[18] Chapters critically analyze materials showing how queer and trans migrants and allies experience that their intimacies are conditioned by migration-control infrastructure, including deportation, and how they countermobilize intimacies to challenge these arrangements. I use a broad understanding of *intimacies* as entailing "a sense of self in close connection to others."[19] I provide a fuller discussion of intimacies below. Queer, trans, and ally struggles against deportation exemplify that infrastructure involves numerous elements that interact with intimacies in shifting ways—which opens up multiple possibilities for contestation. Rather than offering a general theory of abolitionist intimacies, the book invites readers to consider how infrastructure and intimacies, when taken together, may open up possibilities for contestation and transformation in readers' own contexts.

Not all of the work discussed is abolitionist—for example, chapter 2 shows the logics and compromises that may be required when working within the system to save a loved one from deportation. Yet, that information helps to clarify the necessity for abolition as a horizon for action. Without blueprints or guarantees, the queer and transgender migrant and ally antideportation work discussed in this book comprises "an incremental politics of small [and big] happenings, acts, and events which come to cohere and sustain a radical intent" to realize a different world.[20]

The remainder of this introduction is divided into three sections. The first section provides historical and political context for understanding the struggles I discuss in the book. The section discusses, first, why I conceive migration controls that depend on deportation as an infrastructure of chokepoints; then, how deportation reproduces global apartheid, denial of Indigenous sovereignty, and inequalities among the citizenry; next, a brief history of the emergence of the US deportation system; and finally, how logics of crimmigration, attrition, and national security have dispersed deportability throughout everyday life in recent decades. The second section discusses common conceptions of *intimacies* and how I use the term to understand writings about the work done by queer and trans migrants and allies who contest deportation. The final section describes the methods and materials on which the book is based and provides an overview of the upcoming chapters.

Historical and Political Context

US Migration Control as an Infrastructure of Chokepoints

Deportation is a critical element of the US migration-control system, which I characterize as infrastructure.[21] The migration-control infrastructure includes individuals, institutions, discourses, laws, policies, practices, built environments, and funding streams.[22] Federal laws and policies establish the infrastructure's broad parameters, but migration control also works in tandem with state and local governments, private corporations, civil society, individual citizens, and shifting discourses to generate different configurations in specific locations.[23]

Thinking of migration control as infrastructure not only highlights the multiple, interacting elements involved but also, as Lauren Berlant explains, "helps us see that what we commonly call 'structure' is not . . . an intractable principle of continuity across time and space, but is really a convergence of force and value in patterns of movement that's only solid when seen from a distance."[24] When seen up close, gaps, sutures, corrosion, and parts that fit poorly become evident, presenting possibilities for contestation. For years, migrant-justice groups have focused on infrastructure: for example, they have analyzed the infrastructural arrangements that are steadily pipelining people into deportation, situated these infrastructures in historical context, provided resources that help individuals and organizations to resist, and demanded changes or an end to the infrastructures.[25]

I conceive the migration-control system not just as infrastructure but as an infrastructure of chokepoints through which some noncitizens' deportation and deportability—along with other noncitizens' admission and conditional residence and citizens' belonging or not—become produced and contested. I take the term *chokepoint* from Mark Krikorian, the former director of the right-wing Center for Immigration Studies. Krikorian narrowly understood chokepoints as institutional filters within social and economic life that enable the identification, criminalization, and deportation of undocumented people from the United States.[26] This book uses a broader conception than Krikorian's, arguing that the migration-control system overall comprises an infrastructure of chokepoints that are expected to produce varied outcomes depending on the rules that govern noncitizens' possibilities for legally entering and remaining and officials' and others' understanding and implementation of these rules.[27] As rules change, noncitizens often transit in and out of different statuses.[28] My conception of chokepoints builds on the scholarship about checkpoints and the relational understanding that state migration controls are never just about restricting some people's movement but are also always about facilitating others' while iterating citizenship norms.

I also conceive migration control as an infrastructure of chokepoints in order to highlight that the system is violent and continually generates violence. National and transnational migration controls that interact with global capitalism force many people into clandestine migration routes around which dense economies of violence have grown.[29] These economies generate enormous profit as migrants become "cargo to smuggle, bodies to prostitute, labor to exploit, organs to traffic, or lives to exchange for cash."[30] Wendy A. Vogt emphasizes that "officials and criminals alike profit" from these economies of violence, which are kept in place by national and transnational migration controls.[31] Migration controls also generate violence and death among people who are living and working without legal status, remain locked in detention, or are forcibly deported. Legally admitted migrants experience the violence of ongoing surveillance and governance that pipelines some into deportation and others into marginality based on class, gender, racialization, and other factors.

Michel Foucault's analysis of biopolitics informs how many scholars theorize the violence associated with migration controls. Foucault coined the term *biopolitics* to explore how life became the object and purpose of politics. According to Foucault, under liberalism, states sought as their raison d'être to foster the lives of (some of) the population, which concomitantly involved letting other populations die.[32] "Letting die" speaks to the ways that, through failing to make available basic resources and creating hostile environments, many people are pushed into the realm of "let die" even when they are not explicitly targeted for death. In the United States, people who are Indigenous, Black, of color, low-income, queer, female, transgender, and disabled are consistently exposed to greater harm, deprivation, and risk of death. Moreover, these groups are more consistently killed outright in a process that Achille Mbembe theorizes as necropolitics.[33] Yet, under the imperative of fostering (some people's) lives, states generally claim deniability and lack of responsibility for (other people's) deaths.[34]

Migration scholars theorize multiple connections between biopolitics and state migration controls. Some explore how migration controls continually generate deaths at sea, in deserts, and elsewhere even as states claim deniability. Scholars connect migrant deaths to state efforts to foster the lives of valued citizens. Jonathan Xavier Inda, for example, suggests that US migration policies enact "the idea that the elimination of the enemy—that is, the undocumented migrant—will make the body politic [citizens] stronger and more vigorous" and shows that these dynamics occur in racist and racializing ways.[35] Claudia Aradau and Martina Tazzioli suggest that in addition to generating elimination and death, biopolitical practices affect migrants in other ways.[36] Tazzioli proposes that choking offers a framework for understanding "political technologies that actively disrupt migrants' movements and their infrastructures of liveability, without necessarily killing or letting them die."[37] As Tazzioli explains, "'choking' indicates on the one hand the physical cramping and suffocating of migrants—along the lines of an asphyxiatory power . . . —and on the other the constant disrupting of migrant movements and the dismantling of their spaces of life."[38] Migrants' movements are disrupted not just through forced containment but also through being forced to keep moving, being rerouted, and being chased away.[39] These processes continually strip away people's grounds for claiming rights that might mitigate against violence and death.[40] Tazzioli highlights that technologies of choking dismantle and destroy migrants' "infrastructures of liveability" and sociality, too.[41]

Focusing on choking does not ignore "power's grasp over life and death" or minimize that migration controls in some cases do directly "govern through death."[42] On the contrary, innumerable migrants have choked to death while navigating US migration controls, whether from thirst and heatstroke while crossing the southern desert or from lack of oxygen in sealed, airless trucks and containers. Moreover, authorities count on would-be migrants knowing that the controls may be fatal in order to deter further migration.[43] Focusing on choking, however, expands the conversation to address forms of violence that not only kill people but also contain, injure, exhaust, and wear them out at every step. Moreover, scholarship underscores the connections between migration controls and other violent systems. Tazzioli suggests that attention to technologies of choking "enables tracing out multiple continuities between biopolitical tactics of choking migrants, the governing of colonised subjects and the racialised violent policing of black people."[44] Her framing painfully evokes the racialized, cisheteropatriarchal violence endured by innumerable Black men and women whose anguished words, "I can't breathe," while being held by police in fatal chokeholds, resulted in deaths that have spurred mass protests and for which there has yet to be an accounting.[45]

Describing migration controls as an infrastructure of chokepoints highlights not just violence but also the infrastructures that materially and ideologically generate, facilitate, and normalize the violence. Hannah Appel, Nikhil Anand, and Akhil Gupta make clear the intimate connection between visceral violence and infrastructure, writing that attention to "infrastructure forces us to rethink governance and citizenship not at a distance but pressing into the flesh. . . . [It] does not allow state power to disavow itself. On the contrary, it is an intimate form of contact, presence, and potential."[46] In the context of migration-control infrastructure that chokes, harms, wears out, and generates deportation, queer and trans migrants and allies create intimacies that demand other ways of living.

Reproducing Global Apartheid, Inequalities among Citizens,
and Erasure of Indigenous Sovereignties

The US migration-control infrastructure is rooted in the late nineteenth and early twentieth centuries when the modern world order composed of sovereign nation-states took shape. That world order, and modern nation-states' boundaries, emerged through processes of settler colonialism, colonialism, capitalism, and racial slavery. Control over movement became crucial to realizing and sustaining national boundaries that, in the case of the United States, were often inscribed on or cut through the boundaries of Indigenous nations.[47] Beginning in the late nineteenth century, nation-states stripped private and local entities of the power to control people's movement across national boundaries and asserted the nation-state's power and authority to determine what counted as legitimate movement and by whom.[48]

Possibilities for crossing international borders came to hinge on the distinction between citizen and noncitizen, which required the development of bureaucratic capacities to identify and designate every living person as being a citizen of somewhere.[49] Citizenship is commonly conceived in liberal thought as a universal and valorized status. Barry Hindess and others, however, characterize nation-based citizenship as a strategy for population management that upholds systemic inequalities.[50] The expectation that everyone should be a citizen of somewhere became the grounds for emplacing everyone within nation-states founded on settler colonial and imperial mappings.[51]

Controlling movement across borders based on citizen/noncitizen distinctions normalizes the fact that the material and symbolic value of people's nation-based citizenship statuses vary precisely because of the effects of colonialism, settler colonialism, racial slavery, heteropatriarchy, and global capitalism. Because of these histories and processes, an individual's legal citizenship "closely corresponds to strikingly different prospects for well-being, security, and freedom of individuals."[52] This includes strikingly different prospects for being allowed to legally cross national borders. Thus, while unequal global relations generate mass displacement and migration, citizens of the Global South face numerous restrictions on travel across borders.[53] At the same time, citizens of Global North nation-states are often the recipients of visa waivers and other arrangements that facilitate their travel.[54] Scholars conceive that these interacting conditions reproduce global apartheid, which Joseph Nevins describes as follows: "The relatively rich and largely white of the world are generally free to travel and live wherever they would like and to access the resources they 'need.' Meanwhile the relatively poor and largely nonwhite are typically forced to subsist in places where there are not enough resources to provide sufficient livelihood or, in order to overcome their deprivation and insecurity, to risk their lives trying to overcome ever-stronger boundary controls put into place by rich countries that reject them."[55] Nandita Sharma underscores that global apartheid involves not only restrictions on movement across territorial borders that leave numerous people unable to move legally but also differential treatment toward all noncitizens living and working within the territorial space of the nation-state.[56] Sharma notes that these unequal conditions "are accepted as either perfectly legitimate or relatively unimportant by much of the population, including those who are otherwise critical of neoliberal state policies."[57]

Deportation is the linchpin that keeps this interlocking system of inequalities in place. Tanya Maria Golash-Boza explains, "Global apartheid would not be feasible without deportation, as deportation is the physical manifestation of policies that determine who is permitted to live where."[58] Deportation or its threat maintains the unequal global distribution of wealth and resources.[59]

Deportation also reproduces inequalities among the citizenry. This occurs because the global histories and dynamics that generate inequalities between those who hold different national citizenship statuses also generate inequalities among those who hold shared national citizenship status. Scholars explain that nation-based citizenship is composed of two dimensions: legal status and normative belonging.[60] Each aspect coconstitutes yet is distinct from the other one.[61] Since the inception of the United States, possibilities for accessing legal citizenship status have been economically based, racialized, heteropatriarchal, settler, and imperial, and legal citizenship has never guaranteed normative belonging. On the contrary, meaningful belonging has been restricted, denied, cramped, and under struggle for innumerable legal citizens. Moreover, US citizenship was imposed on Indigenous communities as a tool for further dispossession and elimination. United States migration controls, which are "foundationally constituted through and intertwined with anti-Indigenous, anti-Black, and imperialist warfare," contribute to reproducing and normalizing marginalized citizens' nonbelonging.[62] This includes by firewalling against entry or settlement by migrants who were seen as outside of or directly threatening to settler colonial, imperial, white supremacist, anti-Black, heteropatriarchal, and capitalist norms.

Since legal status and belonging are intertwined, some marginalized citizens' nonbelonging also puts their legal status at direct risk or under erasure. Mass deportations in the 1930s included innumerable US citizens of Mexican descent and Mexican migrants, which highlights that in a racist and settler colonial state, nonbelonging may invalidate legal citizenship. That history is not restricted to the past; every year, a number of legal citizens are denied permission to enter the United States or get deported because officials refuse to believe that they are citizens. Rachel E. Rosenbloom argues that these cases "compel us to reconceptualize citizenship as . . . a status that . . . is, in a functional sense, produced by [immigration] enforcement."[63] Since 9/11, numerous citizens who identified as or were perceived to be of Middle Eastern descent (a vast, complex, and changing category) found that their legal citizenship mattered little as they were put under surveillance and detained without due process. Those who identified or were perceived as Latino/a/x (another vast and complex category) also disproportionately experienced being treated as potentially deportable migrants. A continuous stream of bills that try to deny US citizenship to the children who are born on US soil to undocumented people announce not just that marginalized groups' legal citizenship is fragile but that it can be revoked. In 2020, under President Donald Trump, the Department of Justice launched an office dedicated to denaturalizing targeted citizens.[64]

Struggles over belonging that implicate people's citizenship status occur not just at borders but also throughout the United States. This is because migration controls are infused through all aspects of society, continually profiling people and seeking to identify noncitizens for denial of rights and for detention and deportation. Thus, the controls affect not just migrants but also citizens, especially those who are racialized as likely foreigners, security threats, and criminals (further discussed below). These histories underscore that citizens, including marginalized citizens and all citizens committed to justice, have compelling reasons to challenge and demand an end to the US migration-control system that builds on, reproduces, and normalizes inequalities among the citizenry—while sanctioning discrimination toward noncitizens. This does not mean that migrants and citizens have the same histories, struggles, or stakes in abolishing the US migration-control system. Rather, it suggests that there exists much common ground around which migrants and citizens may—and do—organize to abolish migration controls, including deportation, which is this book's focus.

The US border controls, including deportation, also continually assert domination over Indigenous lands. Indeed, the controls' purpose is to normalize settler boundaries and state-making that emerged through genocide and land theft. Moreover, US border controls often further extend domination over Indigenous nations while pushing back on Indigenous sovereignties.[65] For example, the United States actively funnels migrants into the Tohono O'odham Nation, turning the nation into "the epicenter of death for the militarized border zone," where children and adults may encounter the remains of border crossers who have perished. At the same time, "in southern districts of the Tohono O'odham Nation forming the international border with Sonora, Mexico, O'odham communities in Chukut-Kuk and Gu Vo districts experience the loss of respect for their governing institutions, the maintenance of their social organizations, and the control of their communities and peoples."[66] Border Patrol fences traverse the O'odham Nation, watchtowers surveil people as they go about their everyday lives, and members of the nation endure threats and abuse at Border Patrol checkpoints on all roads leading into and out of the Nation.[67] Border Patrol as an occupying force makes it dangerous or impossible to engage in traditional hunting, gather plants used for healing and prayer, or fulfill religious practices. It fails to respect or protect sacred sites and damages waterways. O'odham adults and children "are witnesses to violent acts, made to accept life in a militarized zone, as well as see physical damage caused by the Border Patrol to O'odham lands in order to sustain border militarization. No other jurisdiction in the United States, Indigenous or not, is exposed to such concentrated forms of ongoing violence to local populations."[68]

Creating Deportation

Deportation builds on violent histories of peopling the United States and controlling people's mobilities to sustain white patriarchal settler hegemony and global apartheid. It was informed by practices of forcibly removing Indigenous communities, controlling the movement of enslaved and freed Black people through Fugitive Slave Acts and Black Codes, and expelling the poor. Deportation involved new innovations, too.

According to Kelly Lytle Hernández, the US state had to invent the power to deport since it was not written into the Constitution. Inventing that power unfolded after the 1882 Chinese Exclusion Act—which was explicitly racist, Orientalist, heteropatriarchal, and capitalist—failed to exclude Chinese people on the scale that white nationalists had hoped for. This led to the passage of the Geary Act, which required all Chinese-born people who were legally present in the United States to register with the government or else be arrested, imprisoned for up to one year, and then deported. Hernández summarizes, "The act knotted immigration control to crime and punishment in historically unprecedented and constitutionally questionable ways."[69] Massive challenges to the act, which were spearheaded by the Chinese community, resulted in two key Supreme Court decisions that established the legal and institutional logics of deportation that still guide us today. In one decision, *Fong Yue Ting v. United States* (1893), the Supreme Court upheld Congress's power to expel any noncitizen for any reason, including racial animus, and justified that power as an expression of settler state sovereignty.[70] The 1896 *Wong Wing* decision established that people could be confined while the state tried to deport them but that this was supposedly not the same as criminal confinement.[71] This opinion "invented immigrant detention as a veiled but valid practice of human caging in the United States."[72]

Over time, the grounds for deportation steadily expanded. Moreover, although the law initially allowed only for deportation on grounds that existed before the person was admitted to the United States, in the 1910s, migrants became deportable for acts or circumstances that arose after their entry. The time limits within which a deportation could occur were expanded. Panic over migrant women's involvement in "white slavery" (i.e., sex work) particularly fueled these changes. European women became conceived as victims of white slavery, while Asian, Mexican, and Black women became constructed as "wayward" on racial, sexual, and gendered grounds, illustrating that deportation contributed to producing and enforcing racialized heteronormativity as the basis of belonging to the nation. These norms affected migrants' possibilities and the perception and treatment of marginalized citizens. In 1917, the two sets of deportation policies that had developed—one directed at Chinese laborers and the other directed at everyone else—became folded into one. By 1924, deportation became what Daniel Kanstroom describes as a mode of postentry social control over migrants that lasted until they departed, naturalized, or died.[73] That same year, the Border Patrol was created. Katy Murdza and Walter Ewing summarize, "Since its creation . . . the Border Patrol has been steeped in institutional racism and has committed violent acts with near impunity" as it engages in policing borders and expelling migrants.[74] Hernández notes that enduring racism grounds deportation: "Detention and deportation no longer explicitly target Chinese immigrants but the regime of immigration controls is no less racialized. . . . Latinos [currently] comprise 97% of all forced removals and deportations from the United States."[75] These racist and racializing dynamics inseparably intertwine with gender- and sexuality-norming for the capitalist settler state.

This history laid the groundwork for the post-1965 period on which this book focuses. The Immigration and Nationality Act of 1965 and the Refugee Act of 1980 set the basic framework for admission today. Under contemporary federal law, permission to cross the border requires noncitizens to show that they fit into a narrow spectrum of state-recognized family ties, economic niches, state-approved protection needs, or short-term visa requirements.[76] These limited avenues for entry are administered in ways that reproduce global apartheid, white supremacy, settler colonialism, normative genders and sexualities, and the exclusion of poor and working people. Concomitantly, the laws establish who cannot be admitted, whether because they are explicitly barred or because they are unable to affirmatively match admission requirements.[77] Deportation cements these interrelationships.

Logics and practices of crimmigration, attrition, and national security have proven critical for dispersing deportability into all aspects of everyday life, thereby shaping the events described in upcoming chapters. Data capitalism that captures, packages, and sells massive amounts of personal information that gets used for surveillance and predictive policing has turbocharged these dynamics.[78]

In the 1980s, the legal grounds and practical mechanisms for detaining and deporting migrants began proliferating through "crimmigration."[79] Crimmigration entails "the intertwinement of crime control and migration control" in a spiraling process that continually deepens the equation between migrants and crime and functions to justify detention and deportation.[80] Crimmigration draws heavily on, and further entrenches, histories of criminalization and mass incarceration that target Black and other marginalized citizens.[81]

Crimmigration vastly expanded the deportation of noncitizens who committed crimes and minor offenses. As the War on Drugs funneled vast numbers of Black and brown people and people experiencing poverty to prison, the state faced a shortage of detention beds. Patrisia Macías-Rojas describes how the shortage prompted authorities to explore expelling noncitizens who were convicted of crimes in order to free up bed space to incarcerate marginalized citizens. The 1986 Immigration Reform and Control Act introduced the Criminal Alien Program to deport noncitizens who were convicted of felonies.[82] That same year, the Anti–Drug Abuse Act expanded mandatory sentencing for drug offenses, which further exacerbated shortages of prison bed space.[83] The 1988 Anti–Drug Abuse Act again expanded penalties for drug offenses and included a provision for deporting noncitizens convicted of aggravated felonies.[84]

These dynamics further exploded in 1996, when the Illegal Immigration Reform and Immigrant Responsibility Act mandated the deportation of both authorized and unauthorized migrants who are convicted of any "aggravated felony." The law, however, redefined and vastly expanded what constituted an aggravated felony such that it encompassed even minor violations like theft or failure to appear in court. Moreover, the law applied these revised standards retroactively so that anyone who ever had minor brushes with the law, even long in the past, suddenly found themselves deportable.[85] That same year, the Antiterrorism and Effective Death Penalty Act made any act of moral turpitude (a vaguely defined concept that may be applied to actions as diverse as driving under the influence and mass murder) into grounds for deportation.[86] States and municipalities added a host of laws and ordinances, such as antiloitering, to facilitate the criminal prosecution of unauthorized migrants.[87] These dynamics vastly expanded deportation. The growing detention of asylum seekers further added to the numbers.

Crimmigration also involved the enhancement or literal creation of criminal penalties for immigration-related acts such as crossing the border without authorization or reentering after being deported. Macías-Rojas highlights that at the southwest border, those most likely to be prosecuted are people who reenter after deportation—vast numbers of whom have long histories of settlement and deep ties to families and communities in the United States.[88] Macías-Rojas further highlights that these prosecutions overwhelmingly affect people from Mexico and, increasingly, Central America and their US citizen and legal resident families and communities.[89] Prosecutions for unauthorized (re)entry have become the single most prosecuted federal crime, and it has vastly swelled federal prison populations where prosecuted migrants now serve time before being deported for reentry.

Significantly increased cooperation between federal immigration officials and state and local law enforcement, including through data sharing, provided the practical means for transforming these changes into growing numbers of migrant detentions and deportations. The Criminal Alien Program, the 287(g) Program, and Secure Communities were key.[90] These programs vastly expanded the numbers of law enforcement authorities and mechanisms that monitored not just possible criminal activity but everyone's immigration status, and they multiplied the chokepoints in everyday life where migrants risked capture and being turned over to immigration authorities. Harsha Walia highlights that the "devolution to state and local enforcement not only mimics the design of anti-Black laws, but also disproportionately impacts Black migrants."[91]

CHOKEPOINTS THAT MAY LEAD to deportation also became embedded into everyday life through logics and practices of attrition. *Merriam-Webster* defines *attrition* as "the act of wearing or grinding down by friction; the act of weakening or exhausting by constant harassment, abuse, or attack."[92] Michele Waslin explains that, when used as a tool of migration control, attrition involves doing everything possible to make it "difficult, if not impossible, for unauthorized immigrants to live in American society," including by turning everyday activities that are required to survive into chokepoints that may lead to deportation.[93] Ubiquitous digital tracking that is embedded into all aspects of daily life has strengthened the attritionary dragnet.[94]

K-Sue Park explains that contemporary strategies of attrition have deep roots in colonial conquest and settlement. According to Park, when colonists could not engage in outright warfare, they sought to create conditions that forced Native people from lands that colonists then expropriated for themselves. Colonists targeted everyday life in order to achieve these goals: "They quickly realized their own settlement created hostile conditions that caused native peoples to remove themselves without always being legible as an assault on tribes that would lead them to declare war. Colonists therefore pursued an indirect removal policy by passing laws and building institutions that had the effect of attacking native people's lives from every angle, impacting their health, safety and freedom of mobility, and their ability to find food, shelter, and maintain kinship bonds and political orders."[95]

Contemporary attrition strategies draw from these histories. The Immigration Reform and Control Act (IRCA) of 1986 multiplied the chokepoints around paid employment by requiring everyone—migrants and citizens alike—to document their identities and eligibility for paid employment. The IRCA did not actually prevent migrants from working, but it did make paid employment harder and more expensive to get, and migrant workers more exploitable and vulnerable, while increasing employment-based racial and gender profiling for everyone, including citizens. Raids on workplaces and day laborer pickup sites, the use of E-Verify, and other initiatives sought to further ensure that undocumented migrants' efforts to secure paid employment instead channeled them into deportation.

In the 1990s, federal law sought to turn childbearing, health care, schooling, and other aspects of social reproduction into chokepoints, too. Through these systems, documented migrants were to be disciplined into self-sufficiency or else risk losing their legal status, while undocumented migrants were to be identified and targeted for detention and deportation.[96] California's Proposition 187, the so-called Save Our State initiative that passed in 1994, offered a template on which federal (and much state and local) legislation subsequently built. These efforts drew from, and further strengthened, laws that targeted marginalized citizens' access to social supports.[97] Disgusted and sickened by Proposition 187, Mexican American cultural workers Lalo Alcaraz and Esteban Zul launched a satirical campaign that included faxing media outlets fake news releases that extolled the benefits of (imaginary) "self-deportation centers" and talking up an (imaginary) group, Hispanics against Liberal Takeover, or HALTO.[98] Their satirical concept of "self-deportation," however, swiftly became part of Republican commonsense justifications for attrition policies that targeted everyday life.

Children attending school were also targeted. In *Plyler v. Doe* (1982), the Supreme Court ruled that all children under eighteen are entitled by law to receive public K–12 education, regardless of their legal status. Yet schools became pipelines to deportation as struggling students, particularly in low-income and minoritized communities, became tracked into the juvenile (in)justice system.[99] Parents picking up children from school were sometimes detained and deported, too, even though areas around schools are officially designated as protected areas where immigration authorities are not supposed to operate.[100]

Supporters like Mark Krikorian expect attrition to generate deportation in three ways: by multiplying the choke/checkpoints through which everyone's legal standing gets checked and those unable to prove legal presence get turned over to Border Patrol; by ensuring that the multiplication occurs in ways that target all aspects of everyday life, thereby choking off migrants' possibilities for subsistence and living; and by calculating that these dynamics will compel migrants who are not captured by the state to self-deport anyway. In the face of this kind of systemic violence, undocumented people can call on neither legal citizenship nor universal human rights to defend themselves. Instead, Alicia Schmidt Camacho suggests that the situation "renders the undocumented vulnerable to an almost total social abridgement of their social relatedness as materialized in actual kinship ties and communal belonging."[101] Documented migrants and citizens are affected by being required to prove their status to racist, settler, cisheteronormative institutions when seeking employment or vital support and by being disciplined into exploitative work conditions and diminishing or nonexistent social supports under a system of neoliberal capitalism that treats poverty as an individual failing rather than as stemming from systemic inequality. Through these practices, deportation has become a further entrenched part of all aspects of everyday life.

Living under conditions of deportability means navigating relentlessly attritionary conditions while trying to survive and build life. Becoming deported after living in the United States furthers the experience of attrition as social and cultural capital that people gained and time that they invested in creating a future are forcibly stripped away.[102] Moreover, people are generally deported without any of the assets that they worked so hard to accumulate.[103] Deportation also strips resources and possibilities from families, friends, and communities in countries migrants are deported from and countries migrants are deported to. Deportation as part of neoliberal global capitalism emerges as an important instrument of attritionary stripping away that operates across multiple scales and temporalities.

THE EVENTS OF SEPTEMBER 11, 2001, further multiplied chokepoints and dispersed deportability through concerns about national security. National security is not self-evident, objective, or universal but, rather, a shifting discourse that has been fundamental to the foundation of the United States as a white, settler colonial, and heteropatriarchal nation. National security concerns ensured that racial, gender, Indigenous, and other marginalized "others" became targets of surveillance and control in order to maintain the status quo.[104] For example, "eighteenth century New York City adopted lantern laws that required Black, mixed-race, and Indigenous enslaved persons to carry candle-lit lanterns if they walked around the city unaccompanied by a white person after sunset. The law's intent was to ensure that persons covered by the law could be 'seen, located, and controlled at all times.'"[105] Surveillance and control measures were also incorporated into the immigration-control system from its inception. When granting Congress broad powers to regulate immigration, the Supreme Court "compared Chinese immigrants arriving in the United States to a hostile army invading its shores" and "rationalized that the power to regulate immigration was a necessary part of the power of a sovereign state to defend itself."[106] The idea of immigration control as a matter of national security informed immigration legislation and practices, including deportation, throughout the twentieth century. At the same time, invoking national security significantly shielded discriminatory and abusive practices from being challenged.

After September 11, 2001, the discourse on migrants in general, and undocumented migrants and borders in particular, as potential security threats "set off a self-feeding chain reaction of enforcement . . . [and] contributed to a range of restrictive policies aimed at banishing undocumented immigrants from the national territory."[107] In a move that further conflated migration control with national security, immigration and border control functions were relocated into the newly created Department of Homeland Security, and massive resources were poured into reconceived screening and tracking systems. Information technologies that promised to accomplish "what ICE, the border patrol, white nationalists, English-only policies, Proposition 187, and voters in the borderlands could not accomplish over centuries" played a significant role.[108] Ruja Benjamin explains that expanding technology enables both obvious and less visible yet insidious harms.[109] The United States negotiated new migration and border control arrangements with Mexico, Canada, and many other countries, enforcement at the southern border reached unprecedented levels, enforcement within the boundaries of the nation expanded, and possibilities for challenging abuse remained daunting in the face of government invocations of national security. In new ways, people from Muslim, Middle Eastern, and Arab backgrounds were singled out, surveilled, incarcerated, and otherwise targeted. Young men from majority Muslim and Arab countries became required to register with the government and found themselves subjected to interrogation and, in some cases, detention for reasons that were rarely explained. "Of the 83,000 men who came forward, 13,000 were deported," even though "none were charged with terrorism related crimes."[110]

A spate of legislation reflected and resourced the framework of the "immigrant as threat." Key laws included the USA PATRIOT Act (2001), the National Intelligence Reform and Terrorism Prevention Act (2004), and the Real ID Act (2005). Immigration and Customs Enforcement released Operation Endgame, a plan to detain and deport every single migrant who was deportable on any grounds whatsoever.[111] Anna Sampaio argues that these laws, practices, and security logics, which combined "masculine protectionism and racialized demonization," provided "a template to scrutinize, harass, and encumber immigrants while also reconfiguring citizenship."[112] Detention and deportation numbers continued to skyrocket.[113]

Funding for the migration-control infrastructure skyrocketed too, even while social spending drastically declined. According to the American Immigration Council, from 1993 to 2021, "the annual budget of the U.S. Border Patrol has increased more than ten-fold, from $363 million to nearly $4.9 billion."[114] After 2003, Border Patrol (now called Customs and Border Protection, CBP) and Immigration and Customs Enforcement (ICE) became part of the new Department of Homeland Security (DHS). From 2003 to 2021, under DHS, ICE spending nearly tripled "from $3.3 billion to $8.3 billion," much of this devoted to detention.[115] In the same time period, "the budget of CBP, which includes both the Border Patrol and operations at ports of entry, has also nearly tripled, rising from $5.9 billion in FY 2003 to a high of $17.7 billion in FY 2021."[116] The budget underwrote enormous changes in the built environment and massively expanded personnel and technology.

Crimmigration, attrition, and discourses of national security thoroughly infuse everyday institutions that are increasingly networked through information technology with the migration-control infrastructure. These logics and practices ensure that everyone, but especially precarious migrants and marginalized citizens, continually navigate violence and that migrants face deportability. Deportability has also been further dispersed globally as the US Border Patrol exports its logics and practices through "an interconnected network of partnerships, funding, multinational industries, and international agreements, stretching across every continent and saturating the world."[117]

Intimacies

This book explores writings by and about queer migrants' and allies' struggles against deportation and deportability through the lens of intimacies that involve "a sense of self in [close] connection to others."[118] Intimacy is a tricky concept with multiple meanings. It is commonly understood as involving family ties, sexual relationships, familiarity, deep knowledge, or proximity/closeness.[119] Intimacy is especially associated with the private home, which, in the United States, is seen as separate from the state and market, and connected with domesticity, whiteness, patriarchy, and the civilizing mission.[120]

Feminist, Black, queer, trans, and decolonial scholarship have significantly challenged these common perspectives and offered important insights that inform this book. The insights include that, first, intimacy does not have a preset domain or normative form but instead is produced in changing ways within multiple relations of power.[121] Second, intimacy is a crucial nexus through which states exercise governance in order to reproduce exclusionary nationalisms and unequal transnational fields structured around hierarchies of settler colonialism, empire, race, ethnicity, class, gender, sexuality, and ability—often using discourses of family. Third, anti-Blackness, dehumanization, and violence have been critical to producing normative intimacies.[122]

Slavery required what Christina Sharpe calls "monstrous intimacies" that transformed stolen African people into "things" that could be bought, sold, traded, and abused while reserving concepts of "the human" for those who were white, male, and propertied.[123] Against this backdrop, Ann Laura Stoler shows that calculations about and control over intimacies provided the material means through which imperial states and colonial administrators created multiple distinctions among populations and tied these distinctions to enduring inequalities.[124] At the same time, intimacies became the basis on which marginalized people challenged these distinctions and the inequalities that they upheld. After the imperial order became rescaled into a global order of nation-states that began to assert and enact sovereignty by controlling immigration, states institutionalized efforts to govern migrants through their intimate ties, and these efforts drew on and repurposed older racist, colonial logics and practices while contributing to nation-making in new ways.[125]

Family became a crucial intimacy through which noncitizens claimed rights to admission and settlement, yet *family* was understood and administered by the US state in ways that, as Nayan Shah shows, produced and naturalized the white, settled, "respectable, propertied, conventionally gendered and sexualized family household" as the model for nation-building that was tied into state-sanctioned forms of paid employment, social welfare, and political participation.[126] The model thoroughly shaped the distribution of material and symbolic resources, while rendering illegible and illegal other forms of sociality and intimacy and nullifying innumerable noncitizens' possibilities for claiming admission and long-term residence.

Family remains a key intimacy through which states enact violent migration controls, including deportation, and through which people contest that violence. Thus, this book pays attention to intimacies that are referenced under the term *family*. This includes nuclear families that are normalized by the state, nonnuclear families and kinship forms that affirm Indigenous, Black, POC, and two-spirit presence in the face of histories of violent erasure, and "families we choose." "Families we choose" reflects that queer and trans people, who often experience violence and rejection from biological and legal families, have rich histories of creating alternative families and intimacies that are often illegible under law and social policies or used as weapons against queer and trans folks, yet offer psychological and material support.[127] William N. Eskridge Jr. describes these "families we choose" as composed of "consent-based intimacy among friends, partners, former lovers, children, and others."[128]

While weaponizing intimacies to govern migration and generate deportation, however, the state never restricts itself to family. The previous discussion of attrition highlighted a wide range of intimacies and ties that have been deliberately instrumentalized to serve the state's deportation goals. These include employer/employee relations and ties involved in schooling, health care, renting, and all manner of service provision and community building. Equally, people challenging deportation mobilize intimacies that include but extend beyond family. This book makes space for all of these intimacies. In doing so, it moves away from binary debates about whether queer and trans people should or should not support same-sex marriage toward exploring how a wide range of intimacies—that include but extend beyond those recognized by the state—figure in the production and contestation of deportation.

The book is guided by Ara Wilson's argument that infrastructure—which "conjures up quite physical things" but remains a "fuzzy" construct—and intimacy should be considered together.[129] Wilson suggests that infrastructures "enable or hinder" specific formations of intimacy and that attention to infrastructure allows us to analyze the "concrete forces of abstract fields of power" and the operations of "actually existing systems" that condition intimacies.[130] The book's chapters center on aspects of the deportation infrastructure around which queer and trans migrants and allies have especially mobilized intimacies to contest deportation: the promise of legalization, same-sex marriage, traffic enforcement that pipelines people to deportation, and transgender migrant detention.

The book does not offer a positivist (or necessarily positive) depiction of intimacies; rather, intimacies are understood as emergent, always in process, and multifaceted. Intimacies assuredly include violence, but I focus on intimacies oriented toward enabling survival and livability in the present and animated by a vision of future thriving. Effectively, I'm interested in materials by and about queer and transgender migrants and allies who, centering on deportation, seek to transform the balance between "what forms of life are supported to persist, alter and thrive, and what forms of life are destroyed, injured and constrained" with the goal of creating a future without deportation that supports life and livability for all.[131]

The traffic stop that opens this introduction shows some ways that intimacies get mobilized in the context of the infrastructure of chokepoints. The stop was prompted by an anonymous call claiming that a man was abducting children; this claim evoked long-standing narratives of migrant men of color as dangerous to normative family intimacies. Details of the call were conveyed to law enforcement, who made a traffic stop. The officers did not rescue abducted children; instead, after local police called Border Patrol, they threatened to utterly transform or completely sever the established intimacies among those in the car. The stop turned Huerta into a father who was on track to lose intimate ties to his children and partner (not to mention to his coworkers and communities), ensured that the children's ties to their father were going to be forever affected, and left Huerta's partner, US citizen Perla López, crying on the roadside as she wondered what to do. Media reported that after the stop, López assumed responsibility for Huerta's children in addition to her own.[132] Effectively, Huerta's deportation reconstituted her as a single parent and provider.[133] These experiences—and the vast scholarship on the struggles facing mixed-status families composed of citizens and migrants—underscore that deportation violently restructures or entirely terminates many intimacies and ramifies in numerous ways that reiterate yet traverse citizen/noncitizen status distinctions. Such terrible experiences also show that deportation struggles involve relations between migrants and citizens that are multiple and intersectional rather than binary and that connect through the norm of good citizenship that produces differential dispossession among interconnected migrants and marginalized citizens.[134]

Alcaraz Ochoa's response mobilized intimacy very differently than the state. His response expressed a deeply felt sense of identification and solidarity with a stranger who publicly experienced being routed into deportation—and with the children and partner who cried as someone they loved was being disappeared into the deportation system, and quite possibly from their lives. Alcaraz Ochoa's sense of identification across lines of sexual or gender identity or parental status challenges bounded conceptions of LGBTQ people as existing in one world and presumably normative heterosexual individuals and families in another one. We can conceive his response through the lens of stranger intimacy, which Shah, building on Michael Warner and others, describes as "another model of 'human closeness' that was distinct from family and institutional relationships" and has the potential to "recast the values and practices of association . . . [in ways] that can bring democratic community into being."[135] Shah's conceptualization of stranger intimacy questions the normalization of racialized heteronormativity that underpins public spheres and expected civic intimacies and insists on the possibility or active presence of other, queer intimacies.[136] Queer intimacies include not just intimacies among self-identified queer people but also intimacies that refuse to adhere to normative boundaries, as was evident when Alcaraz Ochoa identified with and acted in solidarity with Huerta and his family.

Shah argues that racialized cisheteronormativity as the model for civic life "aggravate[s] the experience of estrangement for transient migrants" and enhances their vulnerability.[137] The concept of estrangement is especially helpful for grasping the dynamics of the situation into which Alcaraz Ochoa intervened: "'Estrangement' is an active process of forcible dislocation, removing people from 'an accustomed place or set of associations,' souring the grounds of shared 'membership' by sowing feelings of hostility, distrust, and 'unsympathetic and indifferent' regard."[138] Huerta's, López's, and the children's experiences reflect the continual working of deportation logics and processes that actively estrange and remove people from places and associations. For such estrangement to become normalized requires people to buy into and participate in models of racialized cisheteronormativity and the associational ties that these models presume, promote, and enforce. When Alcaraz Ochoa turned toward Huerta and identified with his terrible predicament, he refused dominant associational models that position Huerta as estrangable and disposable. Alcaraz Ochoa's refusal insisted on the possibility of other, queer kinds of associational models where undocumented migrants, racialized citizens, and mixed-status families are not disposable.

Alcaraz Ochoa's turn toward Huerta and the terrified family on the side of the road involved not just identification but action. He tried intervening into the infrastructure of enforcement that "sour[s] the grounds" among people while promoting hostility, indifference, and a lack of sympathy toward situations like Huerta's. His strategy for disrupting the unfolding deportation was simple but effective: he rolled under the wheels of the Border Patrol van, preventing it from leaving. His cell phone offered a critical technology for documenting what was happening and summoning witnesses and supporters. Alcaraz Ochoa's intervention can be conceived as acting in solidarity; solidarities, in turn, both stem from and continually produce intimacies.[139] As Kate Siegfried explains, "Intimacy . . . gestures beyond the individual to a shared relationship," and to feel intimate involves "turning toward" objects, people, or relationships, including those based on political solidarities.[140] Alcaraz Ochoa's work in Tucson had deeply immersed and continually involved him in extending solidarities that problematized the material and symbolic relations of force and violent intimacies that undergirded that traffic stop.

Alcaraz Ochoa's turn toward Huerta and efforts to interrupt the deportation machine were further significant because Alcaraz Ochoa was a legal resident, not a citizen. Norms of racialized, cisheteronormative, good citizenship expect legal residents to distance and dissociate themselves from situations such as Huerta's—not express and enact identification. By acting in support of Huerta and his family, Alcaraz Ochoa not only enacted identification but risked bodily harm. He also risked being charged with obstructing official efforts to arrest and deport a migrant.[141] This is a felony; noncitizens, including legal residents like Alcaraz Ochoa, may face serious immigration consequences, including deportation, for such charges. This risk shows that normative good citizenship is partly compelled by threats of criminalization and deportation directed at noncitizens, which makes Alcaraz Ochoa's actions even more extraordinary.

Methods, Materials, and Upcoming Chapters

This book builds on my previous works, which put Michel Foucault's scholarship in dialogue with critical ethnic, queer of color, and migration studies in order to theorize sexuality as a key axis of struggle among states, migrants, and citizens in the context of migration controls.[142] Together, the works refuse dominant narratives that posit state migration regimes as natural, self-evidently justifiable, and without history and use queer of color and other theory to historicize the emergence of these state regimes, grasp the multiscalar relations of power and violence in which they are implicated, underscore that migrant struggles are integrally related to nation-state citizenship regimes, and demand other ways of organizing the world.

This book continues that trajectory while engaging and extending deportation scholarship, specifically. I incorporate materials by and about queer- and transgender-identified migrants into deportation scholarship that frequently ignores questions of how sexual and gender logics, in their intersections with racial, capitalist, and geopolitical hierarchies, shape deportation regimes. The materials offer snapshots of and information about queer- and trans-identified migrants' experiences of deportation, which I contextualize through reference to broad-ranging scholarship about the migration and deportation systems overall. The book's main purpose, however, is not to provide a representation of individual or collective queer and trans migrant lives. Rather, centering materials by and about queer and trans migrants, the book sketches an argument about the necessity of abolishing the deportation system. To make that argument, I center material by and about queer and trans migrants for several reasons.

First, the materials offer insight, information, and knowledge about contesting and abolishing deportation that deserve serious consideration, which I provide. Second, the book explores insights that emerge when queer and trans people are centered rather than sidelined in discussions of deportation—centered in a manner that does not silo them from everyone else yet does not ignore the ways that self-identifying or being perceived by others as queer or trans makes material differences to one's life and possibilities. By taking this approach, the book refuses to essentialize modernist sexual and gender identity categories that serve the state, including its migration regimes, or to silo people based on state categories; at the same time, the book acknowledges that the categories have deeply meaningful material, symbolic, and psychic effects and honors that people variously claim and mobilize these categories for important, life-building reasons. As chapters show, states also mobilize these categories for outcomes that range from repressive to reformist.

Third, the book offers "infrastructures" and "intimacies" as broad heuristics through which to grasp important work that has been done to contest deportation and to explore various possible interventions. Its analysis draws from well-established migration scholarship concerning the intimacies of families/kin, domestic work, and sex work, but it extends scholarship by centering materials by and about queer- and trans-identified migrants and allies contesting deportation through varied intimacies while inviting readers to imagine and work toward abolition. This approach builds on histories whereby queer- and trans-identified people's intimacies have provided the basis for stigma, criminalization, policing, incarceration, abandonment, and discrimination—and resistance and transformative world-making. Centering intimacies while highlighting writings by and about queer- and transgender-identified people's mobilizations against deportation does not mean replacing a focus on sexualities and genders with a focus on intimacies; rather, it tracks all these together to build bridges between scholarship and broaden how issues are framed. Since few of us live outside the prison house of normative genders and sexualities, the analysis applies not just to queer and trans folks but to people more generally. As Sarah Haley underscores, "Abolition incorporates critique of the heteronormative and white supremacist notions of gender and sexuality that slavery instantiated and that carceral discourses and modes of policing and containment have reproduced and entrenched," including about intimacies.[143]

Each chapter centers key configurations of intimacies on which deportation systems—and related migration-control and citizenship regimes—depend and ways that people have sought to mobilize intimacies to challenge these. In the process, activists and theorists have advanced new visions and configurations of possible intimacies that not only challenge deportation but also rework what migration control and citizenship could mean. This is queer work, where *queer* is understood not as a personal identity or identification but as an analytic and political horizon.

Queer analytics have been rightly critiqued for often ignoring, eliding, or being actively hostile to trans experiences and priorities. Yet *queer* has also been used in trans-affirming and inclusive ways. Marquis Bey and Jesse A. Goldberg's introduction to the special issue of *GLQ: A Journal of Lesbian and Gay Studies* "Queer Fire: Liberation and Abolition" offers a generative example. These authors explain that the special issue articulates abolition and queerness in a radical manner "where abolition is not affixed to certain 'bad' institutions but is a pervasive call for the eradication of carcerality; where queerness is not merely non-het, non-cis 'identity' but a political posture subversive of normativity, hegemony, and power."[144] Bey and Goldberg continue, "Abolition and queerness, taken together, name the eradication of the current terms of order imposed by racial capitalism as ongoing settler-colonial structure," including "the end of gender, sexuality, class, and race as structures of the world as such."[145] In other words, their vision of queerness does not depend on but seeks to dismantle gender and sexual norms that articulate racial capitalist and settler colonial systems. Echoing their framing, this book comprises a queer studies project framed in a trans-inclusive way that interrogates normalized binary genders and pays close attention to not only links between but also distinctions among queer and trans histories of migration. More explicitly than my two previous books, this book argues that abolition rather than reform of the system offers the only possible horizon for a livable future that allows thriving not just for migrants but also for citizens.

I write as a white, queer migrant who came to the United States from the Irish Republic in the 1980s. I had the privilege of legal status while many of my peers struggled with being undocumented, exploitable, and deportable. In an assertion of control over who counted as properly "Irish" that reiterated white, patriarchal gender and sexual norms, queer-identified Irish migrants were barred by establishment Irish Americans from Saint Patrick's Day parades in New York and elsewhere. In the 1990s, lobbying by the Irish government in conjunction with white backlash in the United States opened pathways for undocumented Irish migrants, but relatively few others, to legalize in large numbers. The creation of legalization possibilities underscored that migrant statuses are products of changing configurations of politics and power rather than reflective of essential qualities or characteristics of migrants themselves. The legalization programs, which allowed substantial numbers of Irish but not Mexican or Filipino or many other migrants to legalize, also highlighted the enduring racism that undergirds US migration regimes.

The ways that Irish government lobbying converged with and supported rather than challenged US white backlash underscored that racist migration policies are reproduced through transnational, as well as national and local, relations. The multiscalar injustices that render people undocumented, exploitable, and deportable were illustrated and challenged by Justice for the Undocumented, a campaign by undocumented migrants in Ireland that highlighted that even while Irish politicians lobbied for legalization of Irish migrants in the United States, they failed to create pathways for legalization among diverse undocumented migrant communities in Ireland. In 2015, as an expression of solidarity, undocumented migrants in Ireland participated in a group photograph with a banner that wished happy Saint Patrick's Day to all undocumented migrants, including those from Ireland living in the United States.[146] This book grows from my embeddedness in these histories and my conviction that the (settler) colonial, racist, capitalist, patriarchal relations that undergird settler state migration controls, making people undocumented, exploitable, and deportable, must end.

The book draws primarily on materials from the public domain. Chapter 2 also draws on interviews with six national-level policy and legal experts about the challenges of securing legal immigration status through same-sex marriage. These interviewees provided generous assistance for which I am deeply grateful. Yet, the process led me to decide to not seek further interviews—neither from people enduring the violence of detention and deportation nor from activists, advocates, and policymakers who were frequently overwhelmed by requests to both assist migrants facing peril and provide information to researchers.[147] Instead, I embarked on a deliberate journey to find and showcase materials about queer and transgender migrants contesting deportation that exist in the public domain.

This approach allowed me to grasp how the availability of information about queer and trans migrants has changed over time. Until the late 1990s, it was very difficult to find information about queer and transgender migrants—much less information or accounts *by* queer and transgender migrants—because being known to the immigration service as queer or transgender could disastrously affect one's legal status and future possibilities. How disastrously partly depended on one's gender, economic situation, place in the racial order, and country of origin, among other factors. In 1990, however, the United States repealed its ban on gay migrants. Subsequently, queer and trans migrants became inscribed into asylum and refugee law, the ban on migrants living with HIV was repealed in 2010, and laws began to recognize same-sex and transgender marriage as a ground for rights claims, including admission. A small but significant number of organizations headed by and dedicated to serving queer and transgender migrants emerged, working in tandem with other social justice groups that also incorporated attention to queer and trans migrant issues. Scholarship by M. Jacqui Alexander, Martin F. Manalansan IV, and a handful of others laid the groundwork for queer and trans migration scholarship to grow.[148] The available information has expanded, as Ari Shaw and Namrata Verghese capture in their description of sources of information about queer and trans refugees and asylum seekers: "We comprehensively searched legal and social science research databases including Lexis Advance, Westlaw, EBSCOhost, Melvyl, JSTOR, Hein Online, PsycINFO, ScienceDirect, and Google Scholar. We also searched the websites of international organizations, national governments, and prominent civil society organizations that work with LGBTQI+ refugees and asylum seekers."[149]

At the same time, significant gaps, deep silences, and deliberate obfuscation structure what we know. Immigration and Customs Enforcement and Customs and Border Protection practices of obfuscation and outright refusal to provide basic information about many aspects of their operations are among the biggest causes of gaps and silences. Practices of obfuscation—which are extended to shield private contractors who detain migrants under abusive conditions—directly enable the ongoing, systemic abuses of migrants and marginalized citizens. Further contributing, ICE has sought to ensure that records of assaults, abuse, and deaths that have occurred at their hands are destroyed.[150] For ICE, nontransparency and obfuscation also fuel individual deportations (as when individuals cannot get copies of their case files in order to appeal a deportation order).[151] Official information about queer and trans experiences remains elusive and opaque; chapter 2 notes that the government does not collect or provide such basic data as the numbers of people who receive legal status through a same-sex marriage. Martha Balaguera problematizes the way that immigration officials seek to control who counts as LGBTQ, which raises further questions.[152] Lawyers, human rights groups, and others have employed multiple strategies to compel ICE to turn over records and to collect firsthand testimonies of queer, trans, and other migrants, including in detention. Migrants have also stepped forward to provide critical information, often at great risk.

Thus, the book builds on information that is publicly available while wrestling with silence and unknowability. Chapters especially highlight what queer and trans migrant individuals and organizations have said through press releases, media interviews, reports, and biographies about detention and deportation, treating these materials as key information to which scholars must attend. This approach responds to queer and trans migrants' calls to listen to and be guided by their analysis (similar to calls by abolitionist and other scholars for shifts in what gets recognized as knowledge and who is affirmed as a knowledge producer).[153] Materials also include congressional debates, hearings, and briefings related to detention and deportation; implementation memos, training handbooks, and policy documents that describe how to operationalize current detention and deportation policies; press releases, reports, websites, social media posts, and YouTube videos by queer and transgender migrant individuals and groups challenging detention and deportation; materials by major pro- and anti-immigrant groups; news articles; reports about detention conditions; and information from lawsuits against the government. Chapter 1 is also informed by the year that I spent as a volunteer instructor for a citizenship course at Pima Community College in Tucson, Arizona. Creative and artistic works remain largely beyond the book's scope. Rather than claiming to represent anyone or reveal personal experiences, the book seeks to raise questions and reframe critical debates.

The chapters particularly center materials by and about queer and trans migrants from Mexico and Central and South America, while making reference to migrants from other regions. That focus reflects the fact that, from 2014 to 2018, when I drafted most of the book, materials that were most visible and available in the public domain particularly concerned deportable queer and trans migrants from Mexico and the Americas. That does not mean that queer and trans migrants from other regions were not also enduring the struggles described in this book; they were. Emerging activism and scholarship—such as the work by the Black LGBTQIA+ Migrant Project and reports on the racist abuse, detention, and deportation of Black migrants who do not conform to or identify with gender binaries—contribute knowledge about other histories and their connections to and differences from the histories described in this book.

The overrepresentation of materials about migrants from Mexico and the Americas also reflects that, historically, US deportation has overwhelmingly focused on people from these regions and the Caribbean. Immigration laws since the 1920s and asylum laws since the 1980s have made it especially difficult for people from these regions to get legal status, while at the same time, the deportation system further developed racist, repressive, and abusive norms by targeting them—not just at the borders but also from within the United States.

The vast amount of materials in the public domain concerning migrants from Mexico, the Americas, and the Caribbean, and the fact that deportation has disproportionately fallen on these groups, reflects interlinked processes; media and politicians continually focus on Mexicans and people from the Americas and Caribbean as constituting what Mae M. Ngai describes as "iconic illegal aliens," which keeps enforcement and deportation especially focused on these groups in a self-perpetuating, racializing, and neocolonial spiral that gets extended to other groups, too.[154] The materials most available to me reflect these dynamics—and from within these, I selected materials that engage the dynamics.

A note of caution is warranted, however: people coming from Mexico, the Americas, and the Caribbean are included in official records, most media, and congressional materials based on their countries of origin and state-generated racial/ethnic taxonomies. As Shannon Speed describes, this approach "disappears" the fact that the migrants include people from Indigenous nations: "The erasure of Indigenous migrants' identity as Indigenous people is one of a long series of technologies used by settler states to eliminate Indigenous people."[155] The materials I used for the book have, in some instances, likely encased Indigenous and other histories within settler nation-state categories, and future work will urgently need to address how to critically open up this issue.

Chapters in the book center on key chokepoints in the migration-control infrastructure around which queer and trans migrants and allies have particularly mobilized to contest deportation while revisioning intimacies. Chapter 1 analyzes a 2013 bipartisan proposal to provide a pathway to citizenship to many of the estimated 11 million undocumented migrants living in the United States at that time. I argue that the proposed pathway, as a cultural logic and material infrastructure, seemed generous but nonetheless cemented interconnections between citizenship as an imagined intimacy among strangers and mandatory migrant deportability. The *Blue Ribbon Commission Report on Deportation*, which was produced by undocumented and formerly undocumented migrants, including queer people, comprised a queer counterproposal that refused the logic of a linear pathway toward an imagined future of citizenship that would likely never come for most people, while demanding an immediate end to deportations.[156] As pathway proposals continue being debated in Congress, the *Report*'s arguments remain critical.

Chapter 2 focuses on marriage, a privileged and recognized intimacy that the state actively fosters to reinforce normative citizenship and nation-making. Centering a citizen man (Tom Swann) trying to prevent the deportation of his undocumented husband (Guillermo Hernández), the chapter extends marriage migration scholarship by exploring how immigration laws mandating that marriages must be grounded in love enable attrition, detention, and deportation logics and infrastructures to flourish. The Swann/Hernández case, which involved the first-ever same-sex wedding in an immigrant detention center, highlights that deportation logics differently affect migrant and citizen spouses within a marriage and that married love often does not prevent deportation.

Chapter 3 explores traffic-related interactions, which have become key infrastructures through which vast numbers of people become routed into deportation. Drawing on Sara Ahmed's concept of an affective economy, the chapter explores how attrition and deportation logics turn driving into an experience of risk and jeopardy that fosters fear, isolation, and hopelessness while materially wearing down bodies and stripping away ties and resources.[157] In response, undocumented migrants, many of them queer-identified youth of color, innovated a logic of "undocumented and unafraid" to counter experiences of fear and terror while driving and undertaking other activities in the public sphere. The UndocuBus project, in which more than forty undocumented people rode a bus from Arizona to the Democratic National Convention in Charlotte, North Carolina, in the summer of 2012, used both the bus and riders' bodies to circulate "undocumented and unafraid" as a framework that summoned new, queer, affective economies, intimacies, and collectivities into being.

Chapter 4 analyzes a 2016 public hunger strike that demanded the closure of the government's LGBT immigrant detention pod in Santa Ana, California, and the release of all detained transgender and queer migrants around the United States. Centering migrant transgender women of color, the hunger strikers connected the abusive conditions that detained migrants endure with the suffering and deprivation experienced by many Santa Ana residents in their everyday lives. They further identified city officials and institutions as having a critical role in addressing these interlinked struggles. This chapter takes up the protestors' questions about what cities can do to foster intimacies that allow thriving rather than only exhaustion, wearing down, expulsion, or death for migrants and marginalized citizens.

The conclusion offers final reflections on deportation infrastructures, queer and trans intimacies, and future directions in the struggle to end deportation and realize a different world.

1

PATHWAYS
Coproducing Citizenship and Deportation

As a queer, undocumented immigrant who was placed in deportation proceedings for over three years, despite having a clear pathway to citizenship, I am concerned that without continued escalation [of antideportation activism], the effort to stop deportations would leave certain members of our community behind. —PRERNA LAL, from #Not1More Deportation, *Blue Ribbon Commission Report on Deportation Review*

Centering on S.744, the Border Security, Economic Opportunity, and Immigration Modernization Act, a bipartisan bill that offered a pathway to legal status and eventual citizenship for undocumented people in the United States, this chapter explores how nation-state citizenship requires deportability even when governments seem to be doing generous things like providing pathways for migrant admission, legalization, or naturalization. S.744, which passed the Senate in 2013 but died after House Speaker John Boehner refused to introduce it for debate in the House, was a significant effort at immigration reform. The bill offered a means to address the predicament facing some 11–12 million undocumented migrants who lived, worked, had families, and belonged to communities in the United States, often for more than a decade, but who remained deportable. The bill offered migrants a pathway to overcoming undocumented status and eventually becoming citizens.

The quote by Prerna Lal, who was an undocumented queer migrant when s.744 was introduced and has since become a naturalized citizen, highlights that possibilities for deportability and citizenship may coexist in a person's life. Her experience suggests that whether someone ends up as undocumented or with citizenship is not predetermined and does not reflect any person's essential character or worthiness. Instead, these possibilities shift depending on larger political forces, laws, and policies; how laws and policies are interpreted and implemented; and how these become modified by struggles—including as queer and trans migrants and other groups work toward change.

In this chapter, I critically analyze pathways as imaginaries and infrastructures that produce deportability for many even while promising legalization and citizenship. I focus especially on s.744, which, although it did not pass, nonetheless reflects logics that are common to pathway immigration processes and bills that had been introduced before and since, including by the Biden administration in 2021. First, I briefly situate debates over s.744 in terms of the histories of state migration controls that coproduce citizenship and deportation. Next, I argue that s.744's vision of a pathway to citizenship for undocumented people built on routine processes for selecting and admitting migrants to the United States. These processes are conceived as lines that are open to anyone, but in reality, there are no lines for millions, who remain undocumentable and deportable. Following that, I argue that the naturalization process remakes some migrants into citizens while simultaneously producing others who are deemed unable, unwilling, or unfit for citizenship and, thus, deportable. I suggest that linear processes like naturalization are especially effective at remaking people in these different ways because they promise a desired outcome at the end—without necessarily delivering. Next, I give details of s.744's pathway to legal status, which built on models of admission and naturalization that sought to discipline eligible migrants into neoliberal subjectivity while at the same time treating them like criminals on probation. Yet, the proposed pathway would have ruled out millions on economic grounds, further strengthened enforcement logics, and left eligible people vulnerable to deportation for more than a decade. I conclude the chapter by considering the 2014 *Blue Ribbon Commission Report on Deportation Review* (hereafter *Report on Deportation*), produced by undocumented and formerly undocumented migrants, including Lal, that critiqued s.744's pathway and offered a different approach. Their approach took into account structural inequalities, systemic state violence, and migrants' perspectives and opened up possibilities for reconfiguring the relationship between deportability and citizenship. As the Biden administration's efforts to create a pathway to citizenship for undocumented migrants stalled, the *Report*'s recommendations remain deeply prescient.

Janus Faces: Citizenship/Deportability

Citizenship was originally associated with propertied males who lived in the city-states of ancient Greece. The contemporary citizen, by contrast, is associated with the territorially bounded nation-state rather than the city and emerged after the French Revolution. As described in the introduction, in the nineteenth century a global system of nation-states began to emerge from processes of colonization and global capitalism, and all people became emplaced as citizens of specific nation-states or territories. Nation-states began asserting control over migration across their territorial borders as an expression of their sovereignty. These controls required states to develop the administrative ability to differentiate "their" citizens from noncitizens, the power to treat noncitizens differently, and technologies to reinforce the division between citizen and noncitizen, including through deportation.[1] William Walters explains, "The modern order of citizenship—in which population is divided and distributed between territories and sovereigns, and in which rights depend mostly on national membership within territorial polities—does not reproduce itself naturally" but requires deportation, among other tools.[2] Walters emphasizes that "deportation is more than an unpleasant, coercive aspect of immigration policy"; it is "a constitutive practice, a technology" for producing modern citizenship.[3] Through migration controls, including deportation, states actively cultivate citizenship as an intimacy that binds people into shared nationalist projects, feelings, and orientations that normalize inequalities.[4]

By the twenty-first century, this system, which allows the United States to regulate migration across its borders without addressing its role in generating displacement and migration in the first place, resulted in some 11–12 million undocumented people living within US borders. Many had been in the United States for more than a decade, had deep ties to people and places, and yet lacked a basis to apply for legal status according to US immigration policy. Consequently, they lived under the continual shadow of abrogated rights and possible deportation any time. s.744, a bipartisan bill that offered a pathway to legal status and eventual citizenship for undocumented people, sought to address this situation. Similar bills had previously been introduced and failed; bills seeking to provide a pathway to legal status and eventual citizenship specifically for young people who had been brought to the United States as children (called DREAMers) had also been introduced and failed.

S.744's proposed pathway built on long-standing logics and processes for selecting, admitting, and naturalizing some noncitizens. The next sections argue that these processes rely on straight lines as cultural imaginaries and practical infrastructure that reproduce but naturalize deportability while celebrating openness and inclusion.

Lines: Imaginaries and Infrastructures for Producing Citizenship/Deportability

For the mainstream United States, immigration is envisioned as entailing progress along a linear pathway that culminates in naturalized citizenship. In this imaginary, immigrants apply to be admitted, submit themselves to inspection and registration, and then undergo a probationary period after which they become eligible to apply for citizenship. This kind of imaginary informs both the common charge against undocumented migrants—"Why don't they just get in line?"—and S.744's logic of offering a pathway to citizenship for undocumented people.

Queer, postcolonial, ethnic, and feminist studies theorists and migrant rights organizers have extensively critiqued hegemonic straight-line cultural imaginaries and associated governmental technologies, arguing that these stem from, reproduce, and naturalize hierarchies of gender, race, class, sexuality, and geopolitics that are integral to nation- and state-making. For example, Siobhan B. Somerville shows that nineteenth-century sexology posited homosexuality as an arrested formation that failed to develop along a normative teleology that supposedly culminates in heterosexuality.[5] Somerville demonstrates that these logics drew on scientific racism, thereby cementing the equation of whiteness, heterosexuality, and national progress. Jules Gill-Peterson further shows that white norms of binary gender were reconsolidated in the process.[6] Scholars and activists thoroughly explore how these kinds of linear temporal logics are harnessed to state- and nation-making projects and economic rationalities that reproduce racialized, heteronormalized, settler, capitalist distinctions between citizens and noncitizens.[7]

Despite their embeddedness in histories of power and subjection, straight lines, queues, and pathways are popularly associated with openness and fair play. In the United States, United Kingdom, and Canada, lining up, or queueing, is a powerful cultural symbol of "decency, fair play, and democracy."[8] As

MIT professor Dick Larson, known as "Dr. Queue," describes, "With a single serpentine line, you have the idea of enforced fairness because first-come, first-serve, and that's how it works."[9] Since lines are symbols of fairness and democracy, moral judgments (that are racial and cultural) are made about those who do not follow the line. The pervasiveness of moral judgments associated with linear imaginaries is captured by the common argument against regularizing undocumented migrants: "Why don't they just get in line?"[10]

This question expresses belief that legally immigrating entails merely entering into a line and following the prescribed process, and it makes negative cultural and moral judgments about prospective migrants who do not "get in line." The American Immigration Council's briefing "Why Don't They Just Get in Line?" debunks the idea that US immigrant admission merely requires waiting in a line to be admitted.[11] Instead, the briefing makes clear that historically, immigration lines were never open to all; and even after the removal of explicitly discriminatory provisions from the law, the lines are still not open to all but are structured to reproduce and naturalize the hierarchies that undergird the nation and citizenship.

Historically, US immigration criteria explicitly precluded people from being considered for admission based on imperial, racial, sexual, gendered, economic, and health grounds. Over the second half of the twentieth century, explicit racial, gender, and sexuality exclusions became significantly eliminated from the law yet reproduced through institutional norms and practices. Explicit economic and medical exclusions still remain, and those coming from regions deemed to be security threats are subject to heightened scrutiny that is highly racializing and heteronormalizing.

Along with legally codified exclusions, the United States began to develop criteria for actively selecting those deemed to be desirable immigrants who could contribute to the national interest. As described in the introduction, current US immigration preferences focus on normative family ties combined with meeting an income/asset threshold, employment that is generally in professional and highly skilled fields, significant levels of capital to invest, or meeting stringent refugee or asylum criteria. Each of these preferences constitutes a separate "line" for admission, and anyone who cannot actively position themselves within one of these lines effectively cannot be considered for admission. Thus, for many, there is no line to get into.

Those who manage to fit into an admission line discover that the line moves more quickly for some than for others—including those with $1,050,000 to invest in a business or who are the spouses of US citizens.[12] Conversely, people may also fall out of or become pushed from a line. For example, an estimated half of the undocumented people living in the United States entered legally but their status expired, was not renewed, or else became revoked. Minor children who applied for admission through their legal resident parents may "age out" (reach twenty-one) before their admission is processed, which means they have to start again using a different criterion for admission—if they can find one. This happened to Lal; her parents' process for getting lawful permanent resident status took so long that she aged out by the time they were approved.[13] Moreover, structural inequalities prevent some from being able to remain in line, especially as the length of waiting and the requirements increase.

Overall, if there are lines for immigrating, they are only open to some. Those who do make it into a line may fall out of, be pushed from, or drop out of that line for many reasons (or get left to languish while preferred migrants skip ahead).[14] Effectively, the idea that immigration processes entail an orderly line that is open to anyone is a fantasy. It belies messy trajectories that intersect with structural inequalities, ensuring that deportability twins with admissibility at every step. Patricia Landolt and Luin Goldring suggest that even for those who seem to meet immigration eligibility requirements, the childhood game of chutes and ladders provides a more apt metaphor than the straight line.[15] David J. Bier characterizes the immigration process as "a labyrinth that few can navigate," as shown by his map of the requirements (fig. 1.1).[16]

Naturalization: Coproducing Citizens and Deportable Migrants

Lines and linear processes also compose infrastructural mechanisms for remaking some migrants into naturalized citizens while simultaneously producing others who are deemed unable, unwilling, or unfit to complete the process, which may leave them deportable. Michel Foucault's *Discipline and Punish* offers a classic study of the effectiveness of lines as technologies of governance that remake (or, in his terms, subjectify) people in relation to larger objectives.[17] As Foucault describes, lines striate space and organize people within it. Lines enable authorities to oversee the space and those within it, move people around to normalize and discipline them, inscribe people into records that will follow them and condition their future possibilities, and act on people not just as individuals but as population groups. All of these insights are relevant to understanding the naturalization process.[18]

Naturalization is effective at remaking people not just because of the dynamics that Foucault describes but also because following or staying in a line promises to deliver desired objects or outcomes at the end.[19] That promise keeps people in line even when the promise is never delivered on or there is

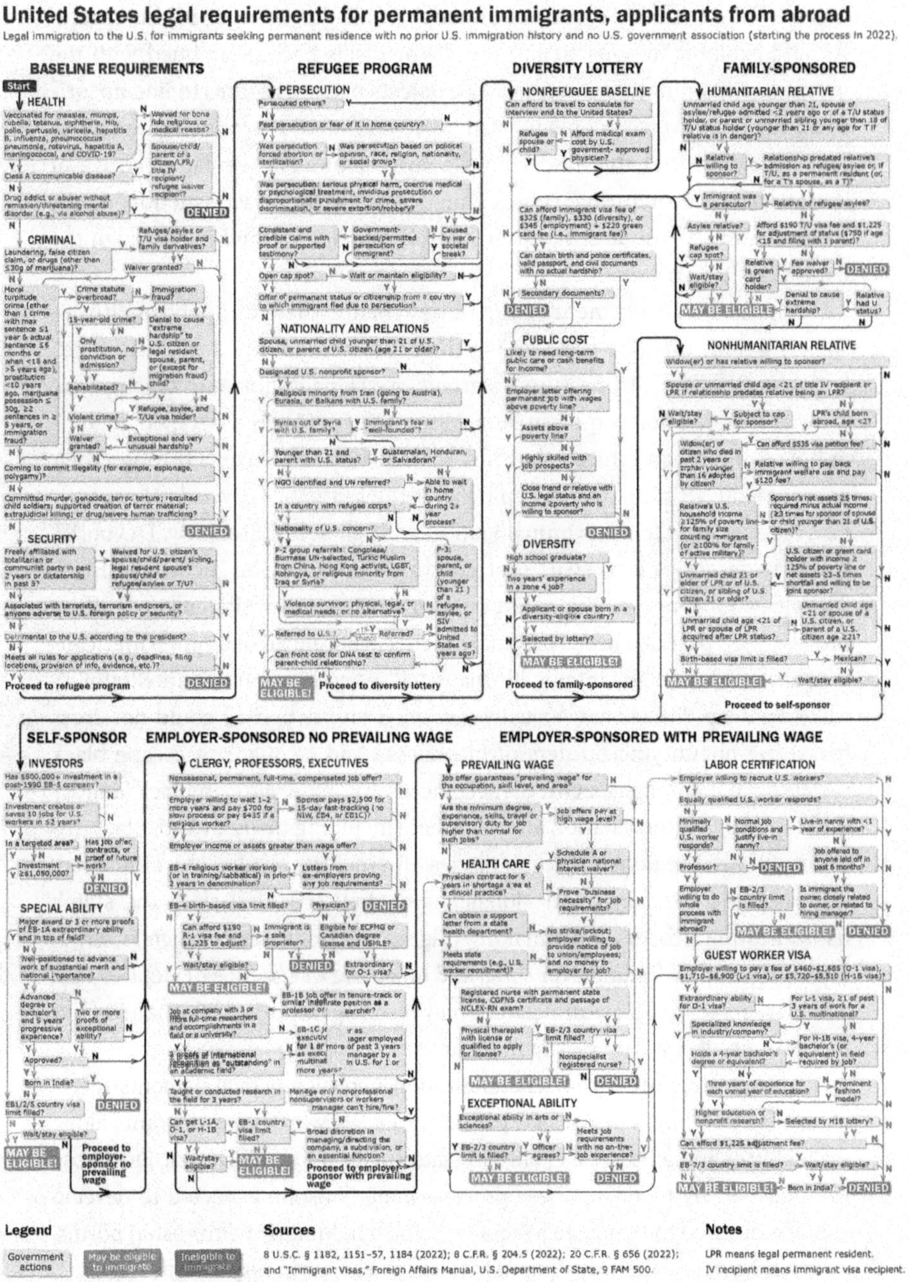
United States legal requirements for permanent immigrants, applicants from abroad
Legal immigration to the U.S. for immigrants seeking permanent residence with no prior U.S. immigration history and no U.S. government association (starting the process in 2022).
BASELINE REQUIREMENTS
REFUGEE PROGRAM
DIVERSITY LOTTERY
FAMILY-SPONSORED
Start
HEALTH
CRIMINAL
SECURITY
PERSECUTION
NATIONALITY AND RELATIONS
NONREFUGEE BASELINE
PUBLIC COST
DIVERSITY
HUMANITARIAN RELATIVE
NONHUMANITARIAN RELATIVE
Proceed to refugee program
Proceed to diversity lottery
Proceed to family-sponsored
Proceed to self-sponsor
SELF-SPONSOR
EMPLOYER-SPONSORED NO PREVAILING WAGE
EMPLOYER-SPONSORED WITH PREVAILING WAGE
INVESTORS
SPECIAL ABILITY
CLERGY, PROFESSORS, EXECUTIVES
PREVAILING WAGE
HEALTH CARE
EXCEPTIONAL ABILITY
LABOR CERTIFICATION
GUEST WORKER VISA
Proceed to employer-sponsor no prevailing wage
Proceed to employer-sponsor with prevailing wage
Legend
Government actions
May be eligible to immigrate
Ineligible to immigrate
Sources
8 U.S.C. § 1182, 1151–57, 1184 (2022); 8 C.F.R. § 204.5 (2022); 20 C.F.R. § 656 (2022); and "Immigrant Visas," Foreign Affairs Manual, U.S. Department of State, 9 FAM 500.
Notes
LPR means legal permanent resident.
IV recipient means immigrant visa recipient.

FIGURE 1.1. Legal immigration as a labyrinth. From Bier, "Why Legal Immigration Is Nearly Impossible," figure 4. An enlarged version of this image is available at https://www.cato.org/policy-analysis/why-legal-immigration-nearly-impossible.

no end.[20] Sara Ahmed's analysis of happiness is illuminating in this regard. Ahmed explores how particular objects or ideals become imbued with the promise of happiness. Pursuit of those objects or ideals serves to line up, orient, and align diverse people in particular ways while reproducing and naturalizing inequalities that underpin the current order.[21] We can conceive of this process as structuring, conditioning, and enabling state-sanctioned intimacies. Ahmed's framework can be usefully applied to thinking through the naturalization process.

From the US government's point of view, before they can apply for citizenship, migrants must be remade (which is commonly framed as "integrated" or "assimilated").[22] To be sure, migrants are remade not only through the state's naturalization requirements; Aihwa Ong provides a detailed analysis of how Cambodian refugees become remade into US citizens through their engagements with the racist, capitalist, gendered logics of workplaces, welfare regimes, medicine, criminal justice, and religion.[23] Similarly, Devon W. Carbado describes how structural racism ensured that he "became a Black American long before [he] acquired [legal] American citizenship."[24] That process was "part of a broader social practice wherein all of us are Americanized and made socially intelligible via racial categorization. My intelligibility was skin deep. Epidermal. Visually inscribed on my body. I could not cross (pass) the phenotypic borders of blackness. And I could not escape black racial social meaning. . . . Out of racial necessity, my American black identity developed one interpellation after another," including through anti-Black encounters with the police.[25] These modes of remaking involve objectification, dispossession, othering, and violence, and they articulate with the state's naturalization process for remaking migrants into citizens, which is structured as linear, unfolding over time, and involving a sequence of steps to take and markers to meet. Naturalization may promise improved life chances, but that promise is not necessarily fulfilled.

Remaking migrants through naturalization involves practical elements: meeting measures along a prescribed pathway, officials who assess migrants along the pathway, and a juridical change of status (naturalized citizenship) for those who make it. By following these processes, migrants are expected to develop and demonstrate the capacities required to match dominant citizenship norms. Citizens, however, are not required to adapt or change in response to migrants, even as many citizens don't particularly approximate citizenship norms.[26]

The United States Citizenship and Immigration Services (uscis) sets the rules for citizenship eligibility and the process to follow and makes final determinations about whether migrants qualify.[27] Those who meet eligibility requirements must file a form (the N-400) that asks for extensive biographical detail, pay a fee, be called for a "biometric appointment" at a USCIS-approved site,[28] and then get called for an interview during which they must demonstrate the ability to read, write, and speak basic English and knowledge of US history and civics.[29] Applicants must also respond to questions based on their N-400, including details of family relationships, residence, employment, ability to be self-supporting, payment of taxes, use of social benefits, and encounters with the law. Applicants receive a written notice of the results of their interview; those whose applications are approved receive notice of the date, time, and location for their naturalization ceremony.[30]

Joseph Turner describes how these requirements ask migrants to engage in "responsibility, self-improvement and empowerment" in order to become naturalized citizens.[31] They are asked "to pay, to learn, to better themselves . . . to work on themselves; to be responsible, to 'improve,' to do what is 'necessary.'"[32] Consequently, Turner argues, "the very practice of learning is more meaningful than what is learnt," precisely because it's about activating capacities and dispositions that are desired by the neoliberal state in the ideal citizen.[33] Migrants engage in these practices because they're promised that this will lead to naturalized citizenship (which they have diverse reasons for seeking).

Like migrant selection and admission, the naturalization process does not explicitly privilege any particular population group, understood in state-sanctioned national, racial, ethnic, class, gender, ability, or sexuality terms. Nonetheless, it rewards those who already have certain capacities, dispositions, and resources. For instance, since applicants must pay application fees (and, in some cases, pay for English, US history, or civics classes) and devote time to studying, the process demands the sacrifice of time and money. Those who already speak English (who tend to come from particular geographic regions and class backgrounds) are already advantaged. The process "works to privilege elite applicants such as highly skilled workers who tend to have access to English and educational opportunities. . . . This privileging of skills and socio-economic capital is compounded by the nature of the examination itself, as it requires a certain level of educational merit, literacy, and communication skills."[34] Turner does not address that racial, gender, sexuality, ability, and geopolitical dynamics also condition who is likely to have the means for undertaking and completing the process, or the judgments made by officials, but there's no doubt that these are fundamental, too. Finally, Turner emphasizes that the process demands sacrifice—in other words, the demonstration of moral capacities that are deemed an important aspect of citizenship.[35] As we know, logics of morality and worthiness attach more easily to some bodies than to others.[36]

In Ahmed's terms, the naturalization process involves producing shared alignments and orientations between populations categorized as distinct and, thus, refiguring proximities and distances (with migrants imagined as becoming more proximate to and less distant from normative citizens over time).[37] The process becomes a means for producing convergence whereby migrants can be safely (from the official point of view) merged into the body of the citizenry. Thus, the official citizenship process is expected to make migrants convertible rather than indigestible or, in security terms, safe rather than risky.[38] Moreover, as Turner describes, "acts of responsibility and improvement" are asked of migrants not just in the name of producing them as particular kinds of individuals but also to show their commitment to the good of the citizenry as a whole.[39] "Would-be citizens are put to work . . . to better themselves, for the health and security of the political community they are 'entering.'"[40] Such convergence and conversion are facilitated by the shared focus on citizenship as a status that supposedly reflects and facilitates intimacies with other citizens.

All of this takes place on terms that are set by the citizenry. As Ahmed explains, "The terms of conditionality are unequal. If certain people come first—we might say those who are already in place (such as parents, hosts or citizens)—then their happiness comes first. For those who are positioned to come after," they are expected to follow the terms that were set by the earlier group. Reluctance or failure to do so can mean that migrants do not get naturalized, and moreover, they become deemed to cause unhappiness or even harm the citizenry.[41] This reveals crucial information about the socialities—and hierarchies—that are re-created in the linear process of citizenship acquisition. The terms on which migrants are expected to acquire citizenship (as a legal status and way of being) are set by those who came before. Migrants are expected to take up and follow these terms, even if they don't agree or find themselves subordinated as a result. Refusal to do so "would threaten the very reproduction of the social form"—in this case, the bounded nation and citizenry—and may lead to rejection of migrants' applications for citizenship and, indeed, result in deportability.[42]

Overall, the naturalization process reiterates that there is a line or distinction between citizens and noncitizens and that the distinction matters in different ways. The process reproduces the hierarchies associated with hegemonic norms of nation, state, and citizenry, even while allowing some noncitizens to alter their positionality and claim the intimacy promised by nation-based citizenship.[43] Noncitizens are expected to alter their positionality through a linear process that orients, aligns, makes them more proximate, and converges them with normative citizens. That process also produces noncitizens who fail in their efforts at convergence and who therefore experience ongoing risks of deportability.[44] Furthermore, many noncitizens are not eligible to undertake the naturalization process, leaving them at risk of deportability.

The model of remaking noncitizens into citizens through a linear process informed how s.744 conceived the pathway to citizenship for undocumented migrants who were living in the United States.[45]

"Earning" Citizenship While Undocumented: The Basics

In 2013, when s.744 was drafted, an estimated 11–12 million undocumented migrants lived in the United States.[46] s.744, crafted by the so-called Gang of Eight comprising four Democratic and four Republican senators, sought to provide undocumented migrants with a pathway to legalization. Legalization was one of four interrelated elements (called "pillars" by the senators) in s.744, which also included reforming the system for legal admission, strengthening systems to verify who has the right to work, and admitting new workers while protecting workers' rights. s.744's proposed pathway built on but also differed from the standard admission or naturalization processes.

By the time s.744 was crafted, restrictionists had pushed the discourse on immigration far to the right. Walter Nicholls describes how "the immigrant threat and borders first" had become the shared consensus.[47] The events of 9/11 and accelerating securitization and criminalization processes had further "unleashed an important expansion of measures to reinforce the southern border and accelerate the deportation of undocumented immigrants."[48] Continually escalating enforcement became the only legitimate strategy, which, as Muneer Ahmad explains, was directed toward "zeroing out the undocumented population and ensuring that a new one was not created."[49]

Those seeking to reform immigration by providing a pathway to legal status shared this eugenic perspective. They differed from restrictionists primarily by viewing "total banishment through blanket enforcement as unrealistic and insufficient" and instead arguing for a seemingly straightforward pathway to legal status for undocumented people who were already in the United States.[50] They did not contemplate that all undocumented people would benefit; rather, the proposed pathway was imagined as offering a means to separate "deserving" from "undeserving" undocumented migrants. The pathway would make good, compliant, safe legal residents and citizens out of the former, while allowing identification and deportation of the latter.[51] The other interlinked pillars of reform, meanwhile, were expected to prevent future undocumented migration.

Even this relatively modest proposal generated significant Republican opposition. Accordingly, advocacy for S.744 became organized around a contrast between amnesty and so-called earned citizenship. The 1986 Immigration Reform and Control Act (IRCA), under which some 3.2 million undocumented migrants acquired legal status, became the most commonly cited example of an amnesty. The American Immigration Lawyers Association explains that an amnesty became understood as "an automatic pardon or free pass, granted to a group of individuals" without asking anything in return.[52] Not only was IRCA described as "rewarding lawbreaking" and demanding nothing in return, but opponents also believed that amnesty actually incentivized, rather than erased, undocumented migration. In order for S.744 to have traction, therefore, advocates needed to separate it from IRCA, which they did by claiming that S.744 was "neither an amnesty nor an automatic fix; it requires undocumented immigrants to *earn* legal status."[53] Moreover, advocates insisted, the process involved a substantial penalty (in addition to regular procedures, which were not framed as penal).[54]

Muneer I. Ahmad describes how the framework of "earning" was deeply flawed because it "tacitly accepts the restrictionists' claim that the presence of an undocumented population is the result of millions of individual decisions to disregard U.S. law" and the outcome of "individual moral failings" rather than produced through structural dynamics that generate migration combined with nation-based laws that ignore the United States' role in fostering such migration.[55] Ahmad summarizes, "This is a pathological understanding of migration."[56] In this context, earning citizenship became not just about eligible migrants showing they could learn and perform citizenship on dominant neoliberal terms but also about showing acquiescence to a narrative that they had done something wrong for which they needed to atone.

The basic process for earning citizenship under S.744 involved a prolonged, highly conditional, and precarious pathway.[57] Migrants first had to apply for a newly created legal status category called "registered provisional immigrant" (RPI). If they received the status, they could renew it again after six years. After ten years, and conditional on border security measures being met (which was something over which migrants had no control), they could apply for lawful permanent resident (LPR) status. If they received LPR, they could apply for naturalization as citizens after three more years. In total, migrants would remain in highly vulnerable legal statuses for at least thirteen years, and likely for considerably longer, since processes of applying for change of status, even when one meets the requirements, generally take years.[58]

The requirements for getting onto and remaining on the pathway concerned continuous presence; continuous employment, education, or income and assets that reached at least 125 percent of the federal poverty levels; payment of fines, fees, and back taxes; and knowledge of the English language and US civics and history in order to transition from RPI to LPR.[59] These requirements not only ignored structural factors that generate migration but also thoroughly ignored structural inequalities in the United States that make it impossible for millions to become eligible for such a pathway, even when they're not explicitly excluded. For example, Peter Schey with the Center for Human Rights and Constitutional Law estimates that the employment and income requirements alone could immediately disqualify up to 40 percent of otherwise eligible migrants who worked in low-wage occupations where turnover is high and employment is seasonal.[60] He further notes that the requirements would likely have a gender-disparate impact, since women remain overwhelmingly responsible for unpaid household and childcare responsibilities, which affects their participation in the paid labor market. Schey's analysis can be expanded to take into account that employment opportunities and pay rates remain deeply stratified by intersecting race, ethnicity, sexuality, gender, ability, and legal status, which also affects eligibility. His analysis also estimates that fees and fines would rule out up to 10 percent; the requirement to pay back taxes, even if these could be estimated accurately, would rule out more.[61]

For those who met eligibility requirements, the pathway process sought to discipline them into demonstrating good neoliberal subjectivity while treating them like lawbreakers on probation. The employment and income requirements, in tandem with the requirements to demonstrate basic knowledge of English and US history and civics, clearly involve ensuring that the pathway produces good neoliberal subjects. But the requirements also involve a conception of exchange that is intended to counter the claims of legalization as something-for-nothing and migrants as free riders.[62] Ahmad describes how the requirements "bear a striking resemblance" to the work requirements imposed on those seeking welfare assistance after the 1996 welfare reform: "The catchphrase for welfare reform, 'welfare to work,' captured the notion not only of a pathway from poverty to self-sufficiency but from moral failure to social respectability. Work was both the method and the goal, a process and an identity."[63] This framework also informed the pathway to legalization. The requirement to pay fines, in addition to steep fees, even more clearly reflects penal logic, a view that those who get on the pathway have done wrong for which they must atone.

The extremely protracted timeline of the pathway was also a significant aspect of penalty. The prolonged timeline was understood both as a penalty in itself and as a practical technology to inculcate "responsibility" into undocumented migrants who were associated with criminality and moral failing simply because they were undocumented. Reflecting this, a White House report described the protracted pathway as a means of both holding migrants and making migrants responsible. The very lengthy process meant that when migrants fulfill these requirements, "there will be no uncertainty about their ability to become U.S. citizens."[64] Marco Rubio, one of the Gang of Eight, described that during this protracted timeline, which would last at least thirteen years and likely much longer, migrants would be "treat[ed] like lawbreakers who need to watch their step" and deported if they set a foot wrong.[65]

Waiting longer and steadily working to earn status were also the means through which migrants were expected to publicly acquiesce to the narrative that they had done something wrong and to show their willingness to make it right. Waiting symbolized public atonement that allowed migrants to become reconciled with the imagined moral community of the citizenry. The expectation of atonement was explicit in the requirement that, after six years minimum as RPIS, they had to go to "the *back* of the line" to start applying for LPR status, behind all those who already had applications in process.[66] Going to the back of the (imagined) line was a symbolically important aspect of accepting negative judgments and publicly demonstrating remorse and renewed commitment to the rules.[67] Yet, the "back of the line" phrase suggests how moral logics were entangled with racial, gender, and economic logics, since the phrase evokes the US history of forcing people of color to sit at the back of the bus and occupy segregated spaces, requiring servants and the poor to enter through the backs of houses, and expecting women to eat after men and children, which underscores that this moral economy is inextricable from multiple forms of hierarchy.[68]

Overall, the regularization process, including its protracted timeline, was presented as a moral logic and practical technology to, in Ahmed's words, "turn" migrants away from "lawbreaking" and toward following the rules (that have been set by citizens and their political representatives).[69] In the process, the idea that citizens set the rules that others must follow (including where entry into the nation-state is concerned) is reinforced. Adhering to a process of regularization that was conceived as linear demonstrated migrants' willingness and ability to engage in fair play and democracy, as defined by those rules. The fact that the overwhelming majority of citizens in whose name these rules were proposed had not earned their citizenship status but inherited it through either birthright or descent was ignored and implicitly affirmed. As Joseph H. Carens describes, "Being born a citizen" in a Global North nation-state is a form of inherited privilege that "greatly enhances one's life prospects."[70] Programs like pathways to citizenship thoroughly reproduce and naturalize these inequalities even while claiming to offer opportunities. Moreover, by never questioning the moral logics of unearned citizenship, yet questioning the morality of migrants who are required to earn legal status and citizenship, the process enables the ongoing racialization and criminalization of migrants.

As if this were not problematic enough, the proposed pathway would not just reproduce but further sharpen the distinctions between citizens and noncitizens through heightened extraction. Migrants who embarked upon the pathway were not just required to maintain continuous employment under exploitative conditions; they were also barred from accessing public benefits, including health insurance through the Affordable Care Act, even though they paid into and helped to sustain these services through their taxes. Schey argues that these conditions, in tandem with the protracted timeline of the pathway, "will create a long-standing and large sub-class of families and workers living in conditions akin to apartheid, unable to vote, with many tied to exploitative employment situations they cannot leave for fear of becoming ineligible for renewal of temporary status or adjustment to permanent resident status in the future."[71] Thus, we can understand the pathway process as one that does not necessarily erase citizen/noncitizen distinctions but instead may sharpen them.[72] Earning citizenship through such a pathway entails prolonged stripping away and dispossession rather than earning, as conventionally understood.

The proposed pathway was also linked to the other three pillars in ways that further expanded enforcement, detention, and deportation practices that operated with little oversight or accountability. s.744 required "major increases in high tech enforcement along the US-Mexico border, elimination of certain family-based visas, no amelioration of highly punitive provisions adopted by Congress in 1996 (that among other things block long-term residents with U.S. family members from legalizing their status), a sprawling new DHS data network collecting information on almost every worker in the country regardless of citizenship, and huge new domestic enforcement, all in effect amounting to a 'zero tolerance' policy for undocumented immigrants going forward."[73]

Because the pillars were interrelated, migrants could not begin seeking LPR status until certain "triggers," which had nothing to do with migrants' actions, were met. The triggers involved certifying that various southern border security measures were in place and working and that there were systems of employment verification and entry/exit in place. It was very likely that the "triggers linked to successful border enforcement [would] never be activated" no matter what migrants did or didn't do. This meant that migrants were very likely to never get to try to follow the arduous pathway toward the promise of citizenship, even if they wanted to.[74]

In all these ways, the proposed pathway to legalization and citizenship made clear how thoroughly deportability is intertwined with citizenship that is grounded in white, settler colonial, heteronormative, and capitalist relations. The pathway process would continue to materialize and normalize these relationships while legitimizing the deportation of millions by either finding them ineligible to apply or else ensuring there was no possibility of successfully completing the pathway while blaming them for being deportable. At the same time, the pathway would further expand the state's enforcement and deportation capacities and sharpen the citizen/noncitizen distinction.

Yet even this narrow and problematic proposal, which accepted the restrictionists' pathologization of migrants and ignored root causes of migration and structural inequalities facing migrants and marginalized citizens, was too much for the political establishment. Republicans in the House of Representatives opposed the bill, and Speaker John Boehner refused to introduce it for discussion, thereby ensuring its demise.

Not1More: Queering the Pathway

The *Report on Deportation*—issued in April 2014 by undocumented and formerly undocumented migrants, including self-identified queer folks who collectively describe themselves as a blue-ribbon commission—offered a vastly different approach.[75] The *Report* did not engage questions about pathways to citizenship at all, though its authors strongly supported opportunities for as many people as possible to get legal status. Rather, the *Report* focused on stopping deportation—which would significantly transform intimacies, possibilities, and lifeworlds. In contrast to the pathway proposals, the *Report*'s temporal frame was not progressively linear but immediate.

The *Report* reflected the extraordinary activisms that had been occurring and the split that had emerged between those seeking a pathway to citizenship and those primarily seeking an end to deportation. As Gabriela Marquez-Benitez and Amalia Pallares explain, the latter group "have changed the target of activism, challenged normative schemes that make distinctions between 'good' and 'bad' immigrants, and expanded the presence and voices of those previously absent. They have rendered explicit and public the shared vulnerability of the undocumented community and high-lighted the precarious status of those excluded from deferred action."[76] The Not1MoreDeportation campaign, under which the blue-ribbon commission released the *Report*, reflected these approaches. That campaign coalesced in 2013 under the auspices of the National Day Laborer Organizing Network. Marisa Franco, a self-described "freedom fighter, woman of color, and bad-ass dyke," directed the Not1More campaign.[77]

After Speaker Boehner refused to introduce s.744 for debate in the House, thus ensuring its failure and continued mass deportation, antideportation activists further stepped up their efforts, including by calling for President Obama to resolve the situation through executive action. In spring 2014, President Obama asked the Department of Homeland Security to explore how to make deportation "more humane," an oxymoron that was widely panned.[78] Nonetheless, President Obama began inviting diverse groups to the White House to solicit their advice. As the *Report* describes, those most affected by deportation were not consulted or meaningfully included in the process. Instead, most politicians continued using undocumented migrants' lives, communities, and struggles to advance their own agendas.[79] In response, currently and formerly undocumented migrants who had deep roots in diverse communities, including Prerna Lal, came together to develop recommendations for the president and the nation in the form of the *Report*.

The *Report* was accompanied by pictures of ten commissioners. Lal and Cecilia Sáenz Becerra, both of whom identified as queer, were among the ten. Another commissioner, Angel Hernandez-Gomez, was tenderly pictured with another man, and his statement included that "a marriage license should not be an ultimatum for the thousands of undocumented LGBTQ and queer people wanting to live free from detention and deportation."[80] Other members of the commission may have identified as queer or trans but did not represent themselves as such for the *Report*. The public presence of self-identified queer migrants working in coalition with non-queer migrants is significant and reflects years of organizing through which bridges had been built.

The *Report* can be considered a queer, antiracist, and decolonial document because of its critique of hegemonic knowledge production and its insistence on foregrounding marginalized people's knowledge as a basis for creating a different world. Indeed, the *Report* reflects long histories and strategies whereby marginalized communities reveal and challenge the role of official knowledge production in justifying and normalizing structural inequalities and discrimination. The *Report* particularly reveals and challenges the norm that knowledge produced by citizens from a citizen-centric stand-point should set the terms for US immigration policies and processes. As described in the introduction, that norm has generated and sanctioned global apartheid, circuits of transnationally displaced and criminalized people, the negation of Indigenous sovereignties, and inequalities among the citizenry. By demanding that currently and formerly undocumented people who are directly "impacted by potential upcoming policy changes" must get to weigh in and be heard by the president, policymakers, and the general public, the *Report* sought to radically transform the epistemological relations of power that generate and normalize these inequalities.[81]

In a 2002 review, Nicholas De Genova argues that scholarship largely treats the category of "undocumented" as self-evident rather than as a product of history, law, and power and that it treats the people to whom the category attaches as objects. De Genova argues that this approach normalizes and reproduces the violence of the state and capital and urges that undocumented status, and the lives of people to whom the category attaches, must be critically addressed as "an epistemological, methodological, and political problem."[82] Since De Genova's review, there have been important shifts in how undocumented people's lives are studied, and several initiatives that create space for undocumented people's voices, perspectives, and analysis have formed.[83] Nonetheless, it remains rare for undocumented migrants' words to be treated as theory or used for policymaking. Underscoring this absence, Leisy J. Abrego and Genevieve Negrón-Gonzales's introduction to their edited collection, *We Are Not Dreamers* (2020), explains that the collection breaks new ground because "it is not a collection of testimonies, narrative reflections, or first-person essays" but rather a collection of "empirical and theoretical work by undocumented or recently undocumented scholars."[84]

The *Report*, too, broke new ground by centering recommendations made by noncitizens who were directly affected by the policies that were being considered. In so doing, it directly challenged the dominant system for producing knowledge that underpins and legitimizes US migration policy. The form in which this intervention took place is also significant. The *Report*'s authors cast themselves as members of a blue-ribbon commission and the *Report* as the result of the blue-ribbon commission's work. Wikipedia defines a blue-ribbon commission as a group of "exceptional people appointed to investigate, study or analyze a given question."[85] The "blue-ribbon" element refers to the idea that members are experts who are the "best and brightest" for the task. Presenting antideportation recommendations in the form of a blue-ribbon

commission *Report* that is authored by currently and formerly undocumented people thus reversed the hierarchy of authority and knowledge that
underpins almost all immigration policymaking. Producing and disseminat-
ing the *Report* through social and mass media, and including a "request to
meet with the President to discuss the findings" and to let him "hear directly
from those who are impacted by potential upcoming policy changes," radically challenged the norm that knowledge produced by citizens or from a
citizen-centric point of view should set the terms for US migration policy.[86]

Like s.744, the *Report* offers a way forward. Unlike s.744, the *Report*'s approach is based on addressing power, violence, and structural inequalities.
Arguing that "the President must take action to address the root causes of
migration to the United States," the *Report* describes how free trade agreements like NAFTA cause "massive displacement of workers," who run "the
gauntlet of immigration enforcement" only to "face precarious, often exploitative working conditions in the U.S." if they manage to enter.[87]

Further reorienting audiences away from dominant imaginaries of a linear
pathway to citizenship, the *Report* instead highlights pathways to deportation that have grown exponentially since the 1990s. The recommendations
name specific mechanisms that ensure that, under the United States' enforcement agenda, people who are displaced into migration but cannot get legal
status become transformed into deportable noncitizens living under highly
abusive conditions. The *Report* offers recommendations for changing or entirely rolling back these mechanisms: ending collaboration between local law
enforcement and ICE; ending Secure Communities, the Criminal Alien Program, and 287(g) agreements that involve collaboration; ending agreements
between rogue sheriffs and local law enforcement agencies that undermine
civil, labor, and human rights; ending ICE home and community raids; ending Operation Streamline; terminating federal contracts with private prison
contractors; eliminating the detention bed quota and curtailing the use of
detention; improving "deplorable" conditions in detention facilities; and expanding protections for vulnerable detainees, including pregnant women,
people living with HIV, transgender people, and people with disabilities, who
"face especially horrific and dehumanizing conditions."[88] The *Report* also
recommends reining in Customs and Border Protection and taking action
to end migrant deaths on the border. The *Report*'s detailing of the specific
mechanisms through which migrants are being made detainable and deportable reflects the authors' intimate knowledge of the migration-control system.
Their analysis underscores that deportability stems not from any inherent

characteristics of migrants, which is the dominant narrative, but from state policies and practices.

The *Report* urges a generous expansion of relief from deportability for as many people as possible. Thus, it recommends revisions to ICE's enforcement priorities; an expansion of those deemed low priority for deportation; an end to expedited removal for Special Immigrant Juvenile Status–eligible youth (i.e., youth who are eligible to seek immigration status after having been abandoned, neglected, abused, or mistreated by one or both parents); deferred action for people who have filed civil, labor, or human rights complaints; and expanded use of humanitarian parole so that people who have already been deported can return. Moreover, the *Report* urges a very different process for deportations in general.

In the *Report*'s preamble and during the press conference that launched it, commission members acknowledged that the most difficult question they faced concerned who should and should not be deported and on what grounds. They did not want to participate in the dominant logic that divides immigrants into "good" and "bad" (which drives the pathway to citizenship framework), since the division is generally founded on and further legitimizes state violence. For example, the mainstream framework generally accepts that migrants with criminal records should be deported. Yet, policing, and who ends up with a criminal record, reflects the dynamics of a racist, cisheterosexist, anti-poor state. For these reasons, the *Report* authors argued, "instead of allowing a criminal record to be a categorical bar to inclusion, it must be weighed within the entire consideration of a person's contributions and community and be discounted in the context of a biased criminal justice system that impacts communities of color and low-income people at higher rates resulting in their disproportionate presence and more likely contact with law enforcement."[89] In a significant reorientation of the state's authority to deport, the *Report* authors instead put the burden on the state to justify each deportation: "Removal proceedings should . . . *begin* with a presumption that an individual will face hardship if deported, weighing family and community ties first, rather than drawing a hard line of deportability at criminal records. Each individual should have the opportunity and due process to make their own case for relief, but the burden of proof of what makes a person a priority for deportation should be with the government."

Finally, different from the protracted timeline of s.744's pathway, the *Report* demands that these changes be made now. The conditions that maximize people's precarity, exploitability, and deportability require immediate change.[90]

Conclusion

Citizenship is one of the core intimacies of nation-states. Many nation-states have mechanisms that allow select noncitizens to alter their legal status, yet the change must occur in ways that uphold distinctions between citizens and noncitizens and subjectify potential future citizens into the unequal terms of belonging that characterize national citizenship. The pathway logics that undergird US processes for making legal status changes, as reflected in practices for selecting, admitting, or naturalizing migrants, are commonly framed as generous. Yet, these logics demand and normalize white, settler colonial, capitalist, and heteronormative intimacies within and beyond families as conditioning access and belonging to citizenship. By ignoring structural dynamics that generate migration across borders and systemic inequality within the United States, and by asserting that only citizens may decide the terms for progress along the pathway, the pathway process reproduces and legitimizes these intersecting inequalities, which are backed up by deportability. s.744's proposed pathway to legal status for undocumented people in the United States reflected these features, and its protracted length threatened to further sharpen citizen/noncitizen distinctions as a basis for dispossession and unfettered state violence. Proposals for pathways to legal status for undocumented people that were introduced but stalled in 2021 also reflected these features.[91]

The *Report* offered a very different framework.[92] It did not directly engage questions of citizenship or debates about a pathway to citizenship at all. Instead, centering structural inequality and state violence, it demanded changes that would materially and significantly transform the lives of millions of noncitizens who, to varying degrees, live under the threat of deportability. In making these demands using knowledge produced by currently and formerly undocumented people, the *Report* affirmed the radical purposes and fierce dreams that fuel challenges to dominant knowledge production. The volume *Imagining Queer Methods* asserts that such challenges seek to create conditions for making life livable and for queer, feminist, antiracist, and decolonial world-making to occur.[93] Through producing and circulating the *Report*, which is grounded in knowledge from those whose voices are generally silenced as a condition for normalizing the US migration system, the blue-ribbon commission sought to end deportation, which would enormously contribute to transformative world-making and livability.

Although the *Report* did not directly engage questions of citizenship, its implications for citizenship are substantial. Walters shows that deportation is directly constitutive of normative citizenship; Bridget Anderson, Matthew J. Gibney, and Emanuela Paoletti argue that struggles over deportation symbolically and materially redefine the meanings of citizenship as legal status and belonging.[94] Thus, the *Report*'s recommendations for stopping deportation, if implemented, would deeply change what citizenship means—in ways that we can't fully know in advance. At the very least, ending deportation would change the dynamics that seek to continually sharpen the distinction between citizen and noncitizen and to produce new, protracted modes of dispossession and sanctioned violence. In these ways, the *Report* offers possibilities for aligning and distributing socialities, intimacies, communities, and life chances in ways that differ radically from the current dominant model. These changes could lay the groundwork for a world where citizenship is not coanchored by and reproductive of global apartheid, the denial of Indigenous sovereignty, and the marginalization of innumerable legal citizens, which are all backed up by deportation. The *Report* thus creates space for imagining and creating a transformative queer, decolonial, antiracist future—for migrants and citizens alike.

2

LOVE, MARRIAGE, AND DEPORTATION

For Tom Swann and Guillermo Hernandez, their first marriage. For Hank Kuiper, his first time performing a gay marriage inside a federal immigration center. For the United States, the first same-sex marriage of someone in detention awaiting a deportation hearing.

"This is the happiest day of my life," said Swann, 58, shortly after he wed Hernandez [21]. "Happier than the day I graduated boot camp in the Marine Corps." . . .

Hernandez's next deportation hearing is March 23 [2016]. Swann hopes the marriage increases his husband's likelihood of staying in the United States or coming back shortly after he is deported. —GUSTAVO SOLIS, "Gay Couple Wedding a First in US Immigration Detention"

Queer and trans migrants have contested deportation by seeking legal residency through the US immigration preference system. That system offers residency to migrants who demonstrate state-recognized family ties, including marriage, or high degrees of financial or cultural capital, or fit with the state's definition of *persecution*.[1] Centering on Tom Swann and Guillermo Hernández, this chapter focuses on migrants who seek residency through marriage in order to challenge deportation.

Marriage remains a core intimacy for reproducing the US state, nation, and citizenry as reflected in the priority the preference system gives to married couples. Historically, migrants seeking residency through marriage were evaluated in terms of their conformity to settler colonial, racist, capitalist, and patriarchal norms. Over time, explicit exclusions based on race, ethnicity, gender, and sexuality were eliminated from immigration law, even though these logics remain integral to the immigration system as a whole. The law contains explicit economic restrictions, however, that reserve marriage migration for those who meet income or asset requirements and that particularly disadvantage disabled people who, as migrants, are often presumed liable to become public charges or who, as citizens or legal residents, may not have the resources to sponsor a migrant spouse.[2] Migrants must also satisfy requirements regarding health, safety, security, and noncriminality. Officials assess migrants' fit with the requirements through gendered, racializing, and neocolonial logics, including demanding proof that their marriages are based on love.

Queer and trans migrants have experienced difficulties gaining residency through marriages that satisfy normative understandings of love and meet other requirements. These difficulties are exemplified by the experiences of Richard Adams, a naturalized US citizen, and Anthony Sullivan, an Australian citizen, who, in 1975, obtained a marriage license from the county clerk in Boulder, Colorado, held a wedding ceremony, and then petitioned the immigration service for residency for Sullivan. Their petition was rejected in a letter saying that they had "failed to establish that a bona fide relationship can exist between two faggots."[3] A revised letter explained that a marriage between two males was invalid for purposes of seeking residency. Only since 2013 can all same-sex and trans couples receive residency through marriage, and only when they can affirmatively show that their marriages were entered into for love and they meet other normalizing requirements, too.

Given this history and the current requirements, gaining residency through marriage effectively involves participating in a "devil's bargain."[4] Frances S. Hasso explains:

> Reliance on states [including state immigration laws] as the primary sources of protection and support in intimate life has largely worked to rearticulate gendered, economic, and other inequitable power relations, bolster states, reconstitute state authority over intimate domains, and limit possibilities for gendered, sexual, and kin subjectivities and affinities. This dynamic may be metaphorically described as a "devil's bargain" since state-delivered rights and protections in these realms are often

attached to important restrictions and foreclosures. . . . I use the verb "bargain" to capture the active and complex agencies, power dynamics, economic exchanges, and negotiations that exist between state-affiliated actors, activists, regular men and women, and others as these pertain to intimate life.[5]

Centering on Swann and Hernández, this chapter extends marriage migration scholarship by exploring how the devil's bargain involved in gaining residency through marriage is inseparable from histories and practices of migrant deportation.

In this chapter, I first discuss the history of love as a technology for governing migration. I show that the demand to demonstrate love legitimizes not just some migrants' incorporation into dominant norms but also other migrants' inability to acquire or retain legal status and their experiences of deportation. Next, I discuss the 1986 Immigration Marriage Fraud Amendments (IMFA) that mandated that only state-sanctioned marriages grounded in love may lead to admission as a legal resident. The IMFA, however, was unable to affirmatively define what a loving marriage was; rather, loving marriage was defined through contrast with imaginaries about sham marriages that involved crime, exploitation, abuse, or unearned benefits. These imaginaries offered grounds for the intensification of moral and penal logics within which practices of detention and deportation flourished. Couples seeking to use marriage as a ground to contest deportation orders must navigate the fact that their marriages were often interpreted as being entered into for benefit rather than love.

Next, I discuss the 1980s as a time when LGBTQ groups began demanding recognition of same-sex and trans marriage. I detail how marriage equality was often envisioned as incorporating same-sex and trans couples into dominant norms without challenging the systemic, inequitable distribution of power, property, and social value that marriage subtends. By the second decade of the twenty-first century, the national marriage-equality movement switched from emphasizing the inequalities of excluding same-sex and trans couples from mainstream marriage to emphasizing the need to recognize love. After same-sex marriage became recognized under the law, same-sex and trans couples became eligible to apply for legal immigration status based on their marriages on the same terms as heterosexual couples.

Tom Swann and Guillermo Hernández's experience illuminates how requirements that married couples must adhere to dominant norms, including love, connect with migrant deportation struggles. Drawing from media materials about their experiences, the fourth section examines how deploying marriage to contest deportation involves negotiating a devil's bargain. The state's interest in promoting marriage, while sustaining a migration regime grounded in criminalization and deportation, sets the terms within which citizens like Swann must mobilize love and marriage to try to bargain to prevent a partner's deportation. The fifth section describes how the balance of power within which couples bargain for legal status based on loving marriage further shifted toward state investment in detention and deportation under the first Trump regime. In the conclusion, I discuss Jesús I. Valles's play *(Un)Documents*, which asks whether a different bargain, founded on a model of radical love, is possible.

Love as a Technology to Govern Migration

Political scientist Anne-Marie D'Aoust describes how "love is often assumed to be the liberal hallmark of a universally and individually experienced freedom, a homogenising social force that bridges difference."[6] But, she notes, what counts as love and how love is experienced are not universal. Rather, love ties individuals into culturally and historically specific modes of subject formation, as well as broad social, economic, and political relationships. Effectively, love functions as what Michel Foucault describes as "a dense transfer point for relations of power" and an object through which governance is organized.[7] This includes in terms of organizing whose migration becomes authorized, on what grounds, and the relations of governance into which these migrants become inserted.

Since the nineteenth century, love in the United States is expected to become channeled into romance and marriage, which remains the core intimacy through which citizenship- and nation-building occurs. Marriage has always organized and legitimized the inequitable distribution of material goods, legal rights, and social value. Elizabeth Freeman explains that, in addition to codifying gender and sexuality inequalities, "marriage law . . . is implicated in the property relations, racial hierarchy, immigration policy, and colonialist projects that have determined national membership."[8] Marriage therefore not only ties two people together in cisgendered, heterosexualized, class-specific, and racialized ways but also provides the form through which hierarchal social, political, and economic relations are organized and naturalized. In all these ways, the model of romantic couple-love channeled into marriage reproduces what Elizabeth A. Povinelli calls "the uneven distribution of life, goods, and values in liberal settler societies."[9]

Romantic love is commonly understood to reflect consent and choice by both parties in a marriage, and consent and choice are believed to provide the foundation for democracy. As Freeman describes, "The founders of the United States saw marriage as a template for the ideal society in which people freely consented to leadership rather than submitting to a hierarchy."[10] Yet, the ability to consent and make choices was understood in racialized, gendered, class-specific, and colonialist ways.[11] Since its inception in the late nineteenth century, federal immigration law reflected and further contributed to these ideas about which migrants were capable of choice and consent leading to loving marriage and, therefore, whose marriages should provide a basis for legal admission. The Page Act of 1875, which was foundational to the creation of the modern federal immigration system, barred the admission of convicts, contract laborers, and women being brought from Asia to the United States for prostitution. As Nancy F. Cott describes, the law established a contrast between migrant marriage based on consent and choice and migrant sex work based on coercion.[12] Moreover, the law was implemented in a manner that presumed most Chinese women migrants were coerced sex workers. Only Chinese women who could convince officials of their modesty, often because of their relatively privileged class status, gained admission.

The Page Act and its implementation vividly exemplify how ideas about marriage based on consensual, freely chosen romantic love were foundational to US immigration controls that articulated racial, ethnic, gender, sexual, class, and colonial logics. The act not only delimited which marriage migrants could be considered eligible for admission and on what terms but also contributed to the development of state technologies of surveillance and exclusion that later became expanded to a general system of migrant deportation. The act's role in exhorting love-based marriage as the anchor for normative nation-building and citizenship was evident in the widespread discourses claiming that the act was vitally necessary to protect white, properly gendered and sexualized married couples and families.

Subsequent immigration laws further encoded cishetero-gendered, racializing, class-specific, and colonialist understandings of who was capable of consent and choice within marriage and linked those understandings to changing inspection processes, exclusion laws, and a burgeoning deportation apparatus.[13] The laws reflected and reproduced differential migration possibilities for noncitizens and differential belonging among citizens: gender, race, and class shaped who could petition for spouses and on what terms. Asian, Jewish, and Mexican migrant marriages, and citizen women trying to reunify with migrant men, were particularly singled out.[14] At stake was the concern that "if marriage produced the polity, wrongfully joined marriages could be fatal . . . [and] could infect the whole body politic."[15]

These histories undergird contemporary immigration-control processes that bureaucratically distinguish between marriage migrants and labor migrants, even though that distinction often does not hold up in the lives of actual people. Nonetheless, the distinction creates different paths for legal admission, which are associated with different regimes of state assessment and governance and divergent future possibilities.

Those who seek legal status through marriage must prove that their marriage is valid according to the state where it is performed and that it is based on love, not coercion or an instrumental search for benefit, as well as meeting other requirements. As D'Aoust explains, "Good marriage migrants are expected to reunite with their partners for the sake of love, not for the sake of other material benefits."[16] The expectation has given rise to elaborate processes for assessing whether marriage migrants' relationships are based on love, withholding or granting legal status accordingly, and, for those who do get status, incorporating them into neoliberal social relations and nation-making projects. Yet it is important to recognize that there is no universal standard for what constitutes a loving marriage, and no way to objectively determine whether a marriage is loving or not. Instead, couples seeking admission know that they need to curate information and engage in performances to match officials' expectations about love. Thus, Melissa Autumn White describes how binational same-sex couples seeking immigration status in Canada work to produce "intelligible intimacy" for officials.[17] Overall, assessments about love function as chokepoints in the ongoing "biopolitical regulation and creation of a national population" by ordering and sorting among potential migrants.[18]

Scholarship explores how migrants who are able to make their marriages legible to officials on the terms that the state demands become incorporated into neoliberal relations of rule. The demand to demonstrate that one's marriage is based on love, however, also underpins other migrants' inability to acquire or retain legal status and their experiences of attrition and deportation.[19] The 1986 Immigration Marriage Fraud Amendments significantly defined the terrain for that struggle in the contemporary period. Though formed around the model of normative male/female marriages, the IMFA became extended to all marriage migration after 2013.

The 1986 IMFA mandates that those seeking immigration status through marriage must show that their marriage is "genuine." A "genuine" marriage is one that meets state eligibility criteria and is based on love, which is difficult to define exactly. Under the 1986 legislation, a marriage of love was primarily defined through contrast with "sham" or "fraud" marriage, which is described as marriage that was entered into "for the sole purpose of obtaining permanent residence."[20] In a chapter from a practitioner's manual, US Citizenship and Immigration Services (USCIS) acknowledges that Congress recognized "the inherent difficulties faced by the [Immigration] Service" in determining whether a marriage is genuine.[21] The chapter then lists evidence that may be treated as showing that the marriage is genuine rather than "entered into for the purpose of evading the US immigration laws of the United States": joint ownership of property, joint tenancy, commingled finances, and birth certificates of children born to the marriage. Of course, these are measures not of love but of capacity to adhere to middle-class economic and reproductive social norms; yet, these were—and, in slightly modified form, still are—the measures used to guide USCIS decision-makers, since love per se defies measurement. Income/asset and health requirements further ensure that legal status through marriage is available only to those who meet a government-mandated financial threshold and who do not have medical conditions that might involve public costs, even when the marriage is loving. Taken together, these requirements, as well as USCIS's ability to demand information about people's adherence to the requirements and to make judgments about whether a marriage is genuine, tie migrants seeking legal status through marriage into normalizing forms of governance and subjectification that involve not just the state but also their citizen partners.[22]

The norm of "genuine" marriage is produced and stabilized through contrast with "fraudulent" or "sham" marriage.[23] This contrast offers a fertile ground for moralizing logics and penalizing practices of detention and deportation to flourish. As a category, "fraudulent" marriage is as amorphous as a "genuine" one, but it functions as a catchall for shifting anxieties about crime and exploitation that authorize deportation. Under the IMFA, those who marry "for the sole purpose of obtaining permanent residence" are cast as criminal. The crime is twofold: "perverting" the institution of marriage by marrying not for love or the intention to reproduce normative social life but for legal status, and acquiring legal status, which immigration officials describe as a "benefit" to which one should not be entitled without genuine marriage. The discourse of migrants using marriage to gain a legal status to which they are not entitled seamlessly merges with discourses about migrants' supposed abuse of other kinds of benefits, including claims that migrant women birth children not because of love but because they intend to engage in cynical, calculating benefit-seeking through the children.[24]

Under the 1996 Defense of Marriage Act (DOMA), Congress explicitly reserved love and marriage for male/female couples. As federal law, DOMA presented an insurmountable barrier to same-sex couples that included a migrant, since immigration is governed as a federal matter. Thus, even when individual US states recognized same-sex marriages, migrants could not acquire legal status that way because federal law refused to recognize the marriages. However, DOMA provided no guidance about who legally counted as male or female. Until 2002, marriages involving male/female couples where one or both people had sex-reassignment surgery were generally recognized for immigration purposes if the marriage was considered valid in the jurisdiction where it occurred.[25] Beginning in 2002, however, USCIS began denying immigration visas based on these marriages. That year, Gia Teresa Lovo-Ciccone, a transgender US citizen who had gender-reassignment surgery and amended her legal documents, petitioned for her husband, José Mauricio Lovo-Lara, a citizen of El Salvador, to migrate based on their marriage. USCIS denied their petition and the couple appealed. In the *Lovo-Lara* decision,[26] the Board of Immigration Appeals reversed the denial and ruled "that a marriage is valid for immigration purposes so long as it is considered a valid 'heterosexual' marriage between two people of the opposite sex according to the law of the state where the marriage was celebrated. Furthermore, USCIS had a policy that, in marriages where both people were assigned the same sex at birth, the agency would approve I-130 petitions only where a transgender spouse had undergone 'sex reassignment' surgery *and* the surgery had resulted in a legal change of sex under the law of the place of marriage."[27] Tristan Josephson underscores that the decision demarcates trans people as legally and conceptually distinct from lesbian and gay people and "marks a moment in which legal institutions reproduce and reify medical and cultural discourses of sex, gender, and sexuality as distinct and definable normative categories."[28] The decision opened the door to selectively incorporate some trans people into state-sanctioned heteronormativity (when they had the means to pay for surgery and lived in jurisdictions that allowed gender markers to be amended on birth certificates and driver's licenses) while casting out everyone else who couldn't match the rules. The decision also radically failed to recognize the complexities of trans identifications and embodiments. As Em Puhl writes, the decision "led to absurd and discriminatory results."[29]

In 2009, USCIS incorporated *Lovo-Lara* into its *Adjudicator's Field Manual* but interpreted the decision as requiring that trans people must undergo sex-reassignment surgery in order to be reclassified according to their identified gender.[30] In April 2012, USCIS abolished the requirement of sex-reassignment surgery and instead allowed a licensed physician to attest to change of sex.[31] According to USCIS, a marriage was valid for immigration purposes if the person changed their gender and subsequently married a person of the other gender, the marriage was recognized as a heterosexual marriage under the law of the jurisdiction where it took place, and the jurisdiction where the marriage took place did not explicitly bar marriage between a transgender person and "an individual of the other gender."[32]

In different iterations, then, a state-recognized marriage under DOMA remained anchored in (and an engine for reproducing) binary gender norms and racialized heteronormativity, thereby preventing all same-sex couples and many trans couples from getting immigration status through marriage. Moreover, DOMA passed in the same year that migrant criminalization and deportation provisions were significantly expanded, and welfare was restructured to further demonize and immiserate citizen women of color with low incomes while promoting heterosexual marriage instead of economic transformation as a solution to poverty.[33] In a move that further sharpened the citizen/noncitizen distinction, long-term legal residents were also cut off from welfare access. All these changes redefined norms of belonging and possibilities for acquiring legal status or future legal citizenship, including through marriage.

In setting the terms of marriage migration, Congress was concerned not just about enforcing normative heterosexuality and love while preventing fraud; USCIS describes how "Congress was particularly moved by the testimony of numerous citizens whose alien spouses had left them shortly after obtaining residence, as well as the testimony of Service representatives concerned with 'marriage for hire' schemes."[34] This sentence evokes the ways that, in recent decades, norms of love, sex, and intimacy have been utterly transformed by global capitalist commodification and transnational mobility, generating significant anxiety; the IMFA can be read as seeking to shore up marriages in response to these kinds of transformations.[35] But the USCIS sentence also establishes that the IMFA was motivated by concern for citizens, primarily women who fit hegemonic gender, racial, and class norms and who could be seen as supposedly unwitting victims of migrant men who divorced them after acquiring legal status. Migrant women were also positioned as potential victims.

The International Marriage Broker Regulation Act of 2005 reflected further concern with migrants as potential victims of male/female marriages that did not match norms of love. The act sought to protect migrant spouses (generally figured as normative women) from abusive and homicidal US citizen spouses (generally figured as normative men). Subsequent legislation sought to expand the protection of migrant women from traffickers who lured or forced them into marriages or sex work.[36]

Ensuring that migrants are not exploited or abused, including through marriage, remains an urgent goal. Yet, critical trafficking scholarship and scholarship about the ways that humanitarian protection regimes generally serve nation-state border enforcement and security apparatuses rather than individuals offer compelling reasons to be suspicious of claims that demanding love will provide a bulwark against abuse, exploitation, or crime.[37] That scholarship makes clear that we cannot expect the immigration system to meaningfully address experiences of exploitation and crime, or offer significant protection, when that system is itself an important producer of exploitation and crime. For example, Jill Williams describes how, as numbers of deaths at the southern border grew in response to the immigration service's Prevention Through Deterrence strategy, Border Patrol incorporated so-called rescue objectives into its recruitment materials and enforcement mission. In that context, migrant capture became reframed as migrant rescue, which was increasingly figured as rescuing and thereby protecting migrant women who were trapped in situations of severe abuse and exploitation.[38] After rescue, however, most were quickly processed for deportation. Border Patrol's claims to provide rescue enhanced its credibility, garnered more resources, and enabled it to further criminalize citizens who assist migrants—without requiring it to address the US immigration policies that were routing people into these exploitative and abusive situations in the first place.

History has shown that policing marriage migration by demanding proof of love, which is the presumed antithesis of and expected bulwark against crime and exploitation, legitimizes enforcement and deportation, which have been expanding. This is consistent with the ways that liberal love has historically reproduced and naturalized inequalities of belonging and legal status. Without addressing the system of global apartheid, the United States' role in conditions that generate migration, or US laws that leave millions unable to access legal migration status, claims about preventing crime and protecting victims by demanding proof of love are simply not credible. Rather, these intersecting conditions can be understood as promoting rather than ameliorating crime, exploitation, and trafficking.[39]

Hegemonic norms of love and marriage remain engines for reproducing and normalizing not only citizen/noncitizen distinctions that deportation reaffirms but also unbelonging among the citizenry, including when citizens confront the deportability of their migrant spouses. The Swann/Hernández case illustrates these issues.

The Struggle for Same-Sex Marriage: Contextualizing Swann/Hernández

The Swann/Hernández case must be situated within the ultimately successful effort to secure recognition for all same-sex and trans marriages, including as a basis for acquiring legal immigration status. Historian George Chauncey provides a sympathetic framework for understanding how the drive for what was called "marriage equality" began gaining traction in the 1980s. He describes how growing numbers of gay men were becoming ill and dying from AIDS-related complications, yet their significant others often remained unrecognized during struggles with health-care providers and hospitals and at funerals, and their material assets were disposed of as if they were single.[40] By the 1990s, there was also a lesbian baby boom, yet, nonbiological mothers (and, in some cases, the biological mothers, too, when they were known by hostile spouses, social workers, and others to be lesbians) had few grounds to legally assert their ties to the children or their right to have a say in vital aspects of the children's lives.[41]

In this context, marriage equality was often framed as a matter of ensuring that same-sex couples should be able to get married, have their relationships recognized, and access the same rights, benefits, and social legitimacy as married normative male/female couples.[42] In other words, it was a struggle to gain belonging to dominant norms without challenging the systemic, inequitable distribution of power, property, and social value that marriage enables. Nor did it involve extending the material benefits and social legitimacy of marriage to those who were unmarried or participated in households and social groups, including intergenerational ones, that involved love and care without conforming to the logics of the privatized, married couple.

The dominant version of marriage equality generated significant opposition, critique, and counterorganizing. Priya Kandaswamy notes, "The most visible advocates of same-sex marriage . . . often employ a liberal narrative of progressive inclusion that positions same-sex marriage at the inevitable end of America's long march toward equal rights for all and participates in the production of US national identity as grounded in progress, equality, liberty and freedom."[43] Lisa Duggan indicates that such a strategy contributed to homonormativity, which is a logic that links the state's recognition of relatively privileged gay-identified people to neoliberal restructuring.[44] The dynamics offer selective incorporation to some trans-identified people, too.[45] Jasbir K. Puar underscores the link between homonormativity and modes of dominant nation-making that recapitulate racism, gender normativity, economic exploitation, and colonialism: "The narrative of progress for gay rights is thus built on the backs of racialised and sexualised others, for whom such progress was either once achieved but is now backsliding or has yet to arrive."[46] The editors of and contributors to *Queer Necropolitics* critically explore how these logics leave less privileged LGBTQ people—and those who did not channel their intimacies, socialities, and survival networks into the form of the state-sanctioned privatized couple—available for violence, wearing down, and premature death.[47]

Nonetheless, advocates of same-sex and trans marriage equality highlighted the unfairness of excluding these couples from the dominant marital norm and from the privileges and social value associated with that norm. By 2012, however, according to Myrl Beam, the national marriage-equality movement, drawing on market research, switched its strategy from emphasizing unfairness to emphasizing love:

> After years of utilizing a strategy focused on equality that centered the unfairness of a ban against same-sex marriage, the national marriage movement went another direction, and Minnesota was the launching pad for this new strategy. Based on significant focus-group research on messaging conducted by the national organization Freedom to Marry and the centrist think tank Third Way in the four years after Proposition 8, the four marriage equality campaigns in 2012—the ballot initiative in Minnesota, and marriage referendums in Maine, Maryland, and Washington—instead chose to centralize love, freedom, responsibility, and sameness. As a result, the proposed ban on same-sex marriage in Minnesota was successfully defeated, and voters approved referenda legalizing gay marriage in Maine, Maryland, and Washington. Love, apparently, *does* win.[48]

Narratives emphasizing love rather than unfairness may have become dominant by 2012, yet love narratives were significant in earlier efforts, too. These included efforts to gain support for same-sex marriage as a basis for acquiring legal immigration status. *Family, Unvalued*, published in 2006, was one of the most significant reports to seek such support. The report argues:

> When two people fall in love and plan to live the rest of their lives to-gether, they may depend on the state to acknowledge and safeguard their union: never more so than if they have different nationalities. United States policy is to help foreign spouses and fiancé(e)s immigrate and live with their U.S. partners. But not if that partner is of the same sex. . . . An American man, faced with the expiration of his Venezuelan partner's tourist visa, wrote us: "I am very proud to be an AMERICAN. . . . We are trying to find other options to allow Jorge to stay in the country—we do not know what options we have but with our faith in God—we believe we will find the answers. I respect the laws of the United States and will continue to do so if Jorge's visa expires. . . . We have no intention to break up or separate—this is not an option—it has never been an op-tion for the heterosexual couples. Jorge dreams about being an Ameri-can citizen, celebrating the incredible freedom afforded to Americans, and to once again be proud of a country he strongly believes in."[49]

This normalizing narrative, centered on love, conveys uncritical endorse-ment of dominant settler colonial nationalism, the state's migration regime, citizen/noncitizen hierarchies, and a marriage regime that reproduces in-equalities of gender, sexuality, race, and class. The report's plea to recognize same-sex couples who perform dominant norms of love echoes the logics of the IMFA and affirms an immigration system that coproduces deportation alongside couples whose love has been verified by the state.[50]

Appeals to normative love were indeed successful. On June 26, 2013, in the *United States v. Windsor* decision, the Supreme Court struck down section 3 of DOMA, which defined *marriage* as a relationship between one man and one woman.[51] US Citizenship and Immigration Services swiftly responded that it would accept applications for green cards (i.e., legal residency) based on same-sex marriage. On June 28, 2013, USCIS notified US citizen Julian Marsh that it had approved the green card petition for his Bulgarian hus-band, Traian Popov.[52] On July 1, 2013, Secretary of Homeland Security Janet Napolitano issued a statement saying, "Effective immediately, I have directed U.S. Citizenship and Immigration Services (USCIS) to review immigration visa petitions filed on behalf of a same-sex spouse in the same manner as those filed on behalf of an opposite-sex spouse."[53] The statement was accompanied by a list of frequently asked questions about how the process would work. More-over, those who had in the past applied for and been denied green cards on the basis of a same-sex marriage were allowed to reopen their cases at no charge.[54] Trans couples no longer had to present and be validated as "opposite sex" in order for their marriages to count. Two years after *Windsor*, on June 26, 2015, in *Obergefell v. Hodges*, the Supreme Court struck down discriminatory marriage laws in all fifty states, making same-sex and trans marriage legal across the nation.[55] President Obama tweeted, "#LoveWins."[56]

These changes meant that all same-sex and trans couples became eligible for legal status through marriages on the same basis as normative male/female couples.[57] Effectively, some married same-sex and trans couples would be incorporated into the system's production of acceptable, privatized, responsibilized, neoliberal married couples who are deemed to match the norm of love. Their incorporation was inseparable from the coproduction of same-sex or trans married individuals who are deemed to not match norms of love or are unable on other grounds to get legal status despite their marriages and thus face deportability.[58]

The experience of Tom Swann and Guillermo Hernández, who married in an immigrant-detention facility in California, helps us to understand how requirements that couples adhere to dominant norms of married love connect with migrant deportation struggles. As a binational couple composed of a citizen and a migrant, their experiences involve one common model of how inequalities of legal status and belonging intertwine in these struggles.

"With This Ring, I Thee Wed"

Media accounts relate that on March 14, 2016, US citizen Tom Swann married Mexican citizen Guillermo Hernández at a detention center in Calexico, California. They had met through a mutual friend in May 2015, and Hernández moved into Swann's home shortly thereafter.

Swann was a US veteran who served when LGBTQ military service members were required to be silent about their sexuality or else risk dishonorable discharge under the Don't Ask, Don't Tell policy that prevailed from 1994 to 2011. Swann had a considerable record of activism around demands to recognize and honor LGBTQ military service members. Newspapers wrote that he was legally blind, living with HIV, and often depressed.[59] Hernández assumed a significant caretaking role in Swann's life. Swann shared, "He makes me laugh, and smile, and brings joy to me. He's a very happy person."[60] On December 24, 2015, which was Hernández's twenty-first birthday, they got engaged and planned to marry on Valentine's Day 2016 at a Palm Springs golf course.

Hernández had lived in the United States since the age of seven. Media did not discuss the circumstances that impelled Hernández's family to migrate, although the larger global dynamics impelling Mexican migration are well documented.[61] The ways that US immigration policies leave many like Hernández's family without possibilities to get legal status have also been well documented. News accounts describe that Hernández attended and graduated from high school in California.[62] Between the time of Hernández's arrival in the United States and his engagement to Swann, at least a half dozen major immigration reform bills—that would have opened up a path to legalization for young undocumented people like Hernández or for undocumented people generally—had failed in Congress.[63] He had received Deferred Action for Childhood Arrival (DACA) status, which allowed him to temporarily work and travel within the United States but provided no pathway to permanent legal status.[64] Unfortunately, Hernández became disqualified from renewing his DACA status after he was "arrested once for drug possession and another time after a parole officer found drug paraphernalia in his apartment."[65] He was also banned from the Spa Resort Casino for violating their minimum age policy. Disqualified as a result from even the minimal protections offered by DACA, Hernández was among those affected by the ways that immigration law increasingly focuses on denying status to and mandating the deportation of anyone who has ever had any brushes with the law in a context where BIPOC, low-income, queer, trans, and migrant communities are heavily policed and criminalized.

Four days after his engagement to Swann, on December 28, 2015, Hernández was arrested again, this time on charges of trespassing at the Spa Resort Casino from which he had been banned. In January 2016, Hernández attended a court hearing related to the trespassing charges. The fact that he attended the court hearing suggests his efforts to abide by the law, even while he was constructed as being outside of the law based on his undocumented status. His lawyer had arranged in advance that Hernández would be sent to a one-year drug rehabilitation program to get his life in order.[66] His older sister, María (twenty-four), described that they "were happy" with that expected outcome and that Hernández had brought a bag in anticipation of going from court to rehab: "His clothes, his hair spray, his mousse, all that was in the bag because he thought he was going to rehab."[67]

After his hearing, Hernández entered an elevator with his bag in hand, but instead of being able to leave the courthouse, he was arrested by Immigration and Customs Enforcement (ICE) agents.[68] The fact that ICE was able to arrest him in the courthouse reflects the existence of agreements between federal, state, and local authorities over the ways and extent to which public buildings and spaces can be organized to support immigration enforcement and deportation. These agreements are contested; the ACLU of Southern California had challenged ICE practices of policing in and around courthouses and ICE had promised to back off but clearly didn't.[69] In a news article, Swann speculated that local law enforcement had tipped off ICE about Hernández. Practices of tipping off ICE underscore the pervasiveness of surveillance, including by families, communities, and random strangers, and the ever-present threat of capture.

The ACLU of Southern California argued that based on the federal deportation priorities that were in effect at the time, Hernández should not have been arrested. These priorities, which had been created after significant political struggle, required ICE to focus on deporting those who were considered to be major threats to public safety, security, and health, as well as on recent entrants.[70] Hernández was none of these. The fact that he was picked up nonetheless shows the gap between official rules and actual ICE practices, as well as the large margin of discretion within which ICE operates. This margin of discretion functions as a criminalizing force that creates and sustains pathways away from legal status and toward detention and deportation.

Hernández was initially held for four days in a Customs and Border Protection trailer where he slept on the floor before being transferred to a detention center in Calexico, where he reportedly spent four months.[71] Swann visited Hernández several times while he was in detention. On at least one occasion, Hernández's sister María drove Swann to the detention center, which was two hours away. A news report suggests her support of her brother and the couple: "He [Swann] is devastated about all of this. . . . I know he loves my brother because no person would do this much for him."[72]

Swann decided that they should go ahead with the wedding even though Hernández was detained. After all, he wanted to marry Hernández, and moreover, marriage might offer a means to contest Hernández's deportation. In particular, Swann calculated that marriage would make Hernández into the immediate relative of a US citizen, which might open up leverage for contesting deportation. The fact that Swann was a veteran would further strengthen the argument that Hernández's deportation would cause "exceptional and unusual hardship" to his citizen spouse.[73] Effectively, Swann tried to use his citizenship status and the ways that veteran status was supposed to generate enhanced considerations to challenge the forces of criminalization and deportation that were bearing down on Hernández and affecting them as a couple.[74] In the process, Swann would test out and further learn about the possibilities and limits of his own citizenship.[75]

Swann and Hernández sought and received permission to marry from the warden of the detention facility and ICE officials. Lauren Mack, an ICE spokeswoman, described their wedding as "the country's first same-sex marriage for a detainee in an immigration detention facility."[76] Diverse media ran stories about the wedding. One stated, "For the wedding, Swann purchased two wedding bands for $38 each on sale at Walmart. Hernández, who wore his orange government-issued detention garb to the wedding, gave Swann a rosary that he spent two weeks making out of plastic he found inside the facility."[77] Other stories detailed Swann's clothing and the process of the ceremony, including "'with this ring I thee wed,' the grooms told one another. 'Take it and wear it as a symbol of my love.'"[78]

Swann and Hernández's marriage was widely portrayed by media as an American story of love, dedication, and struggle. For the purposes of getting immigration status, however, officials' judgments are what count. Advocates have worked hard to educate USCIS about ways that same-sex couples might not easily fit expected norms, yet aspects of Swann and Hernández's relationship certainly risked triggering official suspicion.[79] For example, the USCIS's Fraud Referral Sheet lists "unusual or large age discrepancies between spouses (when found in conjunction with other indicators)" as grounds for possible further inquiry.[80] Even if officials were persuaded that their marriage fit norms of love, the fact that marriage might offer Hernández a route to legal status rather than deportation made the marriage vulnerable to charges of being motivated by desire for benefit. Swann's statements to media about his love for Hernández suggest that he was aware of that possibility and was seeking to preempt potential suspicious and negative judgments about the supposed genuineness of their marriage. The fact that he was intentional is not a reason to impute insincerity to him or to assume the position of immigration officials by trying to seek out some "hidden truth" about the relationship.[81] Rather, as Melissa Autumn White describes, couples learn to anticipate and perform to official expectations.[82]

News coverage trailed off after the wedding. One story says that Hernández received support from the ACLU of Southern California and legal assistance from Centro Legal de la Raza in Oakland, which reflects intimacies and solidarities beyond marriage and family. Another story describes how, after an initial denial, permission was given for him to be bonded out of detention.[83] "He had not even set foot outside the Detention Center when the sheriff's office arrested him for not showing up for at a court hearing in Indio while he was under ICE arrest," which was obviously not possible.[84] Five days later, he was given conditional release but was required to report periodically to the sheriff's department regarding the pending case of trespassing at the Spa Casino Resort.

In 2018, he was arrested by the Riverside County Sheriff's Office for failing to regularly report to his probation officer, which was required because of the trespassing charge. Hernández says that while he was imprisoned, sheriff's officials pressured him to sign a notification to ICE that he was behind bars, and as a result, when he was released from jail, ICE took him immediately to the Adelanto detention center, where he spent fifty-three days. Swann paid $3,600 to bond him out in time to celebrate his twenty-fourth birthday and Christmas 2018.[85]

Marriage against Deportation: Bargaining with the Devil

Swann and Hernández's experiences took place in the context of an immigration system that mandates compliance with dominant heteronormative standards of gender, sexuality, race, and class and demands the demonstration of love in a form that is legible and acceptable to officials. For binational couples like Swann and Hernández, the citizen partner must effectively assert rights associated with their legal citizenship to argue for the noncitizen partner's acquisition of legal migration status. Acquiring such status protects against deportation to some extent, though not completely, since legal migrants may be deported on criminal or security grounds. Since Hernández already had a deportation order against him, the couple hoped that marriage would both prevent his deportation and provide a basis for continued legal presence.

The bureaucratic process that citizens and their noncitizen partners must go through when trying to use marriage to prevent deportation does not challenge the system of global apartheid that leaves people like Hernández without status in the first place and normalizes citizen/noncitizen inequalities and deportations. Quite the contrary: by requiring citizens to assert claims based on their legal citizenship status, the process requires citizens to invest in, take up, and mobilize these inequalities. The process also requires citizens to understand which grounds for belonging to normative citizenship are particularly valued and to emphasize their fit with these grounds to try to win status for their noncitizen spouses. Yet, citizens who undergo the process may come to further experience their belonging to dominant citizenship as precarious and insecure as a result.[86] Meanwhile, noncitizens like Hernández remain unrepresented on their own terms and instead are represented primarily in terms of what their possibilities for legal status meant for their citizen partner's status.

Nonetheless, the privileged status of marriage does provide grounds for seeking legal status for a spouse and for trying to preempt or overturn a spouse's deportation order. Such efforts, however, require affirming and participating in dominant logics that produce deportability in the first place. In these ways, marriage and its deployment to generate legal status and preempt or contest deportation can be understood as involving a "devil's bargain."[87] In situations like Swann and Hernández's, the state's interest in a particular model of marriage, into which same-sex couples were incorporated, runs up against the state's investment in a migration regime grounded in criminalization and deportation. Within that space, which sets the terms for bargaining between the individual and the state, Swann tried to mobilize a loving marriage, together with his own status as a disabled veteran citizen, so that Hernández could get legal status rather than face deportation.[88]

The devilish nature of that bargain, where the balance of power remains decisively on the side of the state, which constantly adjusts the rules of negotiation depending on its priorities, was further highlighted when Trump swept into office in 2017 on an aggressively anti-immigrant, white supremacist, patriarchal, and procorporate agenda. The intimacies of marriage emerged as a site of contestation and further enforcement of the administration's focus on all-out deportation.

Media began reporting that marriage, including between long-term partners who had not previously planned to marry, was emerging as a survival strategy. For example, on December 29, 2016, the *Boston Globe* ran a story with the confusing headline, "Is Trump Pushing Immigrants and Same-Sex Couples to Marriage?"[89] The story opens by describing Matthew Sabato, a US citizen, and Pedro Silva, a Brazilian citizen on a visa, who decided to forgo elaborate wedding planning in favor of going to city hall to quickly marry. The story connects their decision to rising numbers of marriage license applications and wedding planners who were busier than usual in New York City and nationally. According to the story, undocumented migrants who had no criminal convictions, long US residency, and strong family ties and who felt deprioritized for deportation under Obama now worried they might be targeted and were marrying to try to get legal status. One respondent told the reporter that marriage offered a way to "take control of your life" when you're being targeted by racism, hatred, and xenophobia.[90]

As these migrants predicted, Trump moved swiftly to expand deportation while further rolling back possibilities for getting or keeping legal status.

One of Trump's very first presidential acts involved issuing a January 2017 executive order that effectively rescinded the Obama-era deportation priorities and, instead, made all undocumented migrants subject to deportation regardless of their family ties and length of US residence.[91]

The intensification of deportation efforts included policies and practices that explicitly targeted immigrants who tried to legalize through marriage, and it used their marriages to try to capture them for deportation.[92] On April 19, 2018, the *New York Times* ran an article titled "A Marriage Used to Prevent Deportation. Not Anymore."[93] The article described that undocumented migrants, including those with jobs, homes, and families, were facing deportation even when they married US citizens. This was especially likely when there was a deportation order on record against them, as was the case for Hernández.[94]

The vulnerability of those with a deportation order reflected changes in policy and practice. In 2016, President Obama had extended the Provisional Unlawful Presence Waiver process to cover migrants who were seeking to legalize through marriage or other family ties and who had old deportation orders on file, if the deportation orders were not based on criminal charges. Under the Trump administration, however, people with old deportation orders who followed the required process for trying to legalize through marriage found that when they showed up for their USCIS interview, USCIS often affirmed the genuineness of their marriages and then turned the migrant partner over to ICE to detain and deport anyway.[95] In some cases, USCIS deliberately exploited intimacies by scheduling marriage interviews to accommodate ICE's ability to send an agent to detain the migrant partner.[96]

The practice was so pervasive that in April 2018, the ACLU filed a class action suit to challenge it.[97] The ACLU stated, "In effect, the government's one hand beckons Petitioners forward, and its other hand grabs them."[98] This description captured the catch-22 involved: when migrants followed the steps that the government laid out for regularizing their status through marriage, they risked becoming detained and deported. But if they did not try to regularize, they also risked being detained and deported. The ACLU further argued that these practices "reflect a consistent desire to drive out immigrants of color and prevent non-white people from becoming American."[99] All the couples participating in the suit include an immigrant spouse from Mexico or Central or South America.[100]

News coverage makes clear that same-sex couples, as much as male/female couples, were being targeted for deportation, including when they showed up to prove that their marriages are based on love rather than the search for benefit.[101] The stories generally focused on couples where the citizen partner fit into nationalist narratives of valued belonging. For example, in 2017, US citizen and army chaplain Tim Brown married Sergio Avila, who entered the United States from Honduras without authorization when he was seven years old. The couple's marriage was deemed bona fide, and they had received a Provisional Unlawful Presence Waiver. Yet, on May 10, 2018, Avila was arrested and detained when he presented himself for what he thought was going to be a routine check-in with ICE.[102] Similarly, US citizen Paul Frame married Mexican national Jose Ivan Nuñez. On January 31, 2018, when the couple attended an interview with USCIS to ascertain the bona fides of their marriage, Frame was asked to leave the room and ICE entered and arrested his husband. Subsequently, USCIS affirmed that their marriage was bona fide. Yet, Nuñez remained detained. Frame described that "his husband . . . was doing exactly what immigration critics demanded—'getting in line,' filing papers 'the right way' so that he could live in America legally"— and that resulted in Nuñez's detention.[103]

Conclusion

In regard to state-recognized intimacies, is a different bargain possible among migrants, US citizens, and the US nation-state? High school teacher, playwright, poet, and actor Jesús I. Valles has been exploring that question through the lens of the immigration system's impact on families composed of married couples and their minor children. Like married couples, parents and minor children are given preference under the US immigration system, yet that system often ends up transforming, devastating, or destroying many of these intimate relationships through deportation, too.

Valles's play *(Un)Documents* explores being an undocumented person, then a documented person, and then a naturalized queer migrant from Juárez, Mexico. Their undocumented older brother, however, gets picked up in a workplace raid, detained for months, and then deported. When Valles and their mother visit him in Juárez, they find that he is struggling and suffering. The play traces the rhythm of official processes, documents, questions, and normalizing judgments within which these experiences of interrupted intimacies unfold. It underscores that these official processes—the kind that this chapter highlights—constitute state-sanctioned forms of brutality that terrorize and destroy, as much as incorporate, migrants and their loved ones, even while claiming to value families. The play's title, *(Un)Documents*, and publicity for the play explicitly link state documentation processes, and the relations of power in which these processes are embedded, with transforming and often destroying individual, collective, and familial intimacies, whether these are based on law, biology, or choice. The play's message echoes the news stories about same-sex couples who filed the paperwork and attended mandated interviews only to have ICE appear to arrest and deport the migrant partner.[104]

(Un)Documents not only reorients the audiences' attention toward pathways to detention and deportation by highlighting the impacts of official documentation requirements; it also promotes Valles's call for practices of "fierce love" that resist and remake the brutal conditions engendered by state migration regimes. Valles's understanding of love is very different from norms of romantic love, possessive individualism, and the privatized couple or family that are central to the structural reproduction and cultural normalization of inequality through US immigration processes required of married couples and nuclear families. Asked what they hoped audiences would take away from the November 2020 performances of *(Un)Documents* put on by Teatro Audaz in San Antonio, Texas, Valles provided an extended statement on love:

> I always hope that the show will leave audiences with the hunger to find new language to talk about citizenship and migrations. I would love for audiences to imagine a world where we care for one another far more than we care for the nation-states that so often hurt us or exploit our labor and our bodies. I want us to choose to love each other better and far more than we love our countries. A country, a law, a border— all of these things are fictions that cannot love us back. What might it mean to choose each other every day instead? For those audience members directly impacted by immigration policy, my hope is that the performance will help to ease some of the loneliness and silence that so often becomes part of our contract with this nation. I hope, more than anything, that the performance encourages us to make a home, a new country, in and with one another.[105]

Valles's vision echoes a tradition of community organizing, critical thinking, and cultural work, including by Lauren Berlant, bell hooks, María Lugones, and Chela Sandoval, who explore political possibilities for love to bring about personal, collective, and social transformations.[106] Valles's call extends these works by connecting them to the urgencies of transforming an immigration system that is rooted in global apartheid and reproduces unbelonging, exploitation, suffering, and deportation that differentially affects migrants and citizens.[107] The model of love that Valles envisions helps us to apprehend the violence of the current system and to believe that a different future—a different bargain—is possible.

Innumerable couples like Swann and Hernández still face navigating the preference system that positions normative marriages and nuclear families as core intimacies through which official nation-building and production of good citizens take place. Scholars theorize that marriage migrants are incorporated into nation-building and citizenship on terms that reproduce normative gender, heteropatriarchy, racism, capitalism, settler colonialism, and citizen/noncitizen distinctions. I extend this scholarship by highlighting that the preferences also generate and normalize detention, deportation, and deportability and that migrants and their citizen partners mobilize marriage preferences to contest risks of deportation.

Swann and Hernández's experiences reveal the uncertainties and limits of maneuvering from within the preference system to contest deportation. Such maneuvering requires accepting the deeply unequal terms of the bargain set by the state and ensures that contestations cannot easily go beyond seeking official discretion regarding an individual case. Because of these limits, scholars and activists are often deeply critical of how the recognition of same-sex and trans marriages constitutes a reform that sustains rather than challenges multiple inequalities, including the immigration regime.[108] Yet, Swann and Hernández's experiences also suggest that individuals and couples often decide that they cannot *not* try to contest deportation from within the system, even when doing so reproduces the system. As Melissa Autumn White explains, "cannot not" marks noncitizens' complex positionality that cannot be grasped through the political logics associated with the liberal subject of rights; these logics undergird many of the criticisms.[109] Pooja Gehi and Gabriel Arkles offer a way forward by suggesting that the burden of dismantling the US immigration regime, including the preference system that coproduces selective incorporation for some in tandem with deportation and deportability for others, cannot fall primarily on the backs of migrants and citizen relatives.[110] Instead, as the state deploys its normalizing model of married love against couples, collective action grounded in visions of radical love must continue to be mobilized to transform and abolish that system.

3

DRIVING WHILE UNDOCUMENTED

Circulating Fear and Fearlessness

One day when I was 16, I rode my bike to the nearby D.M.V. office to get my driver's permit. Some of my friends already had their licenses, so I figured it was time. But when I handed the clerk my green card as proof of U.S. residency, she flipped it around, examining it. "This is fake," she whispered. "Don't come back here again." Confused and scared, I pedaled home and confronted Lolo [my grandfather]. . . . Lolo was a proud man, and I saw the shame on his face as he told me he purchased the card, along with other fake documents, for me. "Don't show it to other people," he warned. —JOSE ANTONIO VARGAS, "My Life as an Undocumented Immigrant"

Jose Antonio Vargas, a Pulitzer Prize–winning journalist who publicly came out as an undocumented gay migrant, had expected to participate in a common rite of passage among US teenagers: getting his learner's permit, learning to drive, and moving through the world. Instead, the rite revealed that he was undocumented, which left him scared, confused, and ineligible for a driver's license.[1] Vargas's ineligibility and fear connect to a history of how immigration chokepoints that build on the targeting of marginalized citizens have become embedded into everyday routines and activities.

In the United States, which provides limited public transportation, driving is crucial for everyday activities and intimacies such as working, shopping, picking up children, getting health care, and much more. Yet, traffic interactions, which are one of the most frequent ways that marginalized citizens engage with state officials in racializing and (cishetero)patriarchal encounters, have also become a major pipeline to migrant deportation. The connections between driving a car and becoming deported highlight how thoroughly attrition practices that are intended to fuel deportation are interwoven into everyday life. Centering on driving, this chapter explores how attrition practices not only target everyday activities in an effort to make life unlivable but also foster fear. The purpose is both to identify and deport migrants and to compel migrants to decide to self-deport.

In this chapter, I first provide contextual information for understanding how traffic enforcement has become a crucial means for identifying, criminalizing, and deporting migrants while they engage in everyday tasks. Next, I argue that targeting driving, which people often cannot avoid doing, fosters fear and anxiety. Fear and anxiety keep migrants exhausted, stressed, and debilitated even when they are not captured through traffic enforcement. The architects of attrition policies hope that deliberately creating constant fear, in tandem with making it difficult to fulfill everyday tasks, will push more migrants to self-deport.

Struggles over everyday activities, fear, and deportation have played out intensely around questions of access to driver's licenses. Therefore, I then center struggles among states over whether to make driver's licenses available regardless of legal status. A video released by Causa, an immigrant rights organization in Oregon, featured Latinx queer and trans people, many of them migrants, who advocated for making driver's licenses available to all Oregon residents regardless of legal status.[2] The video offers a glimpse into how the lack of access to driver's licenses in a context where traffic enforcement has become a pipeline to deportation affects everyday lives and intimacies among queer, trans, and migrant Latinx people.

In a direct challenge to the use of driving as a means to expand deportation and spread fear, undocumented migrants, many of them queer youth of color, pioneered a logic of "undocumented and unafraid." I describe the emergence of "undocumented and unafraid," which thoroughly contested how the US government uses fear to realize attrition and offered concrete strategies for challenging deportation laws and practices. The UndocuBus project, which is my final focus, exemplifies how the logic of "undocumented and unafraid" summoned new kinds of intimacies, collectivities, and political projects into being. The UndocuBus involved over forty undocumented people riding a bus from Arizona to the Democratic National Convention in Charlotte, North Carolina, in summer 2012. The side of the bus was painted with the bold assertion "Sin Papeles Sin Miedo: No Papers No Fear," and the riders, who risked being stopped and turned over to immigration officials at every stage, used the ride to circulate "undocumented and unafraid" as a framework to build networks, intimacies, and demands for change.

Everywhere, Everyday: Criminalizing and Deporting Migrants through Traffic Stops

Federal officials regularly assert that they are deporting dangerous criminal migrants, which fosters safety and security for citizens. Media and watchdog groups counter these claims using Immigration and Customs Enforcement's (ICE) own data, which shows that significant numbers of deported people have been convicted of minor infractions, including traffic-related violations, or no infractions at all. For example, a report by the Transactional Records Access Clearinghouse (TRAC) showed that between 2008 and 2013, "the most serious criminal charge for half of those deported was for an immigration or traffic violation."[3] Clearly, traffic interactions have become a major pipeline to deportation. However, ICE's characterization of traffic violations as "crimes" that justify deporting "criminal aliens" who would otherwise threaten the United States is not accidental. Rather, as TRAC describes, ICE deliberately "uses an exceedingly broad definition of criminal behavior. . . . For example, anyone with a traffic ticket for exceeding the speed limit on the Baltimore-Washington Parkway who sends in their check to pay their fine has just entered ICE's 'convicted criminal' category."[4] In that instance, paying a speeding ticket, which is commonly viewed as exemplifying good citizenship, becomes reinterpreted by ICE as a de facto admission of having committed a crime. Of course, not paying a speeding ticket is also taken as evidence of criminality. The situation highlights that ICE has extraordinary latitude to create chokepoints in everyday life through which criminality becomes laminated onto migrants, which is then used to justify deportation.

The "terminological sleight-of-hand" whereby a traffic violation becomes a crime that justifies deportation reflects that immigration has become increasingly framed and governed as a matter of crime.[5] Grounds for excluding would-be migrants or deporting migrants after entry have proliferated through a dynamic of "crimmigration."[6] Jennifer M. Chacón explains that crimmigration entails "the intertwinement of crime control and migration control" in a spiraling process that continually deepens the equation between immigrants and crime and justifies growing detention and deportation.[7] Crimmigration builds on a long history whereby policing has systematically subordinated people who are BIPOC, queer, gender nonconforming, and/or low income.[8] What counts as a crime "lies not in the content of the behavior itself but in the social response to the behavior or to the persons who engage in it."[9] That response is greatly shaped by the "social and moral standing" of the people involved and the degrees of power they are able to mobilize.[10] In the United States, white supremacy, settler colonialism, capitalism, and patriarchal privilege have always shaped the designations of what counts as a crime; ICE builds on that history, including by using traffic enforcement to generate migrant deportation.

Traffic enforcement remains the most common basis for interactions between law enforcement officials and everyday people and has long been a lightning rod for reproducing and resisting inequalities.[11] In the 1980s, as traffic stops became a crucial element in the state's War on Drugs, Black and brown drivers became disproportionately targeted. Once stopped, they were disproportionately likely to be searched. Stops and searches became opportunities to attach criminality to BIPOC, impoverished, and queered bodies using pretexts from the vast menu of driving rules regardless of how the person had actually been driving.[12] As police became increasingly militarized and heavily armed, traffic stops resulted in deaths even as terrified drivers sought to avoid being killed. Sarah A. Seo notes that "27% of police officer killings of unarmed [civilians] began with a traffic stop, according to one survey."[13] The Supreme Court sanctioned these practices, making it virtually impossible to challenge discriminatory profiling or patently illegal actions by officers even when these resulted in injury and death.[14] Traffic stops also became an important means for cash-strapped municipalities to generate revenue, frequently by disproportionately targeting Black, brown, and low-income residents.[15]

As links between local law enforcement and the Department of Homeland Security (DHS) became increasingly institutionalized and deepened throughout the first decade of the 2000s, traffic stops also became an important tool for immigration enforcement and deportation. The links include 287(g) agreements that deputize local officials to act as immigration officials and data sharing through Secure Communities, which is a mandatory nationwide program that connects local law enforcement, DHS, and FBI databases. Thus, anyone booked into jail, including on a traffic-related matter, is automatically screened for immigration violations, which may result in

ICE sending a request to local officials to put a hold (a "detainer") on someone whom they plan to take into custody. Some states have further links; for example, Arizona's SB 1070 authorizes local authorities to inquire about people's immigration status including during a traffic stop based on "reasonable suspicion of unlawful status" and to contact Border Patrol accordingly.[16] The Supreme Court upheld this provision, which legitimizes racial profiling.

These kinds of links mean that any engagement with local law enforcement, including over traffic, may lead to deportation. Eddy Arias, a gay, formerly undocumented migrant who became a high school teacher, offers one account of his experience of detention and threatened deportation stemming from a traffic stop: "My nightmare in local and federal jail began in October 2011, when I was driving home from work and was stopped by a Houston Police Department officer for passing a yellow light. The officer asked me if I was from the United States and I honestly replied, 'No.' The officer then laughed and said, 'I knew it.' I can only infer that I was profiled because of my accent. I was taken into custody and charged, without cause, with driving under the influence."[17] Arias spent forty-five days in the Harris County Jail even though lab results showed he was not intoxicated. Since Harris County participates in the 287(g) program, he was then detained at the Polk County ICE detention center. There, "because I honestly answered that I was gay when asked by an officer," he was placed in solitary confinement for a week. Arias eventually saw an immigration judge and was bonded out, but "it cost me more than two months of my life. It caused me emotional and psychological trauma and stress on my family and friends. It cost me my job."[18]

Yet, there is great variation in whether and how traffic stops lead to deportation since laws and enforcement practices vary significantly. Under Arizona's SB 1070, for example, officers who suspect someone may be an unauthorized migrant are expected to perform an immigration check, including during a traffic stop, and may call Border Patrol.[19] In Texas since 2016, ICE has a standing request with the Department of Public Safety (DPS) to share details of any traffic stops related to driving while intoxicated or driving without a license, which may lead to deportation. In some cases, DPS has called Border Patrol directly after pulling over drivers.[20] In other states, failing to pay a traffic ticket may lead to an arrest warrant being issued; for noncitizens, these warrants are easily interpreted as evidence that they are deportable criminals. Yet, people going to local courthouses to pay traffic tickets have sometimes been arrested there by ICE and detained and deported. Unpaid traffic tickets, or misdemeanor charges related to driving, can add up to grounds for deportation not just for undocumented migrants but also for legal residents. Traffic data are also used by ICE when it creates lists of people to target during immigration raids.[21] The Migration Policy Institute (MPI) emphasizes the importance of state and local cooperation or not with ICE, especially through 287(g) agreements, on the differential fates of migrants who get stopped for traffic violations.[22]

In sum, there are multiple, unpredictable ways that a traffic enforcement interaction may or may not lead to detention and deportation. That unpredictability adds to the stress and fear that people experience while driving.

Attrition through Enforcement: Fostering Fear

The multiple, unpredictable ways that traffic interactions can result in deportation, combined with the fact that people often have no choice but to drive, means that driving has become fraught with fear, worry, and anxiety. This is deliberate; attrition practices want to make everyday activities like driving difficult in order to foster fear.[23] Sara Ahmed explains that emotions do not reside in and originate from sovereign individuals.[24] Instead, she argues, emotions function as an economy, sliding between figures and signs and sticking to certain figures around which intense emotions accumulate. Through circulation, emotions do particular work.[25] For example, they stick certain people together through shared orientation toward an object or imaginary and differentially surface (i.e., materialize) bodies, worlds, and possibilities. Attrition through enforcement involves an affective economy that deliberately cultivates and circulates fear among the citizenry toward migrants and among migrants. The fear that undocumented migrants are expected to feel when driving a car exemplifies this.

Nicholas De Genova provides a helpful starting place for historicizing how migration enforcement depends on fostering fear to be effective.[26] De Genova points out that migration enforcement "is never simply intended to achieve the putative goal of deportation. It is deportability, and not deportation per se, that has historically rendered undocumented migrant labor as a distinctly disposable commodity."[27] In other words, rather than taking literally the attritionists' stated goal of deporting all undocumented migrants, De Genova offers a historically grounded analysis of how enforcement ensures that some migrants are deported while others become fearful, anxious, vulnerable, and exploitable labor.[28] The latter live under conditions of "deportability," the ever-present possibility of their own capture and deportation, in which affect intertwines with material conditions to heighten their exploitability and disposability. As Tania A. Unzueta Carrasco and Hinda Seif describe, "The state of deportability, of always being vulnerable to being separated from one's job, family, and daily life, and the fear, hopelessness, and vulnerability this produces, has been highly successful in disciplining and subjugating many undocumented people."[29]

Immigration enforcement strategies have long relied on cultivating migrants' fear in order to achieve their goals.[30] Thomas Homan, who served as Trump's first acting director of ICE, made explicit the federal government's expectation that undocumented migrants should feel fear because their status makes them deportable. In an interview, Homan pronounced that undocumented immigrants "should be afraid."[31] When asked about his comment, Homan extrapolated: "And by me saying you should be worried, you should be afraid—if you lie on your taxes, you've got to be worried, 'Is the IRS going to audit me?' . . . When you speed down the highway, you've got to worry, 'Am I going to get a speeding ticket?' You worry. It's natural human behavior."[32]

Homan's perspective reflects a widely shared view that undocumented migrants should feel worry and fear because they have engaged in individual wrongdoing. This view is countered by the argument that undocumented status reflects not millions of individual acts of wrongdoing but systemic violence and inequality that leaves millions of people undocumented and exploitable.[33] The argument that migrants should feel fear also involves moralizing judgments: that migrants have done wrong for which they should feel fear and that migrants who do not internalize the expected sense of themselves as lawbreakers and wrongdoers are not properly human (and therefore deeply threatening to the nation and citizenry).[34] Cristina Beltrán suggests that such judgments have deep roots in the United States' history of Indigenous dispossession, chattel slavery, empire, war, and Asian exclusion. Faced with contemporary challenges to these histories, "a growing share of GOP politicians and voters . . . desire visible displays of cruelty and suffering" to be inflicted on migrants who are expected to be fearful.[35] Beltrán suggests that "such cruelty [offers] not only an experience of community and delight; it's fundamentally a return to a particular civic experience" of white patriarchy as the bedrock for hegemonic citizen subjectivity.[36] "For nativists . . . targeting migrants makes them feel stronger, freer, and more agentic, transforming acts of racialized violence . . . into feats of heroism, democratic redemption, civic engagement, and virtuous sovereignty."[37] These logics sanction tactics of abuse, violence, and cruelty that are central to attrition.[38]

Struggles over everyday life, continual fear, and possible deportation have played out intensely around questions of access to driver's licenses. In the early twentieth century, when driver's licenses were first introduced, they included racial and gender designations. Mandatory racial designations provided a means for white officials to reassert control over Black mobility despite the abolition of slavery.[39] Gender designations, which have been strongly challenged by trans communities, were used to sanction the surveillance, discrimination, and immobilization of people who do not fit binary gender norms. Since gender norms are inseparable from racial and other norms, those who are targeted include but extend beyond self-identified trans and gender-nonconforming people. Cassius Adair argues, "Driver's licenses are a key site through which techniques of racial subjugation—personal data collection, racial and sexual categorization, and mobility surveillance—became rearticulated as privileges of white and male citizenship over the first four decades of the twentieth century."[40] In the late twentieth century, struggles over whether drivers' licenses should be restricted to those who could prove legal residence or citizenship turned these documents into instruments for enacting migrant attrition and deportation, too. "Licenses have now become overdetermined icons of national belonging, a belonging from which many trans people, people with disabilities, immigrants, and people of color are excluded," including through barriers to accessing these documents.[41]

Driving without a license puts people at risk of being charged with a misdemeanor, which heightens their deportability.[42] It also announces to law enforcement that the person may be undocumented and provides grounds for one's car to be impounded, which involves significant cost. A license not only reduces these risks but also enables everyday activities. For example, driver's licenses function as IDs that enable people to secure employment, rent housing, open a bank account, turn on utilities, return merchandise, buy a drink, and much more. Yet, many states do not allow people to acquire driver's licenses unless they prove they are legally present, which makes these everyday activities immeasurably difficult. In 1993, California became the first state to ban undocumented migrants from acquiring driver's licenses, and numerous states quickly followed suit.[43]

Arguments in support of banning undocumented migrants from getting driver's licenses significantly rely on discourses about security and safety for US citizens and claims associating undocumented migrants with crime and terrorism. As we will see, groups have sought to work within these discourses to create windows of possibility for migrants. The dominant discourses were given a significant boost by *The 9/11 Commission Report*, which argued, "For terrorists, travel documents are as important as weapons" because these documents enable them to "meet, plan, case targets and gain access to attack."[44] Anti-immigrant and white supremacist groups like the Federation for American Immigration Reform and the Center for Immigration Studies seized on 9/11 to deepen arguments about why undocumented migrants should not have access to driver's licenses. They insist that allowing undocumented migrants to acquire driver's licenses poses national security risks, opens the United States to terrorism, enables fraud and crime, and encourages undocumented migration. They also oppose driver's licenses because driver's licenses facilitate rather than hinder everyday tasks.

The regulation of driver's licenses is a state-level rather than federal matter, however, and some states disagree with these arguments for restricting driver's licenses. Like those that oppose allowing undocumented migrants access to licenses, these states center issues of security, safety, and well-being. But they reach different conclusions. The National Immigration Law Center offers a comprehensive summary of common arguments in favor of allowing undocumented migrants to acquire driver's licenses.[45] These include claims that allowing everyone to acquire driver's licenses will make the roads safer because everyone will know the rules and be able to seek insurance and that people will also be less likely to flee hit-and-runs.[46] Moreover, access to driver's licenses will enable and encourage interaction with local law enforcement authorities on matters of crime and safety, which improves safety for everyone. Driver's licenses will allow more accurate tracking and identification of everyone, which speeds up the identification of terrorists or serious criminals. Related arguments center on revenue that will be generated by issuing driver's licenses and by increasing car sales and claim that driver's licenses will further enable migrants to work, which generates tax revenue and boosts consumer spending. Some arguments in support of driver's licenses explicitly support offering driver's licenses because they enable migrants to perform everyday tasks more easily and safely, but many avoid this argument because it might reduce support for making driver's licenses available to all.

Arguments in favor of issuing driver's licenses to everyone regardless of legal status run up against the 2005 REAL ID Act. This federal law set standards that IDs, including driver's licenses, must meet in order to be recognized as valid when boarding an airplane or entering a federal facility. These standards include establishing one's gender and showing proof of legal presence in the United States. Trans and gender-nonconforming communities and allies have strongly mobilized against the gender requirement, which is premised on and mandates a binary gender system and invites suspicion toward anyone who is not immediately legible within it.[47] The requirement to show proof of legal presence in order to get a driver's license, meanwhile, has become what Lina Newton describes as an "area of expressive conflict" between the federal government and individual states, with twelve states and the District of Columbia now offering driver's licenses to people regardless of legal status.[48] Those latter states generally offer two versions of driver's licenses: those that are REAL ID compliant and those that are not.[49]

In the battles over driver's licenses, discourses about citizens' safety set the horizon within which struggles are waged (even while actual Black, brown, low-income, and queer citizen drivers often experience anything but safety because of barriers to accessing driver's licenses and discriminatory traffic enforcement). Yet, these battles show that there actually are disputes about whether citizenship should be understood strictly as a matter of one's legal status or as a matter of practical connectedness to a specific place.[50] While the federal government asserts the primacy of legal status, states and municipalities that extend various rights, recognitions, and protections to everyone regardless of legal status exemplify the workings of other models of citizenship. The states that allow everyone to get a driver's license reduce undocumented migrants' risk of being criminalized for driving without a license and enable their everyday activities that require official IDs. This may reduce—but does not eliminate—fear and worry, too.

Understanding the stakes, groups have formed to lobby more states to make driver's licenses available to all.[51] Fran Ansley, who participated in one such migrant-initiated campaign, explains that while participants understood the urgency of ensuring driver's licenses were available to all, they believed that putting migrant rights or well-being at the center of their messaging would be "the kiss of death," so they instead highlighted US citizens' well-being and safety.[52] Their strategic decision to work within the dominant discourses "was not uncontroversial" but "was made easier by our knowledge of the difference that [access to driver's licenses] could make in the lives of people we knew. It would magnify freedom and decrease terror for sizeable numbers of people."[53]

Some in Oregon adopted a similarly strategic approach in their effort to get Measure 88, also known as the Safe Roads Measure, on the ballot in 2014. Measure 88 would have allowed the Department of Transportation to issue "driver cards" to Oregon residents without requiring proof of their legal presence in the United States. Causa, which describes itself as "Oregon's Latino immigrant rights organization," released a video that featured Bamby

Salcedo, a nationally known trans migrant organizer, and local LGBTQ Oregonians who were "both immigrant and not" to explain the impact of not having access to driver's licenses and to advocate for Measure 88.[54] In the absence of systemic studies, the video offers important insight about how a lack of access to driver's licenses and traffic enforcement as a pipeline to deportation affect everyday lives and intimacies and foster fear among queer and trans Latinx migrant communities.

Without a license, people either don't drive, which presents significant challenges when taking care of the basic necessities of life, or else they drive without a license, which is deeply stressful and puts them at risk. Luis describes, "I see my friends struggling. Just the difficulties in the daily things that should not be a problem, it becomes a huge problem, an issue. Like, you're trying to go to work and you get stopped and then you have a ticket, and some people, I have heard stories that because they get stopped by a cop when they are driving, and end up in deportation when they don't have any other problems other than they just don't have a license. All that they were doing is just driving to work."

In addition to risking deportation for engaging in "daily things," Nadia describes how lacking a driver's license makes it impossible to get car insurance. This puts people at risk of catastrophic expenses: "I know of a person who was in a car accident. She didn't have a license or insurance, then she had to pay the bill, she ended up paying about $25,000." Those who are caught driving without a license risk having their cars impounded, too.

To reduce the chance of encountering law enforcement or facing catastrophic expenses, people often severely curtail their driving. Yet, curtailed driving sets limits on people's connections to and interactions with important institutions and people. Oscar describes how this may affect children's schooling: "I'm constantly hearing from parents that they would love to attend events at school or they could drop off their children off at school if they missed the bus, *if* they had access to drive legally on the roads. And a lot of families haven't. So I see constantly that families struggle to be engaged in their children's education." Inability to legally drive may have deeply attritionary impacts on children's education while also affecting parent/child relationships.

Nadia describes another significant effect on relationships: worry. Whenever she has to drive to work, her wife and kids worry "if I am going to be okay, if I would get stopped by the police." Being stopped could lead to deportation, so she worries too. "I don't know when will be the last day when I will see them." Erick describes "fear" because one of his brothers ended up in deportation, and his whole family has "felt the fear of that happening again."

These narratives show the multiple intimacies and life-making possibilities that interviewees are embedded in, which involve natal and chosen families and various workplaces and public spaces. They echo the findings from numerous studies about the attritionary impact of traffic enforcement and driver's license restrictions on undocumented people's ability to carry out everyday tasks, which greatly affects their intimate ties, connections, and ability to live, while fostering fear. Citizen and legal resident relatives and friends experience the spillover effects, including additional driving responsibilities and constant worry and fear. The fact that immigration enforcement activities are conducted in racist and racializing ways also means that every driver who is perceived as Latinx or Black, regardless of citizenship, faces the heightened likelihood of a traffic stop and of discriminatory and violent encounters with local law enforcement in the course of that stop.

These individual testimonies make clear how a lack of access to driver's licenses has deeply attritionary effects.[55] The harms are not just individual but also cumulative and compounding in their effects on biological and chosen families, communities, groups, and places. Conversely, small changes may have positive impacts not just on individuals but also on all those who are connected to them—as Leisy J. Abrego shows from her research about the impact of getting Deferred Action for Childhood Arrivals (DACA) status. Even though DACA is a deeply temporary and insecure status that offers no pathway to more secure residence, it allows holders to live, work, and drive legally in the United States. One of the most common outcomes of receiving DACA status is the ability to apply for a driver's license. Abrego argues that "even though DACA targeted only single members of families," it temporarily benefited whole families in seemingly mundane but cumulative and powerful ways.[56] This included what it meant to have someone in the house who could drive legally.

The converse is also true: when traffic enforcement becomes a pipeline to deportation, entire families and communities, in addition to the deported person, are deeply affected.

"Undocumented and Unafraid": A Counteraffective Economy

Amalia Pallares and Ruth Gomberg-Muñoz note, "In this context of profound repression and state violence . . . a small but committed group of activists have responded to intensified policing by becoming more visible, not less."[57] These include migrants, many of them self-identified queer youth of color, who resisted attrition and deportation by creating and circulating a stunning counteraffective economy of "undocumented and unafraid."[58]

"Undocumented and unafraid" is particularly associated with undocumented youth activists, including LGBTQ-identified youth, who organized to advocate for the DREAM Act. First introduced into Congress in 2001, the DREAM Act provided a pathway to legal status to those who were brought to the United States as children, could show continuous presence, met educational standards, did not have a record of criminal convictions, and, over time, demonstrated military service, enrollment in higher education, or steady employment.[59] Given these terms, DREAM Act activism was significantly organized around foregrounding youth's deservingness of legal status because of their ability to match dominant norms. Activism generally emphasized a contrast between the youth, who were characterized as undocumented through no fault of their own, and their parents, who were implicitly characterized as undocumented because they broke the law.[60]

The Immigrant Youth Justice League (IYJL) of Chicago has been credited with coining and mobilizing the framework of "undocumented and unafraid" at an event that they organized in March 2010. The event was billed as a "Coming Out of the Shadows" day where several youths publicly came out as undocumented and encouraged others to do so. Coming out as undocumented, which borrowed from the coming-out strategy of the LGBTQ movement, rejected the stigma, dehumanization, and criminalization attached to undocumented status.[61] Tania Unzueta Carrasco, an activist who organized and spoke at the event, publicly self-identified as being both undocumented and a queer woman of color.

In May 2010, coming out as undocumented became linked to civil disobedience when four undocumented students and a high school counselor (Osmani R. Alcaraz Ochoa, whom we met in the introduction) staged a sit-in at Senator John McCain's office to demand passage of the DREAM Act. Three of the four students and the counselor identified as queer, and all identified as people of color. Their courageous action further highlighted that queer and migration struggles are deeply intertwined.[62] Their action further circulated "undocumented and unafraid" as a counteraffective economy that challenged the dominant regime's efforts to produce fear, debilitation, and deportability.

Nonetheless, Unzueta Carrasco and Seif suggest that "stories presented during the first year of 'coming out of the shadows' rallies in 2010" were still largely tied to normalizing narratives of the worthiness of select migrants for legalization.[63] When the DREAM Act failed again in 2010, however, some activists began to reject seeking inclusion on mainstream terms and instead started making demands for deeper change. In this context, coming out as undocumented and unafraid became repurposed for other ends.[64] Reflecting the shift, the IYJL began turning away from seeking legalization on mainstream terms and started focusing on "stopping deportations and fighting for the rights of immigrants to be present in the United States. This emerging activism more directly includes those who do not conform to the classed, gendered, racialized 'model citizen.'"[65]

Unzueta Carrasco and Seif describe how organizing around undocumented status as a collective injustice (rather than as individual wrongdoing for which exceptions should be made for select, supposedly worthy people) redefined who the community was composed of, reoriented horizons of possibility and the kinds of claims made, and enabled new forms of intimacies and connections. The sense of having a community that was built through organizing and would be there in times of trouble "allows us to risk deportation as part of a strategy to challenge the nation state."[66] Coming out as undocumented and unafraid, while "knowing there is a way to fight if we are placed in removal proceedings," became key.[67] Thus, the meanings of "undocumented and unafraid" began to shift, offering new possibilities to more diverse people.

Coming out as undocumented and unafraid was connected to the creation of UndocuQueer as an identity, too. Prerna Lal boldly asserts that "undocumented queer immigrant youth built" the contemporary immigrant rights movement by reflexively learning from and drawing on their experiences at the intersection of multiple struggles, and UndocuQueer emerged accordingly: "In order to acknowledge the intersectional oppression, the spaces being created, and the foundational work of queer undocumented youth, members of the newly formed National Immigrant Youth Alliance (NIYA) coined the phrase 'UndocuQueer' as a political identity. This inspired the creation of the Queer Undocumented Immigrant Project within United We Dream to continue pushing for the inclusion of LGBT issues in immigration reform."[68] The work of artist Julio Salgado, whose *I Am UndocuQueer!* series circulates virally to inspire and encourage, was also critical. In an interview with Hinda Seif, Salgado relates, "I cannot take credit for creating the term [*UndocuQueer*]. I do not remember where I heard it first. . . . But what I knew, undocumented and queer people had been behind many of the actions that led to the first civil disobedience in Tucson in 2010. They were open about being undocumented and queer. Tania, Yahaira. That was a great shift in narrative. . . . To have these youth . . . saying 'this is how we are, this is who we are'—it was historic. I could not *not* pay attention to it."[69] Undocu-Trans also emerged as an important identity and basis for coalitional work.[70]

In sum, "undocumented and unafraid," in various versions, emerged and circulated in ways that challenged the affective economy and material practices of attrition through enforcement. While the materialities and stresses of being undocumented remain pervasive and deadly, "undocumented and unafraid" coexists, contests, and offers possibilities to build life-affirming ties to others and oneself. The UndocuBus journey, in which queer migrants played a central role, offered a genius means to further circulate, disperse, and experience this counteraffective economy and renewed intimacies at local, state, and national scales.

The UndocuBus

The UndocuBus project involved undocumented migrants from diverse walks of life who volunteered to ride a refurbished bus (called Priscilla) from Phoenix, Arizona, to the Democratic National Convention in Charlotte, North Carolina, between July 28 and September 3, 2012, making stops along the way in ten states and over fifteen cities.[71] The side of the bus was painted with the slogan "Sin Papeles Sin Miedo: No Papers No Fear" along with the iconic image of a monarch butterfly. Like a rolling billboard, the bus and its riders displayed the concept of being undocumented and unafraid to everyone they encountered along the journey.[72] Given how heavily traffic stops have become a key means for identifying and deporting undocumented migrants, the riders faced significant risk of being stopped, arrested, and deported; the ride website describes them as "risking everything."[73] Moreover, their path deliberately took them through southern states that had enacted some of the most draconian state-level immigration laws in the nation, which heightened their risk. Their journey evoked the histories and legacies of freedom riders for civil rights who also struggled over movement, mobility, and possibilities to move through public space without violence or criminalization.[74] The journey became a means to further disperse "undocumented and unafraid" as an affective economy that pushes back on the fear that is expected by those crafting and normalizing attrition through enforcement. Dispersion included through community engagements that extended and fostered solidarities and intimacies along the way.

The UndocuBus website explains how the bus journey allowed opportunities to circulate and have people experience "undocumented and unafraid" as a constantly expanding affective economy in a context of attrition through enforcement: "Riding the bus alone is a great risk because of the checkpoints and profiling that has become so common. But the ride is also [an] arena for mobilizing, where we will build with those who have a story to tell, who have realized that the only secure community is an organized one."[75] The website describes numerous stops, interactions, and encounters among riders and others that allowed people to step forward, meet others, make connections, share stories, exchange knowledge and practical help, feel encouraged, and get organized while encountering and experiencing "undocumented and unafraid" as a mode of being, doing, and connecting in diverse contexts of struggle.

As suggested by the website, "undocumented and unafraid" offers its own model of security, one that is very different from the security that the federal government offers. The website describes the dominant approach to security: "There is a rise of collaboration between local police and immigration agents through programs like Secure Communities, implemented in over 98% of counties in the country." This model of security, which is ostensibly directed as serving (while coproducing who counts as) legitimate citizens, brings "deportation, harassment, and death" to migrant people who are "simply looking for a better life." "Undocumented and unafraid" offers a different model of security for those who are on the receiving ends of these policies. The model involves sharing "undocumented and unafraid" as a logic that allows communities to organize themselves and define their own priorities.

Contributing to this reframing of security was the fact that the ride and its website centered not just youth and college graduates seeking incorporation as "deserving immigrants" but a wide array of people, many of whom are treated as disposable under the attrition framework. The website explains: "Riders are undocumented people from all over the country, including students, mothers and fathers, children, people in deportation proceedings, day laborers, and others who continue to face deportation, harassment, and death."[76] On the website, there's no plea for legalization for "the deserving" on terms that are set by elected officials and the general public; instead there is a demand for justice and change (in forms not specified) for all who are affected by the condition of being rendered undocumented. There's also an assertion that those most affected are the most knowledgeable about current security and immigration logics and that they should be given a seat at the table when changes to immigration policy are considered. Finally, there's a firm assertion about not being able or willing to "wait": wait until Congress acts, wait until others set the terms, wait indefinitely for change that has yet to materialize when left to the political process, wait while individuals and communities continue being harassed and deported and are dying. "We can't wait for anyone else any longer."

In this context of urgency, broad collectivity, and DIY security, riders feel able to take risks, speak out, and engage in civil disobedience while risking possible arrest, detention, and deportation. Since a community has their back, they know that if they're arrested or put in deportation, others will step up to demand their release. This not only offers some security but also transforms arrest and being put into deportation by giving them dignity and collective meaning. The website explains that the UndocuBus builds on a history of developing and refining such a model: "Actions by undocumented students, such as coming out of the shadows, civil disobedience, and occupations of electoral offices have shown what happens when our community acts for itself, it changes everything." The bus both reflects and becomes a means to transport this model to multiple other places.

The organizers and riders included significant numbers of self-identified LGBTQ migrants. Marisa Franco of the National Day Laborer Organizing Network, the "badass dyke" we met in chapter 1 and a key organizer of the UndocuBus ride, suggested, "The Undocubus experience was almost split half and half between queer and straight people. We had this mixed group of folks, mixed age, mixed education level, some people spoke English and Spanish, some people didn't." She adds, "One thing that really was a through line between everyone was that they had done this because they decided that they no longer wanted to hide. And the piece that went further for the queer folks is that they were willing to do this, but they were unwilling to do it not being their full selves."[77] Tania Unzueta Carrasco, whose work with the IYJL contributed to launching the framework of "undocumented and unafraid," was among the riders—as were her parents, and her sister who also identified as queer. Julio Salgado, whose *I Am UndocuQueer!* series has inspired and uplifted untold numbers, joined the bus in Atlanta, Georgia, and provided "dispatches" (travel notes and sketches). His biography on the bus website says, "He . . . is riding the bus because '[he] want[s] to make sure other folks know we have to come out and not be afraid.'"

The journey itself, the encounters along the way, the media that followed the bus, and the riders' savvy use of traditional and social media all contributed to circulating "undocumented and unafraid" as an affective economy that invited widespread participation, renewed intimacies, and a turn away from anti-immigrant or liberal reformist immigration politics toward a demand for transformative change. The economy also circulated in other ways. For example, the ride's website opens with a map with icons for each stop; visitors click to read reports and blog posts about each stop, which allows them to follow along and feel like they are participating virtually. The site asks viewers to "ask these leaders to get on board with the riders and support inclusion over exclusion. Click on their image to ask them to get involved. We've come too far to go back." The site includes images of and links to those who are designated as leaders, ranging from then president Barack Obama and first lady Michelle Obama to celebrities, journalists, and talk show hosts. Visitors are also asked to endorse the ride and to "sign up to receive updates and express your support for the ride. Sign up to virtually 'get on the bus.'" Visitors may respond to the prompt, "Add me to the social media squad. I want to spread the word," by filling out a form with contact details. Visitors are also asked to donate.

The site solicits artwork "that inspires fearlessness." When one clicks the link, the site provides an explanation of what they're doing and why and says, "We urge artists, musicians, and writers to take action and create an image, song, or poem to be used as part of our online viral campaign for NoPapers-NoFear.org and to possibly be published as prints to raise funds for the effort with the consent of the artist." Under "Details," potential contributors are told, "Create an image, song, or poem that shows your support for the No Papers No Fear Ride for Justice and especially for the riders who are risking everything and conquering fear. Make sure to include the specific words on the image such as 'no papers no fear,' 'sin papeles y sin miedo' 'levanta tu cara' 'dignity is here' 'we can't wait' 'right side of history.'" This solicitation speaks to many of the savvy ways that "undocumented and unafraid" circulates—through compelling visual imagery that has inspired a generation, through words and songs, through specific words around which affective intensities of "undocumented and unafraid" gather and gain force, and through DIY grassroots fundraising.

The bus materializes the circulation of "undocumented and unafraid," which engages with the ways that traffic enforcement has become a major means to identify, criminalize, and deport migrants. Riders were stopped and briefly arrested at several events along the way—most spectacularly in Charlotte at the Democratic National Convention, when ten brave riders blocked a traffic intersection, unfurled a banner that read "sin papeles, sin miedo," and chanted and told their stories until they were taken into police custody. They spent twelve hours in custody, wearing the rain-soaked clothes in which they were arrested, until being charged with "impeding traffic," a misdemeanor, and released. Tania Unzueta Carrasco's mother, father, and younger sister were among those who were arrested, and she described that she was "worried" about their well-being, but at the same time, she knew they were mentally prepared. She trusted that the community and public's mobilization—which began immediately—would be effective in ensuring their release.[78] The fact that this came to pass affirmed the organizing logics through which "undocumented and unafraid" sought to produce collective security.

Less publicized than the Democratic National Convention arrests but also significant was an action where four riders mobilized "undocumented and unafraid" to publicly challenge several key architects of attrition through enforcement policies, including Kris Kobach and Mark Krikorian. Their challenge took place at a US Commission on Civil Rights hearing in Birmingham, Alabama, on August 17, 2012. The hearing was convened to examine "whether or not the recently enacted state immigration laws foster discrimination or contribute to an increase in hate crimes, cause elevated racial or ethnic profiling, impact students' rights under Plyler versus Doe or compromise the public safety or community policing."[79] The chair of the hearing, Martin R. Castro, made plain that he strongly disagreed with the testimony of people like Kobach and Krikorian and groups like the Federation for American Immigration Reform but could not bar them since, he said, they were exercising First Amendment rights. Castro acknowledged that "peaceful protestors" were present, similarly exercising their First Amendment rights, and he "thank[ed] them for being here and expressing their view."[80]

Kris Kobach, one of the key authors of Arizona's SB 1070 and Alabama's HB 56 attritionist laws, was the first speaker of the day. When he began his testimony, four UndocuBus riders stood up and protested. They included Gerardo Torres, a self-identified gay man who describes what it was like to draw on the logic of "undocumented and unafraid" to challenge the authority of a key architect of attrition through enforcement. Torres begins by noting that Kobach "was sitting at the table like an expert, when we know there is no one who knows the effects of immigration laws in our communities better than undocumented immigrants."[81] Yet, no undocumented immigrants had been invited to testify before the commission. Torres continues:

> I remember sitting there and listening to Kobach speak about the importance of SB 1070, and how people who were not doing anything wrong should have nothing to fear. He said that the law did not lead to racial profiling or to fear. Meanwhile, I remember thinking about the fear and anger that I have felt, and seeing my neighborhood change. Every day in Arizona, I see people leave their homes out of fear of the immigration laws in our state. There are abandoned homes, empty lots, closed stores, and people displaced. I see children with fear, mothers crying, and people without freedom to move around freely in their neighborhood.

The official transcript shows that, using the hypothetical example of a traffic stop, Kobach denied that SB 1070 leads to racial profiling.[82] His refutation conceived racial profiling solely as a matter of individual prejudice, refused structural and historical analysis, and treated the law as neutral. Interestingly, the transcript shows that Kobach did not use the word *fear*. Torres's comments therefore suggest that he associates SB 1070 with amplifying conditions that instill fear, even when fear is not explicitly acknowledged by people like Kobach. Torres lists some of the affective and material outcomes of fear: abandoned homes, empty lots, closed stores, displaced people, fearful children, crying mothers, and confined people. Moreover, he describes these conditions as constituting a "change": SB 1070 changed conditions in ways that further generated these results.

Torres then describes his own fear, intertwined with anger, because of the conditions. He continues:

> I stood up and held up a sign that read "Undocumented." I told them my name, my age, that I am from Arizona, and that I am undocumented, and that I am not afraid. I told them about my community and how I have experienced the effects of SB 1070. Everyone was looking at me, but I don't remember. It was like tunnel vision, I couldn't see anything around me. It was surreal and powerful. I remember feeling like I was taking away the power they had taken from me, without me knowing I had lost it. The power to defend myself and speak for myself.

The video posted online with this story suggests that his telling occurred under difficult conditions.[83] After he stood, three more riders stood with him. They shared their stories, shouting details as security moved in to remove them, members of the commission demanded silence, and the crowd reacted.

> Security came for the three of them first and I was left alone in the room for what seemed like forever, but was a few minutes. Kobach refused to continue talking while I was in the room, and the Commissioners and presenters discussed back and forth whether this was a peaceful protest. Someone called us hateful. But we knew we were speaking for our rights. I must admit that I did feel scared when I was standing there by myself. I didn't know how the security officer was going to react. I thought if I was by myself, they would treat me worse than my friends. But I think when they realized what I was doing was speaking for my rights, and that I was not scared [*sic*]. I think the moment we rise up in public, they realize that they no longer have power.

Torres's experience shifts between being unafraid and afraid. Yet "unafraid" offers a logic for staying strong even while waiting for security to take him away, which feels like "forever." Torres and the other protestors were escorted from the hotel where the hearing was taking place and shared their stories with media who were gathered outside.

The hearing transcript shows that Commissioner Gaziano, who at the beginning of the meeting had spoken of his own immigrant heritage, characterized the protestors as engaging in "hateful freedom of speech."[84] Commissioner Yaki strongly disputed the assertion. Later in the proceedings, Carol Swain, a conservative and controversial professor of political science and law at Vanderbilt University, explicitly engaged the dynamics of fear in relation to the bus riders' protest: "The rule of law is essential for civilized nations. This morning we witnessed a disruptive, staged outburst by illegal aliens who are not cowering in fear. The infringement, they infringed on the rights of the rest of us to peaceably assemble. The rule of law is what separates civilized nations from oppressive regimes like the ones that many of the illegal aliens fled."[85] Her conviction that undocumented migrants are expected to "cower in fear" echoes former ICE director Thomas Homan's comments and is shared by many who advocate for and craft attrition through enforcement policies. It is precisely the kind of logic that "undocumented and unafraid" seeks to inoculate against.

Torres describes how, at the end of the hearing, he and the other protestors were allowed to reenter the hearing, and a person from Alabama and another from Arizona were invited to give additional testimony to the panel. As a result of their courageous actions, "we at least got a corner at the table." Torres concludes, "I am ready for a second round. The experience has prepared me to be more fearless. If I used to look at things through the window, now I know that I can open the door and walk out." Torres notes that "being part of the gay, lesbian, bisexual, transgender and queer community, and knowing our history, has been important," including by teaching him to speak from his experiences and for himself "without fear, without shame, and [to] spread peace."[86]

Conclusion

Chokepoints work not just through spectacular shows of force but also through embeddedness in everyday institutions that are increasingly networked into migration controls, as exemplified by driving. In the United States, where reliable and efficient public transportation remains deeply underfunded, automobility has been central to subject-making and capitalist production. Historically, states have asserted control over driving in ways that materialize white, heteropatriarchal, settler "expectations to continued unencumbered movement as well as a powerful, racialized sense of entitlement to control, critique, and criminalize the movement of others."[87] These dynamics have been extended by using driving to further embed immigration chokepoints into everyday life.[88]

Scholarship explores how the cultivation of citizens' fears of migrants provides a crucial means to further disperse securitizing logics and practices that reproduce exclusionary versions of nation and citizenship.[89] At the same time, attrition through enforcement strategies seeks to cultivate fear among migrants while making their everyday lives impossibly difficult, including through traffic enforcement. Since driving is often unavoidable for everyday activities yet may result in being targeted, criminalized, and deported, migrants experience great stress and fear when driving. Architects of attrition through enforcement expect this fear to unravel people's being, undermine their capacities, weaken their everyday intimacies, cause them to voluntarily stop engaging in life-making practices, and in some cases to self-deport.[90]

"Undocumented and unafraid," a framework that drew on and repurposed LGBTQ histories of coming out, was generated by undocumented migrants of color, many of whom were LGBTQ-identified. The framework was initially tied to Dreamer activism that sought legal status for young migrants who could fit themselves into dominant norms. "Undocumented and unafraid" shifted, however, to include a much broader range of undocumented people and to reject the view of undocumented status as a marker of individual wrongdoing. Instead, activists reframed undocumented status as a collective condition that reflects the outcome of intersecting forms of power, domination, and inequality that demand transformation.[91] "Undocumented and unafraid" circulated as a counteraffective economy that rejected attrition through enforcement's views of undocumented people, forged new forms of individual and collective subjectivities, and engaged in actions designed to foster security and life for those most targeted for debilitation or deportation by attrition through enforcement logics. The UndocuBus project spectacularly exemplified and further circulated this counteraffective economy. And LGBTQ-identified migrants of color and queer histories that were repurposed to address migration struggles were central to these changes. "Undocumented and unafraid" continues to circulate and enable rather than debilitate.

4

CITIES AS CHOKEPOINTS AND RESISTANCE

I am participating in the hunger strike to ensure ICE no longer continues to terrorize our community here in Santa Ana and to end the abuse and detention of transgender undocumented women. We want an end to all raids, we want ICE out of Santa Ana and all of our communities. The Santa Ana City Council members need to cancel the ICE contract now and stand on the rights side of justice. —JORGE GUTIERREZ, Familia: Trans Queer Liberation Movement

In May 2016, three migrants began a public hunger strike to demand the closure of a special "pod" in Santa Ana, California, that had been created to detain transgender and queer migrants. The hunger strikers were Deyaneira García, an eighteen-year-old high school senior and undocumented youth organizer from Mexico City; Jennicet Gutiérrez, a transgender activist and organizer from Mexico; and Jorge Gutierrez, an UndocuQueer organizer born in Nayarit, Mexico, and raised in Santa Ana, California.[1] As well as wanting the pod closed, the hunger strikers demanded the release of transgender and queer migrants, and all migrants, from detention facilities around the United

States. They connected the abusive conditions that migrants endure in detention with the suffering and deprivation that many Santa Ana residents experience in their everyday lives. And they identified city officials and institutions as having a critical role in addressing these interlinked struggles.

The hunger strikers' demands echoed demands that had been made by protestors in January and February 2016 when the city of Santa Ana considered expanding the pod. This chapter centers on the protestors' and hunger strikers' demands to close the pod and release detained transgender and queer migrants and their critical questions about what cities can do to foster intimacies that allow thriving rather than exhaustion, wearing down, expulsion, or death. By asking these questions, the protestors and hunger strikers were identifying how city governments play key roles in sustaining the infrastructure of immigration chokepoints and have the power to make meaningful changes that contribute to the abolition of detention and deportation while fostering material improvement in everyday life.[2]

In this chapter, I first situate transgender and queer detention, which is often a precursor to becoming deported, within the infrastructure of chokepoints that steer migrants away from their everyday lives and into the violent hands of states and private detention contractors. Next, I explain how detention forces migrants into violent, unwanted intimacies while depriving them of wanted and sustaining intimacies. This exhausts and wears them down, reduces their possibilities for fighting deportation, and makes them available for others' profit. Detained people resist these conditions with support from allies. Then I describe trans and queer migrants' experiences of and protests against the detention system, including the pod, and the growing demand to completely end transgender and queer (and all) detention. Such demands extended beyond the pod to call for changed conditions for the residents of the city of Santa Ana. Next, I highlight the difference between reformist and abolitionist approaches to the pod and the migrant-detention system. Then I describe the city's response to the hunger strikers and how the struggle continues. By putting their bodies on the line, hunger strikers highlighted the stakes and importantly contributed to transformation.

Detention and the Infrastructure of Chokepoints

US migrant detention is a key part of what Martha Balaguera describes as transnational circuits of "displacement and confinement" that strip low-income and working-class migrants of claims to rights at every step while making their bodies available to create value for others.[3] Extensive scholarship explores how crossing the US border converts bodies in these ways, especially when people cross without official permission.[4] Detention occurs not only when people are captured crossing the border or present themselves to seek asylum but also when noncitizens become captured or criminalized within the United States. Immigration and Customs Enforcement (ICE) detention further strips away people's rights, possibilities, and social legibilities while keeping them available as captive bodies from which cheap labor and other kinds of value can be extracted.[5] Detention is often a precursor to deportation, which further extends the dynamics of displacement, confinement, stripping away of rights, and exhausting bodies.[6] Alicia Schmidt Camacho underscores that these interlinked processes reproduce and normalize "the interests of global capital, of nation building . . . [and] ruling ideas of cultural value, standards of living, progress, democracy—in short, all the narratives of development and civilization that require the idea of a border."[7]

The United States' capacity to strip migrants of rights and dignity while extracting value from their lives through detention is enormous. The United States has the largest immigrant-detention infrastructure in the world, with as many as 400,000 people passing through that system each year. The detention infrastructure directly borrows from systems of criminalization and mass incarceration that target citizens and relies on these systems to funnel noncitizens into detention. Like mandatory minimum sentencing laws that funnel people to prison, mandatory detention laws have exploded the numbers of detained noncitizens since 1996.[8] Detention Watch Network explains that *mandatory detention* refers to the practice of "automatically imprisoning an individual without any consideration of their individual circumstances," including serious medical conditions, family obligations, experiences of torture, or anything else.[9] Any noncitizen—including legal permanent residents, asylum seekers, and undocumented people—may become subject to mandatory detention. Detention Watch Network further explains:

> There are two types of mandatory detention: Section 235 of the Immigration and Nationality Act (INA) imposes mandatory detention on asylum seekers during credible fear and asylum proceedings and requires the use of expedited removal, under which people arriving in the country must be detained without bond while their cases are reviewed.
>
> Section 236(c) of the INA also imposes mandatory detention on certain noncitizens who have had contact with the criminal legal system, regardless of the seriousness of the offense or the fact that they have already completed any sentence for the offense. Their family and community

ties or the strength of their legal case also cannot be considered. Misdemeanor crimes including shoplifting or petty drug possession can trigger mandatory detention under this provision.[10]

The lack of possibilities for undocumented people to adjust their status, which intersects with the dynamics that fueled displacement in the first place, further keeps the detention system in high gear.[11] So does the expanding array of people involved in identifying and turning migrants over to ICE. These include local and state authorities who have entered into agreements with the federal government to participate in immigration enforcement. "Individuals in daily, routine contact with immigrants—employers, bank tellers, store owners, car salespeople, apartment managers—[also] attempt to interpret [immigration] law and implement it to the best of their knowledge."[12] Educators, health-care providers, social service providers, and private citizens do too, further funneling people into detention and deportation. The unending drumbeat of assertions by politicians and media that migrants pose crime and security threats fuel and normalize these practices.[13] At the same time, the array of people involved in questioning and resisting the system has multiplied.

During the 1980s, an average of 2,000 people a day were detained; by 1995, an average of 7,475 people a day were detained.[14] In 2009, language was introduced into a Department of Homeland Security (DHS) appropriations act stating that "funding made available under this heading shall maintain a level of not less than 34,000 detention beds" for immigrants across the nation on any given day (which, over the course of a year, translates into some 400,000 detained people who rotate in and out of the beds).[15] These beds were available in ICE facilities, state or local jails, or, in the vast majority of cases, private for-profit detention facilities.[16] The bed quota was bolstered by "guaranteed minimums" requiring ICE to pay for a minimum number of beds at key detention centers even when the beds were not used. These rules ensured that private corporations, who provide the majority of detention bed space, and some local municipalities (though Santa Ana, the site of the protests, was not among them) may count on a guaranteed revenue stream regardless of detention levels.[17] These interlocking conditions not only further normalized detention but also kept it in high gear, as ICE feels pressure to fill the beds that it has paid for.[18]

The first Trump administration further intensified and expanded the detention infrastructure. During his first days in office, Trump signed an executive order that declared that no class of migrants was exempt from enforcement.[19]

Detention became the required response to situations that might have prompted alternatives in the past. For example, the fact of being undocumented became grounds for automatic detention regardless of one's circumstances or length of residence in the United States, all people seeking asylum were to be detained, the administration vigorously explored how to expand the indefinite detention of families, and groups that had been designated as vulnerable and generally exempt from detention under the Obama regime, such as pregnant people, were routinely detained.

In 2017, the requirement to fund at least 34,000 detention beds a day was removed from the law, but detention mushroomed anyway. By fiscal year 2019, ICE was detaining an average of 50,000 people a day, and sometimes as many as 56,000 a day.[20] The expansion occurred despite the fact that Congress denied funding to expand bed space to these levels; however, DHS, which is ICE's parent agency, circumvented congressional restrictions by transferring funds from other agencies to ICE.[21] Moreover, ICE continued expanding its detention space using contracting processes that are often opaque and noncompliant with federal guidelines.[22] Guaranteed minimums remained an important part of the process. Through control over bond and parole decisions, ICE further ensures that as many people as possible stay detained while their cases are pending.[23]

When President Biden came into office, funding was appropriated for 34,000 detention beds a day for fiscal years 2021 and 2022. The 2023 budget requested funds for 25,000 detention beds, a decrease of 9,000, but subsequently returned to funding for 34,000 beds. At the same time, funding for alternatives to detention (ATDs) grew substantially. Though ATDs encompass a wide range of programs, ICE primarily opts for programs that increase "surveillance and restrictions" rather than programs that have "proven to be effective in supporting a noncitizen's navigation of the immigration legal system" while living with families and communities.[24] ICE's preferred programs involve "ankle monitors, a smartphone application with facial recognition technology and phones that undocumented immigrants awaiting court proceedings can use to check in with immigration authorities."[25]

Neither Republicans nor migrant advocates support these alternatives. "For Republicans, detained immigrants are much easier to deport than those who are not in detention, regardless of whether they are wearing ankle monitors."[26] Migrant advocates recognize that ankle monitors, smartphones, and other tracking devices may be less terrible than incarceration in detention facilities, but they remain deeply concerned that these programs "put more immigrants under surveillance than before," which also leads to deportation.[27]

For example, data gleaned from migrants' ankle monitors have been used to raid workplaces and homes, leading to deportations.[28] Monitoring devices, which ensure people are constantly "tracked and trapped," also greatly affect people's everyday lives.[29] The devices have other significant impacts, too: "The data gathered from monitoring enhances the capacity of authorities to label and categorize individuals and groups, and use punitive algorithms to inflict collective punishment that limits the freedom and life options of entire communities or groups with common traits or personal histories. . . . The proliferation of [electronic monitoring] across the globe requires that activists . . . situate these devices in the international network of racialized techno-punishment and control, the world of 'e-carceration.'"[30]

Advocates also oppose the use of for-profit contractors to manage the programs. As of February 2022, BI Incorporated, a subsidiary of the GEO Group, one of the biggest private detention companies, was the sole provider of ATD technology and services for ICE.[31] Not only do people have to pay initial setup fees for devices like ankle monitors, but they also face daily fees that can range from five to forty dollars, driving many into debt.[32] The expansion of fee-based ATDs that are managed by for-profit companies is another way that immigrant detention borrows directly from the system of mass incarceration.

Detention Terror and Abuse: Enforcing Unwanted Intimacies, Withholding Wanted Intimacies

Nick Gill suggests that detention subjects people to multiple unwanted and often violent intimacies while depriving them of wanted intimacies.[33] His framework helps us to track how detention further strips migrants of possibilities to make asylum and immigration claims and further renders them as bodies from which labor and other kinds of value can be extracted.[34]

A majority of migrants are detained by for-profit companies or municipalities seeking to make money. This means that detention puts people in situations where profit-motivated relationships condition everything.[35] From the moment someone sets foot in detention, where they are stripped of their clothing and possessions (except for their wedding bands), "power and domination" pervade all relationships.[36] Detained people are given institutional clothing, bedding, and toiletries that depersonalize and degrade them and are functionally inadequate. Power and domination are further manifested by guards' and workers' control over the environment, including lack of adequate, appropriate, or nutritious food (or in some cases, the provision of spoiled and rotten food), significant cold or heat, lack of access to hygiene and other basic products, and lack of control over one's time. Power and domination are also evidenced by consistent reports that ill, traumatized, and psychologically distressed detainees generally receive inadequate, inappropriate, or no medical or psychological treatment whatsoever and are sometimes placed in solitary confinement instead.[37] Cumulatively, these conditions result in preventable deaths, although precise numbers remain disputed. Livia Luan, in an article for the Migration Policy Institute, reports that 179 people died in ICE custody between October 1, 2003, and February 19, 2018.[38] Based on ICE data, Catherine E. Shoichet at CNN reports that 213 people died in ICE custody between 2004 and 2020.[39] "Dangerous and subpar medical practices," the inappropriate use of solitary confinement, and inadequate or no mental health provisions whatsoever are consistently cited as contributing to preventable deaths.[40]

Detainees constantly experience inappropriate and threatening forms of bodily and psychological intimacy, including when they are guarded, strip-searched, or watched while sleeping, showering, dressing, on the toilet, and engaged in other everyday activities. They are also regularly subjected to sexual harassment, abuse, and coercion. In a 2018 report by the *Intercept* on sexual assault, abuse, and coercion in immigrant detention, Alice Speri found "that sexual abuse and harassment in immigration detention facilities are not only widespread but systemic, and enabled by an agency that regularly fails to hold itself accountable."[41] Speri concluded that the data "paint a damning portrait and suggest institutional complicity to sexual abuse on a mass scale."[42] These findings echo multiple reports.[43]

In this context of ongoing and severe bodily and psychic coercion and stress, detained people become worn-down, "captive consumers and coerced labourers" who work for as little as one to two dollars a day under sometimes dangerous conditions.[44] As people must purchase everyday necessities like food, clothing, hygiene products, and nonprescription medicine from the detention centers' commissaries, which grossly inflate prices, their meager earnings go right back to the detention infrastructure.[45] Through coerced labor, detention facilities also save millions of dollars a year that they would otherwise have to pay to nondetained employees who were earning a wage.[46]

Exploitative, dangerous, neglectful, and threatening conditions are deliberately used to pressure people to relinquish their asylum or immigration claims and "consent" to their own deportation in order to end their suffering. Illustrating this, one of the members of a caravan of seventeen transgender migrants who sought asylum in the United States in 2018, Edwin Pérez-Mejía, had survived abuse, torture, and gang kidnappings in Honduras. But conditions in the Hudson County Correctional Center in Kearny, New Jersey, were so traumatic that he requested to self-deport—until Immigration Equality, an LGBTQ-migrant-serving organization, intervened.[47] Pressuring people to relinquish their asylum or immigration claims and to consent to deportation adds a disingenuous veneer of legality to the process, allows the government to claim that asylum seekers are supposedly not genuine, normalizes the continual abrogation of migrants' rights, and adds to the annual deportation totals that legitimize ICE's existence.

Authorities also rely on mandatory detention under abusive and terrifying conditions to try to instill fear that deters future migrations. Shannon Speed describes how, when asylum-seeking Indigenous women and children from Central America sought release from US detention in 2014, ICE argued that their release would constitute a national security threat. The supposed threat had nothing to do with the individual women and their children but instead ICE's concern that their release might incentivize others to migrate. According to ICE's logic, the more migrants who can be detained under terrible conditions, the greater detention's value for deterring future migrations. This thinking is related to the moral and penal logics discussed earlier. Speed describes this thinking as a logic of "deterrence through incarceration" that violates international law, which affirms that people facing persecution have the right to seek asylum elsewhere.[48] In 2015, a federal court issued an injunction against using detention to deter future migrations. In response, ICE resorted to other legal arguments and procedural strategies (like setting prohibitively high bond rates) to keep people detained, while remaining committed to abusive detention as a strategy for deterring others.[49] The strategy persists despite the fact that deterrence based on fear, terror, and cruelty does not stop people from migrating.

Even as migrants endure unwanted intimacies that debilitate their bodies and psyches, wanted intimacies are made difficult to maintain or entirely unavailable.[50] For instance, migrants traveling together are generally separated when they are caught by or turn themselves in to Border Patrol. Noncitizens picked up by ICE from within the United States also become separated from familial and social ties. The Trump administration's policy of separating parents from children and infants at the border, without ensuring any way for them to remain connected and resulting in hundreds of permanently separated families, built on a long history of weaponizing intimate ties in order to govern migration. Ties are weaponized to deter migration, punish those who migrate anyway, and act as "bait" to bring relatives already in the United States out of the shadows so they can be placed in detention.[51] Aspects of Trump's family-separation policy were modified after a national and international outcry. But officials still routinely separate people who are family: "grandmothers from their grandchildren, aunts from their nephews, uncles from their nieces, cousins from one another," family friends from family members.[52] Mary Pat Brady describes the process as "dismembering kin networks."[53]

Sustaining wanted ties while in detention is made very, very difficult. Family and friends may try to visit, but the process is intimidating, difficult, and may involve driving for hours or days (see the visiting rules posted for detention centers for a sense of the challenges).[54] Those who had health care lose ties to their health-care providers. Being detained sharply affects access to legal assistance, too, which is one of the most critical factors in determining whether migrants remain detained or get released, whether they win their case or get deported. Further weakening or entirely ending wanted intimacies, detained people may be transferred to detention facilities that are hundreds and sometimes thousands of miles away, and often in remote locations, without warning. Emily Ryo and Ian Peacock found that among detainees released in 2015, 54 percent had experienced at least one transfer (and sometimes two or three) during their detention.[55]

The institutionalization of violent intimacies combined with the lack of wanted intimacies are reinforced by a near total lack of transparency, accountability, or oversight concerning what happens in detention. Though ICE claims to have an oversight process that allows the identification and correction of abuses or shortcomings in the detention system, the process has been described as a "theater of compliance" whose purpose is to cover up abuses and avoid accountability.[56] Annual inspections that involve preannounced visits allow operators of detention facilities to conceal problems and orchestrate a positive image, rarely resulting in any negative findings. By contrast, "when the DHS Inspector General conducted unannounced visits, it found utter disregard for human life including overly restrictive segregation, inadequate medical care, and nooses hanging in cells."[57]

Immigration and Customs Enforcement officials generally deny, doctor, lie about, and do not act on credible information about harsh and abusive detention conditions. In addition, DHS and ICE stonewall or outright refuse to provide information about what is happening in detention, nor do they require private contractors to provide such information. Indeed, private contractors with records of detainee complaints or deaths routinely have their contracts renewed or even expanded. Furthermore, DHS and ICE take active measures to bury or destroy information about detention conditions. In July 2018, ICE requested to be allowed to destroy detainee records "including those related to in-custody death, sexual assault, and the use of solitary confinement."[58] The request received preliminary approval, but the American Civil Liberties Union sued to block it. In 2020, the Trump administration designated Customs and Border Protection (CBP) and ICE as "security/sensitive" agencies when it comes to Freedom of Information Act requests, further reducing any semblance of accountability and transparency.[59] The federal government's Office of Inspector General provides some oversight, with limited effect.[60] Under these cumulative conditions, detention infrastructures continually seek to strip migrants of already tenuous claims on rights and further reduce them to bodies from which labor and other kinds of value can be extracted—including through suffering, neglect, and degradation.

Migrants have consistently resisted these conditions, however. In so doing, they have forged intimacies that Damian Vergara Bracamontes theorizes as queer migrant kinship. Queer migrant kinship does not require self-identification as queer or trans; rather, Bracamontes explains, queerness stems from the fact that detained people who are variously marked as nonnormative by oppressive regimes make connections, care for one another, protest the system, and demand change.[61] Protesting migrants also forge ties and intimacies with allies on the outside. Scholars document a long history of these alliances, especially since the 1980s, when a crucial expansion in migrant deterrence, interdiction, and detention occurred in connection with the Cold War, US-backed wars in Central America, US support for Haiti's dictator, and the AIDS crisis. In this context, Mariel Cubans, who experienced prolonged detention because of their homosexuality, gender nonconformity, African heritage, and histories of criminalization by the Cuban state; Haitians who faced interdiction at sea, confinement at Guantánamo Bay while US officials tested them for HIV, and harsh conditions of detention and mass deportation; and Central Americans whose asylum claims were consistently denied all engaged in significant protests against detention with the support of allies on the outside.[62] Alliances between detained migrants and people on the outside remain crucial in the struggle for change.

Immigration and Customs Enforcement tries to prevent or sever bonds among migrants and between migrants and allies on the outside, including by placing people in solitary or threatening to transfer them.[63] Thus, ICE seeks to reassert "power and control" that become threatened by the intimacies of queer migrant kinship within detention and ties with people on the outside.[64]

Well before being detained by ICE, transgender and queer migrants frequently experience unwanted, violent intimacies that stem from their positionalities as queer and gender-nonconforming people living at the intersections of racial, gender, economic, colonial, and other kinds of violence. For example, Amnesty International describes how transgender women traveling from Northern Triangle countries in Central America "are especially vulnerable to death threats from gangs; sexual violence and exploitation; human trafficking; and arbitrary detention and abuse by law enforcement authorities. Along their journeys north to seek safe haven in Mexico or the United States, many face the same threats of violence and exploitation as they fled in the Northern Triangle. Upon requesting asylum at the US–Mexico border, transgender asylum-seekers encounter a new set of challenges and abuses, exposing them to heightened risks of ill-treatment in the US system of indefinite immigration detention."[65]

Those who become detained from within the United States rather than at the border also experience intimacies that harm, dispossess, and exhaust—along with wanted intimacies. United We Dream's *No More Closets: Experiences of Discrimination among the LGBTQ Immigrant Community* reports that in their everyday lives in the United States, queer migrants collectively and transgender migrants in particular "experience high levels of discrimination and harassment in multiple areas of life including employment, education, healthcare and housing."[66] These experiences funnel some queer and trans migrants into the criminal injustice system that then routes them into ICE detention. Laura P. Minero and her colleagues found that among thirty Latinx transgender formerly detained migrants they interviewed, nine became detained as a result of criminalization in the United States.[67] The authors describe systemic conditions that contribute to criminalization: "Lack of access to work permits, limited work opportunities due to anti-trans discrimination, and receiving inadequate pay for work all push Latinx trans immigrants toward illicit activity that is necessary for survival."[68] Presumptions of criminality are also regularly imposed on trans women of color in public spaces, which is reflected in the fact that "two individuals were wrongfully accused of trading sex, and one individual was framed by a police officer for theft," which pipelined them into detention too.[69]

Immigration and Customs Enforcement detention extends experiences of pervasive, violent intimacies directed at queer and trans migrants. In 2007, Victoria Arellano, a twenty-three-year-old undocumented, HIV+, transgender migrant woman from Mexico, was detained after a traffic stop and died in detention while staff ignored her medical needs.[70] Fellow detainees cared for her as she grew sicker. Her death sparked public protest, discussion, and efforts to gather information about transgender, queer, and HIV+ migrant detention, which was barely explored until then. In 2011, the National Immigrant Justice Center (NIJC) broke new ground by filing thirteen complaints with DHS's Office for Civil Rights and Civil Liberties and the Office of Inspector General documenting systemic abuse against detained gay male and transgender migrants.[71] As detailed in Sharita Gruberg's report, the complaints concerned "incidents of sexual assault, denial of adequate medical care, long-term solitary confinement, discrimination and abuse, and ineffective complaints and appeals processes.... In addition to the incidents of abuse described in NIJC's complaints, other complaints have documented LGBT detainees being called names such as 'faggot' by guards and being told to 'walk like a man, not a gay man' and 'act male.' Furthermore, detainees are frequently housed with detainees of a gender with which they do not identify. This means that female transgender detainees are detained with men."[72] In 2011, in response to protests and complaints, ICE established minimum standards for detention, processes for addressing sexual assault, and some minimal safeguards for transgender detainees.[73] These changes lacked the force of law and remained primarily honored in the breach.

Immigration and Customs Enforcement also created a specialized facility within the Santa Ana jail in California that was popularly described as the "LGBT pod."[74] The pod had sixty-four beds and housed some—though by no means most—detained migrants whom ICE recognized as transgender women and gay or bisexual men. Pod staff were required to undergo specialized training concerning the needs of LGBTQ detainees.[75]

The pod reflects the state's control over classifying and spatially distributing people, which has consequences. As Martha Balaguera emphasizes, "Transness is not simply an identity that asylum seekers [and migrants] claim for themselves but one that agents of the state who can inflict discretional punishment also ascribe and enforce."[76] Ascription and enforcement also take place in regard to the other identities represented by the pod. State classificatory regimes, which negate the complexity, multiplicity, situatedness, and changing nature of people's identifications and embodiments, affirm some people as being legibly trans, gay, or lesbian while deeming others illegible.[77] Balaguera describes how the *chicas trans* she interviewed had encountered, learned to situationally perform, and variously internalized "permitted transgender identities" through dealing with shelters, caravans, activists, migration authorities, human rights regimes, and detention officials.[78] The pod was an important site through which officials produced state-recognized trans identities that significantly affect people's possibilities.[79]

Officials characterized the pod as a detention model that could be widely replicated.[80] They also affirmed that the pod protected detained people from violence, which was framed as primarily inflicted by other detainees. These affirmations ignored the systemic violence that systematically routes so many migrants into detainability and deportability in the first place. Officials also ignored violence, abuse, and intimidation inflicted by pod staff and staff at other points in the detention system that migrants pass through in order to reach the pod, and they ignored that the immigration enforcement system as a whole is a system of structural violence.[81] Detained transgender women and gay or bisexual men were not automatically transferred to the pod, either; instead, they had to request a transfer, and most remained scattered throughout regular detention facilities. Officials' control over who was and was not placed in the pod underscores that detention constitutes gender and sexuality "with concrete implications . . . in the flesh."[82]

Close the Pod, End Transgender and Queer Detention

Efforts to completely end transgender and queer detention—including by closing the pod rather than treating it as a model—gained momentum as people protested Arellano's death and participated in the #Not1More and #EndTransDetention campaigns.[83] The drive to end transgender detention was especially urgent. All detained people endure neglectful, abusive, and violent conditions, but studies consistently show that detained people who do not conform to binary gender norms are especially likely to be singled out for sexual assault, abuse, and harassment. The Black Alliance for Just Immigration, the Black LGBTQIA+ Migrant Project, the UndocuBlack Network, and Freedom for Immigrants, for example, documented that Black migrants "face a significantly harsher reality inside ICE detention facilities" than non-Black migrants and that "Black non-binary migrants" were 3.5 times more likely to be singled out for violence and ill treatment.[84]

In 2013, the Government Accountability Office reported that although transgender migrants were about one in five hundred of those detained by ICE, one in five substantiated cases of sexual assault and abuse in ICE facilities involved transgender women, many of whom were detained in all-male facilities where they endured terror and abuse.[85] Medical neglect was also very common, as exemplified by Arellano's death. Furthermore, although

"ICE is required to provide hormones to trans people who were already receiving hormone therapy when taken into ICE custody," this frequently does not happen.[86] Trans and gender-nonconforming people were also disproportionately likely to be placed in solitary confinement, even though the use of solitary has been widely condemned and causes deep, lasting harm. Officials justified solitary confinement as a way to supposedly protect trans and gender-nonconforming people from harm. Trans and gender-nonconforming people were also placed in solitary as punishment or because they were experiencing deep psychological distress.[87]

By 2014, a coalition of activists sought to close the LGBT pod. Their efforts included chaining themselves together and blocking an intersection near the jail. Coalition members included Orange County Immigrant Youth United, the Transgender Law Center, and Familia: Trans Queer Liberation Movement.[88] In December 2014, over 115 transgender, queer, migrant, and allied social justice organizations sent a letter to President Obama that described the suffering and abuse endured by transgender women who were detained in all-male facilities, subjected to sexual violence, and frequently placed in solitary confinement supposedly for their own protection. They asked the president to swiftly release detained "transgender women and other LGBT people" and implement a policy against detaining LGBTQ migrants.[89] In March 2015, demonstrations in major cities demanded the release of transgender migrant Nicoll Hernández-Polanco from Eloy Detention Center in Arizona and protested the horrific conditions that detained transgender women generally face. That same month, thirty-five Democratic members of Congress wrote to Jeh Johnson, the secretary of Homeland Security, asking for the release of LGBTQ detainees.[90] In June, undocumented transgender migrant Jennicet Gutiérrez interrupted President Obama at a White House Pride event, demanding the release of detained transgender and queer migrants. She was excoriated and removed. Also in June 2015, ICE released the Transgender Care Memorandum, which recognized the vulnerability of transgender people in detention and announced a new set of transgender detention guidelines.[91]

In early 2016, Santa Ana's city manager proposed doubling the bed space in the LGBT pod from 64 to 128 and increasing the overall available detention beds from 200 to 300. Since the city earned $105 per day for each detainee, the city manager projected that the expansion could earn the city an additional $2.2 million annually and help to pay down the debt that had been incurred to build the jail.[92] The city manager's proposal reflected the neoliberal economics that have fueled criminalization and mass incarceration. As

Ruth Wilson Gilmore explains, jails and prisons became increasingly central to California's and the nation's economies during the 1980s and 1990s in the context of neoliberal restructuring.[93] Cities began building or expanding jails as a means to participate in anticrime initiatives, secure funds, and create jobs. Setting aside beds in local jails to detain migrants became a strategy for cash-strapped cities to further boost revenue, including in Santa Ana.[94]

The protestors in February and the hunger strikers in May 2016 thoroughly understood and pushed back against these penal and profit-driven logics. Although the city manager presented the proposal in neutral, strictly budgetary terms, protestors strongly objected that it was a proposal to profit from the suffering of people who were targeted for dispossession by the intertwining of neoliberalism and crimmigration. Hairo Cortez, the program coordinator at Orange County Immigrant Youth United, argued, "We think it's extremely shameful that the city is looking to in a sense cover its budget holes on the backs of undocumented people."[95] Here, Cortez vividly evokes the ways that budgets depend on the exploitation and wearing down of bodies. Hunger strikers reiterated this argument; their first demand was "that the city of Santa Ana schedule a vote to cancel the city's jail contract with ICE, which allows the city to profit from the detention of undocumented immigrants, including transgender women."[96] Moreover, their form of protest—a hunger strike—viscerally dramatized that bodies are at stake.[97]

The protestors and hunger strikers also linked suffering in the pod to the struggles experienced by city residents. The press release in advance of the city council's February vote on expanding bed space, from Orange County Immigrant Youth United, Resistencia Autonomia Igualdad y Liderazgo, and Familia: Trans Queer Liberation Movement, laid out some of the links: "'As ICE causes panic with its raids and trauma with its abuses inside detention, Santa Ana should be ending any collaboration with the agency not expanding it.' . . . The contract expansion . . . is raising questions if those proposing it are more interested in funding the jail off of those who would be detained than it is in the well-being of its constituents who could be targeted by immigration enforcement activity."[98] In other words, not only was ICE imprisoning people in the city jail, which the city supported and sought to expand, but ICE had a presence and conducted raids within the city that caused panic and trauma. Since ICE operates based on racial and other kinds of profiling, all marginalized people in Santa Ana were deeply affected by ICE presence even when they could prove their legal status or US citizenship. Moreover, ICE's actions were thoroughly interconnected with policing that targets marginalized citizens and migrants alike. Contracting with ICE to detain migrants implicitly endorsed these actions against city residents who experienced stress, trauma, and terror as a result, and some of whom ended up detained and deported.

By linking the suffering of migrants in the pod and the suffering of city residents, the protesters and hunger strikers linked criminalization produced through state migration control with criminalization produced through white supremacist, capitalist, antitrans, antiqueer logics that turn migrants and subaltern citizens into targets in various ways. At the same time, they identified the key role that city council could play in contributing to, or helping to unravel, these interlinked forms of violence and suffering, which condition intimacies and life possibilities.

Abolition

The fact that the pod was described as a model for detaining queer and transgender migrants became a point of conflict between protestors and some members of the city council. The conflict highlighted the difference between a reformist approach that does not substantially change the existing system and an abolitionist approach that seeks to end the system and create new possibilities. Kay Whitlock and Nancy A. Heitzeg explain that reforms function as "cons" when they do not address the "structural inequality and violence that are foundational to the United States" and instead reentrench and even expand existing systems.[99] Abolitionist scholars and activists therefore support reforms that, as Mariame Kaba explains, "are, to use the term coined by André Gorz and popularized by Ruth Wilson Gilmore . . . non-reformist reforms" that contribute to shrinking the system and moving toward an abolitionist future.[100] Activists and scholars have developed criteria to assess whether a proposed reform is likely to entrench or to contribute to the abolition of the existing system.[101]

The LGBT pod was a reform intended to entrench the existing system. The pod was used to suggest that ICE could engage in supposedly humane detention that was sensitive to the needs of vulnerable groups—without acknowledging or addressing that state migration controls and the migrant-detention system stem from and reproduce violent structural inequalities. Thus, ICE consistently described the pod as a model facility with well-trained staff and good conditions that are responsive to detainee needs. Immigration and Customs Enforcement spokesperson Virginia Kice told Tina Vasquez that the Santa Ana pod "is a protective custody environment established by ICE to ensure that transgender individuals who are subject to detention while their immigration cases are being adjudicated can be housed in a safe setting."[102] An ICE statement further explained: "'Officials trained Santa Ana City Jail staff on [LGBTQ] matters in July 2013, June 2014, and again in 2015.'... The training focused on 'ICE policy and procedures addressing sexual assault prevention and response; searches; medical care; privacy; [LGBTQ] sensitivity and transgender detainee care; and specific instruction on the provisions of the Transgender Care Memorandum.'"[103] Concerning claims of abuse facing transgender women in the pod, which were reported by Human Rights Watch in March 2016, ICE responded that "'Santa Ana City Jail, which houses the overwhelming majority of ICE's detained transgender population, has medical professionals on staff who have experience providing health care to transgender individuals, including hormone therapy.' A spokesperson from the federal agency also reported that 'ICE has not received any recent official complaints from transgender detainees regarding medical treatment at the Santa Ana City Jail facility.'"[104] In these and other ways, ICE affirmed its cultural sensitivity while continuing to operate a brutal system. They consistently asserted that the pod proved that detention of vulnerable people could be conducted safely and appropriately, even when all evidence shows otherwise.

The fact that the pod was presented as a model facility sowed doubt about whether to push for completely ending the contract for the facility among some city council and community members. Councilmember David Benavides told the *Orange County Registrar* that before the February vote, he was "wrestling" with an important concern: "'Either way, for us in the city of Santa Ana, folks are going to be detained and held somewhere,' Benavides said, 'and would it be the case where the city of Santa Ana would be able to be a place that would (be known for) providing dignity and a respectful way to be housed?'"[105] Detained migrants also worried that if the pod closed, they might be moved to a more repressive facility rather than released.[106]

Benavides's wording conceives of detention as inevitable and of the pod as a place where detained people are treated humanely and respectfully, which formerly detained people and a Human Rights Watch report from March 2016, *"Do You See How Much I'm Suffering Here?,"* strongly disputed.[107] The respectful treatment that was imagined to occur in the pod contrasted with the abuse that is known to occur there and in the general detention system. The existence of the pod effectively absolved ICE from addressing the fact that detention is abusive, whether in a pod or not.[108] Roberto Herrera from DeColores Queer OC challenged Benevides's reformist logic, arguing that ICE officials and the city of Santa Ana were "'pushing a narrative intended to create fear and doubt in the community, positioning the queer and transgender pods at the jail as "the most humane option" for queer and trans undocumented immigrants in detention.'"[109] Rather than focusing on fears that the pod might close, leaving transgender migrants to suffer in general detention facilities (which was already happening), protestors and hunger strikers offered an abolitionist vision of ending detention altogether. Herrera argued: "'We need city council to shut this program down and we need to work at a national level and advocate to free all queer and trans people from detention. Incarceration will never be the answer.... We can't be complacent. The city can't be complacent. We have to tell the city they cannot adopt or continue implementing this "model practice." First, we need to shut this down locally and then do this nationally. We are advocating for the release of all trans women.'"[110] Hunger striker Jennicet Gutiérrez strongly affirmed that detention, whether in the pod or the general system, could never be the right place for transgender and queer people:

> "You know where the best place for our queer and trans brothers and sisters is? It's with their communities.... In detention, no matter where, we are harassed, we are made fun of, we are threatened, we are misgendered. We are denied medical access. If you complain about this, they put you in solitary confinement and say it's for your 'safety'— and that is punishment. I believe that is torture. Trans women who have been detained verify this. The Human Rights Watch report verifies this. They say they care, that they are doing everything they can to treat trans people fairly, but the reality is a different story."[111]

Gutiérrez connected struggles over detention to global structural inequalities: "Detention has to end because transgender women, globally, are in a crisis. We are being targeted, we are being murdered, we are being discriminated against and denied basic access and rights.... Putting us in detention isn't the solution to that."[112]

A blog post by Isa Noyola on the National Domestic Workers Alliance website put Gutiérrez's analysis into even broader context by calling for the making of a world where not only were transgender women of color not being abused in detention but also conditions existed for them to thrive in the world:

> That doesn't just mean ending the horrifying abuses transgender women face in immigration detention, although that is a huge part of it. It also means ensuring trans immigrant women are able to live and thrive in this country after they are released from detention.... We cannot just shout #FreeNicoll—we must also work towards creating

a system to support her and other trans women as they navigate life post-detention.

Racial, environmental, economic, and immigrant justice work is transgender justice work.[113]

Protestors and hunger strikers explained that working toward this kind of vision served not just transgender women but everyone. For example, Jennicet Gutiérrez told *Vice* that she was working for freedom not just for detained transgender and queer migrants but also for everyone without legal status, "'and that includes our families, our cousins, our uncles who might be undocumented but aren't necessarily part of the LGBT community.'"[114] Jorge Gutierrez, a queer-identified migrant hunger striker whose brother had been deported to Mexico, explained succinctly, "'If we're able to fight for the most vulnerable, then we're actually fighting for everyone.'"[115]

Making Change

On May 17, 2016, a vociferous city council meeting ended with the decision that the city would not end its contract with ICE but would allow it to expire in 2020. On May 19, the hunger strikers ended their protest. In December 2016, the Santa Ana City Council approved a sanctuary city resolution. They also voted to notify ICE that they would reduce the available migrant-detention space in the Santa Ana jail and commissioned a study to explore possibilities for reusing the jail for other purposes.[116] Aviva Stahl reports, "For Jorge and Jennicet, the development exemplified a tangible way that immigration rights activists could support the work of groups like Black Lives Matter, and a broader movement against police violence and what many groups see as racist and reflexive use of incarceration. 'Now, because of our campaign and how we've been pushing, there's a whole conversation to close down the city jail completely and reuse it for something for the community,' Jorge told me."[117]

In January 2017, the city council passed some of the most far-reaching sanctuary policies in the nation.[118] Days later, upon being sworn in as president, Trump signed an executive order that proclaimed, "Sanctuary jurisdictions across the United States willfully violate Federal law in an attempt to shield aliens from removal from the United States. These jurisdictions have caused immeasurable harm to the American people and to the very fabric of our Republic."[119] The order targeted every undocumented migrant for deportation and targeted sanctuary cities, which were seen as impeding deportation efforts, for punishment.

In February 2017, ICE sent the city of Santa Ana a ninety-day notice that it was withdrawing from its contract for detention. Initially the pod was to be relocated to the Prairieland Detention Center in Alvarado, Texas, but in 2017, it was instead relocated to the Cibola County Correctional Center in New Mexico, operated by CoreCivic, a private corporation that has greatly profited from detaining migrants.[120] Tina Shull explains, "Upon the pod's closure, Freedom for Immigrants, Las Crisantemas, and community organizations worked quickly to find sponsors for trans women detained at Santa Ana and to fight for their release rather than transfer. However, a small number of trans women were not released and instead transferred to New Mexico."[121] The pod at Cibola was redesignated as transgender only with capacity for sixty. Balaguera captures ICE's continuing control over who counts as trans while in detention and the consequences of that control. Two interviewees told her that a *chico gay* had been housed in the pod with *chicas trans*. The *chicas trans* viewed him as "of our community" and viewed the pod as an LGBTQ—rather than solely T—space.[122] After eight months, ICE relocated the *chico gay* to an all-male detention facility, which caused concern. His transfer shows the ongoing management of identities within detention and the stakes: "The threat of sexual violence is not the same everywhere, even as it is already extremely high for all LGBT detainees."[123]

Serious concerns continued to be raised about the treatment of people both in the pod and in general detention. In May 2018, Roxsana Hernández, a thirty-three-year-old, transgender woman living with HIV who fled Honduras to save her own life, died after being transferred from a CBP icebox, where she suffered severe cold and a lack of medical care or adequate food, to the pod at Cibola and then to the hospital.[124] In June 2019, Johana Medina Leon, a twenty-five-year-old transgender asylum seeker from El Salvador, died after being detained at the Otero County Processing Center in Chaparral, New Mexico. That same month, twenty-nine trans women and nonbinary migrants detained in Cibola sent a letter to Trans Queer Pueblo outlining harsh conditions. These included failure to provide timely or appropriate medical care to people with disabilities, people living with HIV, or anyone in need, and daily verbal and psychological mistreatment.[125] The letter was sent just days after the media had been given a tour of the facility that showcased detainees playing basketball, gardening, and getting their hair done. Although they feared retaliation, the letter writers courageously signed their names and listed their A-numbers while asking "for the national and international human rights community to launch an official investigation into the facility."[126] In 2020, as the COVID-19 pandemic spread rapidly in migrant detention centers, numerous attempts were made to get transgender, queer, and all migrants released.

The struggle to #EndTransDetention continued through a #NoPrideInDetention campaign that harnessed Pride to resist trans detention. Actions included a funeral service in Washington, DC, that honored and grieved the lives of three trans women—Victoria Arellano, Roxsana Hernández, and Johana Medina Leon—who died in ICE custody.[127] On June 16, 2021, eight advocacy groups sent a letter to President Biden and secretary of Homeland Security Alejandro Mayorkas that summarized the lessons learned from years of struggle and again demanded the release of transgender migrants, as well as migrants living with HIV:

> For years, the Department of Homeland Security ("DHS") has attempted to create conditions of confinement that are safe for these historically disenfranchised minorities. This has been a fool's errand. Under both Democrat and Republican leadership, DHS has wasted millions of taxpayer dollars attempting to overcome a simple and inevitable truth: it is not possible for the U.S. government to house transgender and HIV-positive asylum seekers safely. Every progressive policy, every well-meaning protocol, and every specialized facility has utterly failed. This has to stop. It is in your exclusive power to put an end to this ongoing human rights atrocity.[128]

Abolition Is a Long-Term Commitment

Highlighting the key role that city governments may play in enabling—or challenging—infrastructures of violence and oppression, protestors demanded that Santa Ana stop enabling even when that resulted in lost revenue and punishment from the federal government. Their vision refuted assertions that a carceral state can ever adequately care for transgender and queer migrants, whether through general detention or a specialized pod. They also refused the normative model of nation-based citizenship as an intimacy premised on structural inequalities and that model's definition of who was properly included in the citizenry of Santa Ana. Instead, they asserted forms of belonging based on presence rather than official legal status and visions for intimacies that, by ensuring thriving for economically struggling and working-class transgender migrant women who are overwhelmingly Latinx, Black, or Indigenous, ensure thriving for everyone. Their efforts and organizing that has happened since underscore that thriving is impossible under conditions of criminalization, mass incarceration, and privation that pipeline marginalized citizens and migrants into prisons and migrants into detention. The hunger strikers who put their bodies on the line showed that working for abolition requires responding to continually changing conditions and that city officials and residents have key roles to play in challenging the distribution of resources, possibilities, and futures away from their current entrenched dependence on the exhaustion, exploitation, and wearing down of marginalized bodies toward something else.

CONCLUSION

"At the Edge of the Possible"

The book has centered writings by and about queer and trans migrants of color and diverse allies working to reset human and planetary lives and possible futures by vigorously contesting deportation logics and practices. The writings conceive deportation not as an individual, un/fortunate, or un/deserved event but as a cornerstone in an unjust system of interlocking inequalities that seeks to reproduce and normalize global apartheid, the negation of Indigenous sovereignties, the criminalization of displaced people, structural inequalities among citizens, the normalization of mass incarceration, and migrant terror and subordination. Undocumented and precarious migrants are direct targets of the US deportation regime, but the regime also coproduces the good migrant, the normative citizen, and the marginalized citizen as categories that relationally define one another in structures of inequality. These relationalities offer the basis for queer, trans, and all migrant and citizen allies to work to end deportation and the interlocking forms of violence that deportation depends upon and reproduces, while making space for different possible futures to emerge.

Chapters highlighted that interactions between infrastructures and intimacies provide grounds for challenging deportation and realizing different futures. Rather than offering a grand theory or prescription, the book used "infrastructures" and "intimacies" as heuristics that allow us to grasp the often overlooked, visionary work that has been done and the multiple further interventions that are possible. This conclusion offers final reflections on infrastructures, intimacies, and continuing possibilities in the struggle for what Sarah Haley calls "necessary transformations" to end deportation and realize a different world.[1]

Infrastructures

Infrastructures include personnel, built environments, budgets, laws, policies, practices, and discourses, which together materialize how migration controls are enacted and experienced. Shaped by the federal government and operating in tandem with state, local, corporate, and individual practices, the massive US migration-control infrastructure assumes specific forms in specific locations.[2] Queer and trans migrants and allies are often experts on understanding the overall infrastructure of immigration control and the forms it takes in particular places. Their work includes contributing to broad campaigns like Defund ICE (Immigration and Customs Enforcement), Abolish ICE, Defund Hate (i.e., ICE and Customs and Border Protection), and #FreeThemAll that target big infrastructure.[3] Other initiatives challenge how information capitalism and big tech are expanding surveillance, extraction, exclusion from social programs, detention, and deportation directed at migrant communities and marginalized citizens.[4] Still other efforts target small components of infrastructure that are nonetheless crucial.[5]

Doors, for example, have become deeply contested in the struggle against deportation, as Daniela Vargas's experiences illustrate. News media relates that when she was seven, Vargas and her family came to the United States from Argentina under a visa waiver program that allowed entry for ninety days.[6] They remained beyond ninety days, which meant that they became undocumented. In 2012, Vargas sought and received Deferred Action for Childhood Arrivals (DACA) status, which allowed her to be present and legally employed but did not provide options for permanent legal status. In November 2016, Vargas's DACA status expired, and she struggled to save up the $495 renewal fee. On February 10, 2017, weeks after Donald Trump became president, she mailed her DACA renewal application. Days later, she watched ICE arrest her father and brother while they headed to work. Then ICE came knocking at the Vargas home. Rather than open the door, Vargas called her pastor, who notified advocacy groups and local media. They stood outside the Vargas home for five hours as ICE agents tried to persuade Vargas to open the door. When she continued to refuse, they left, returned with a search warrant, and broke down the door. They found Vargas behind a closet door. Guns drawn, they pulled her out and placed her in handcuffs. She said she held DACA status; they said they knew her DACA status had expired but were giving her a "pass" this time.[7] Vargas went into hiding and, two weeks later, spoke at a press conference in Jackson, Mississippi, that opposed a law banning cities from developing sanctuary policies. Afterward, ICE agents pulled over the car she was riding in, opened her door, hauled her out, and took her to a holding facility and then detention.[8] Vargas's friend who was driving called advocates and attorneys, who immediately launched a deportation-defense campaign.[9] Vargas describes how, while being driven to detention, she gazed out the window, trying to absorb the sight of trees, the road, and unconfined people before she became locked behind the walls, doors, and bars of a detention center.[10] Ten days later, Vargas was released from detention on an order of supervision.

Vargas's experiences show some of the ways that doors are important in the struggle against deportation. The standoff at her family's front door evokes the dense struggles and resulting laws that have cohered around the police executing a search warrant on someone's home.[11] Understanding the importance of doors, migrant activists have created "know your rights" campaigns and materials to prepare individuals and communities for responding when ICE comes knocking at the door. United We Dream, which played a pivotal role in Vargas's defense deportation campaign, offers detailed advice about preparing for the possibility of ICE coming to one's door and what to do when that actually happens.[12] Their materials stress that people should not open the door unless ICE can show they have a warrant. The Transgender Law Center's advisory, "ICE Raids," further cautions that "ICE is allowed to lie to get into your home. . . . ICE may pretend to be police and say they need help, that they are investigating a case, or that they need to verify someone's identity."[13] Once inside the door, they may detain whomever they encounter. For that reason, people should not open the door. Nonetheless, as the Transgender Law Center advises, "be prepared and expect that ICE will enter without a warrant and be aggressive."[14] That aggression may include misgendering people or "say[ing] something offensive about your gender expression, body, and sexual orientation." The Transgender Law Center warns that reacting to ICE's gender, sexual, and corporeal aggression could be used against the person.[15] In Vargas's case, when she refused to voluntarily open the door, ICE left to secure a warrant, perhaps because they were being observed.

Emboldened by the warrant, they broke down the door, searched the house, and pulled a traumatized Vargas from behind the doors of the closet while pointing a gun at her.

It matters what kind of structure the door is part of. Rules concerning doors to a home are different from rules concerning other kinds of doors. For example, private homes are not listed under ICE's "protected areas" (formerly "sensitive locations") policy, but places of worship, schools, and health-care facilities are listed—although ICE can invoke exceptions to circumvent these restrictions.[16] Nonetheless, the protected areas policy, which resulted from struggles against ICE, accounts for why taking refuge in a church may offer levels of protection that are unavailable when taking refuge in a home. The doors to a church are treated differently than the doors to a home. The doors to the closet where Vargas hid offered no protection. After the car she was riding in was pulled over, the car door also offered no protection from being detained and incarcerated.

Doors demarcate and constitute spaces: home versus street, sacred versus secular, detention versus nondetention. In constituting spaces, doors generally organize the flows of people, intimacies, and im/possibilities in ways that reproduce social relations of power. For example, in demarcating the boundaries between public and private, the doors of a home depend on gender, sexual, racial, economic, and legal status arrangements. When ICE broke down the front door after Vargas refused to open it, their action showed that the supposed privacy of the home is primarily available to white, middle-class, cis-, hetero-, or homonormative citizens. Yet, ICE secured a warrant before breaking down the door, which they often do not do. The warrant does not diminish the violence that was involved, but the fact that ICE paused to get a warrant reflects the effects of prior histories of contesting state violence. Struggles over who may pass or refuse to pass through a door, depending on which kind of door, contest and seek to reset the structural inequalities that underpin norms of home/street, off-limits/not off-limits, and safe/detainable. When seeking to contest deportation, every element of the infrastructure, big and small, offers possibilities that deserve attention and action.

Intimacies

Intimacies emerge, cohere around, become reconfigured, or are severed as people and infrastructure interact. The US migration-control regime seeks to condition intimacies in ways that serve dominant nationalism and valorized forms of citizenship. Married, middle-class couple relationships and parent/child ties remain key to state efforts to cultivate a neocolonial, settler, racialized, cisheteronormative nation and citizenry anchored in the privatized home. At the same time, continual efforts to stigmatize and sometimes criminalize citizens and legal migrants who spend time, share space, provide information, or offer food, a ride, or a bed to a person without documented legal presence, including to family members, friends, and strangers, make clear the wide range of intimacies that the state seeks to manage in order to achieve its goals. Teachers, health-care workers, social-service providers, bank clerks, and others have become compelled to inquire into people's legal status during professional interactions. Everyone is encouraged to become a "watchful citizen" who reports individuals to Border Patrol based on everyday interactions and suspicions.[17]

The Trump administration further deepened efforts to manage intimacies in ways intended to enforce white, nationalist, settler colonial, and cisheteronormative ways of being. This included aggressively seeking to further criminalize citizens and legal residents who provided assistance to migrants with irregular status—even when they were injured, ill, or dying—and criminalizing and defunding organizations and municipalities that refused to follow a strictly enforcement-only approach. The Trump administration also ramped up practices of disregarding, severing, or deliberately using state-recognized intimacies against migrants in order to make them vulnerable and deportable, while sanctioning unfettered, abusive intimacies toward migrants who were in state hands. In short, while claiming to offer family-friendly migration policies, the US government also actively engages in "dismantling relationships of solidarity and care that sustain life" and "stripping people of any family, community, or social relationship capable of transcending differences of nationality and legal status" in order to further criminalization, attrition, and deterrence.[18]

I have analyzed writings about how queer and trans migrants and allies have mobilized, created, cohered, and tried out different intimacies as they seek to survive and resist the chokepoints that generate detention and deportation. When Vargas's father and brother were arrested, the intimacies among family members became deeply disrupted. As Vargas sought to shield herself from possible arrest by refusing to open the door to ICE, she activated a network of allies who extended intimacies of care and assistance. When Vargas spoke at a press conference in support of families who were enduring the threat of deportation, she affirmed intimacies across lines of legal and social status. Her words challenged the Trump administration's efforts to further estrange migrants from citizens while deepening other social divisions. After the press conference, ICE pulled over Vargas's car, removed her from her car, confined her within an ICE vehicle, and transported her to the brutal intimacies of the LaSalle Detention Center in Louisiana. Her friend again mobilized allies who organized a successful deportation-defense campaign.[19]

Experiences like Vargas's and chapters in this book illuminate Ann Laura Stoler's argument that the management of intimacies has always been central to state-making and citizenship in a context of empire, slavery, and settler colonialism—and central to resistance and refusal, too.[20] In the crosshairs of deportation practices that maintain stratified nation-based citizenship and global apartheid, queer- and trans-identified migrants of color and allies extend Stoler's analysis by enacting intimacies within, below, and beyond the deportation state's horizons in order to foster survival, well-being, and abolitionist futures.

Futures

Angela Y. Davis and her coauthors stress that abolition is about "building and experimenting as much as it [is] about what must be dismantled."[21] Reflecting this insight, the work discussed in this book involves not just dismantling the existing infrastructures of deportation while cohering intimacies within and beyond the horizons that are set by the state. It also involves imagining and creating different futures through building alternatives. Since there are no road maps for creating a future without criminalization, detention, and deportation, the work of building alternatives is "of necessity speculative" and messy.[22] Organizations not only seek to stop deportation, defund ICE, abolish ICE, abolish CBP, abolish prisons, and defund the police but also offer suggestions for redirecting the extraordinary resources that would become freed up toward fostering human and planetary thriving.[23] For example, #DefundHate's "divest-invest" strategy sought to defund ICE and CBP and redirect the estimated $25 billion a year that's spent on profiling, jailing, and deporting migrants toward "investing in education, housing, green infrastructure, and healthcare programs."[24] Queer and trans migrants and allies also continually experiment with building their own infrastructures.

For example, groups have been working to create housing. Housing is not the same as a home. Will McKeithen explains, "Home is a physical structure (e.g., a house), an imaginary, felt, embodied place, and a contested process of everyday un/making. . . . The modern home has also served as a potent site in the sociospatial politics of heteronormativity" and as a metaphor and material arrangement for compelled configurations of nation and citizenry.[25]

Although it may not be home, housing often contributes to a sense of home.[26] Housing is infrastructure in its own right and part of larger infrastructural arrangements, too.[27]

In numerous ways, access to housing reduces the likelihood that people living in the United States will become deportable. For example, housing may reduce the necessity of engaging in criminalized forms of survival work, one's chances of being criminalized for being unhoused, and the likelihood of becoming the victim of a violent crime that triggers police attention or a hospital stay. Housing also ensures one has a fixed address that is required for getting documents and information and that may provide a base for getting connected to resources and communities.[28] Creating affordable, safe housing is also a crucial part of creating a different future for everyone, including struggling citizens.

Yet, to engage housing is to engage one of the most intractable issues through which deep-rooted, intersecting inequalities materialize in people's lives. As Anne Bonds describes, the history of property ownership, including housing, "is underpinned by the expropriation of indigenous territories, the enslavement of humans legally classified as property, and the exploitation of devalued labor."[29] Moreover, "it is impossible to understand the racial economics of property without attention to gender and sexuality and the ways in which [gendered] bodies and socially reproductive labor were (and are) essential to property making."[30] After slavery was formally abolished, laws and policies steadily institutionalized segregation, thus ensuring continued white access to land, housing, paid employment, public space, and more. These developments were inextricable from the construction and diffusion of a heteronormative order grounded in the white, settled, homeowning, patriarchal family.[31] Throughout the twentieth century, enforced residential segregation; lending practices that discriminated based on race, gender, and sex; housing covenants; redlining; and racist and classist urban renewal projects enforced by violence and terror reproduced this system. Accordingly, housing inequality significantly accounts for the vast racial wealth gap in the United States. Bonds suggests that since the 1970s, white homeowners' fears of declining property values became linked to fears of risk and crime that legitimated the rise of the carceral state, including mass incarceration and migrant criminalization. The subprime mortgage crisis of 2007, fueled by lenders who deliberately targeted communities of color and low-income white people for high-interest-rate mortgages that became impossible to repay, reveals the persistence of housing policies that generate capital accumulation through racist, gendered, and heterosexist logics of economic exploitation and ongoing colonial expropriation. Moreover, the subprime mortgage crisis was inextricable from global capitalist dynamics that drive migrations.[32] The 2020 pandemic, which pushed housing prices to new highs while generating skyrocketing rents and an eviction crisis, continued these dynamics.

Addressing queer and trans migrants' housing needs, which reduces their risk of detention and deportation while capacitating their lives, therefore involves navigating complex histories, deep inequalities, and the constant possibility of reaffirming existing structural inequalities.[33] For example, US migration law and policy offer more avenues to get out of detention and into housing to queer and trans migrants who are legible as asylum seekers than they do to other queer and trans migrants.[34] Prioritizing asylum seekers risks affirming binaries of deserving asylum seekers and undeserving undocumented migrants that legitimate the dominant system. Similarly, ICE's guidelines make release most feasible for migrants who have no criminal record and have a citizen or lawful permanent resident (LPR) relative or friend into whose custody they can be released through sponsorship. These release guidelines seek to institutionalize power and dependency between migrants and sponsoring citizens or LPRs, especially between migrants and socially valued citizens or LPRs who have stable housing and no criminal record, which is very problematic.[35] The guidelines also require that, effectively, the citizen or LPR sponsor must undertake the role of tracking the migrant on behalf of the state until their case is resolved. It also transfers financial obligations to private individuals, which saves the state money, as Jill M. Williams and Vanessa A. Massaro insightfully analyze.[36] Releasing people into private housing also comes with risks of exploitation. For example, Freedom for Immigrants, which formalized a sponsorship model on which others have built, sought to preempt the risk that the relationship could become one of coerced, unfree labor: "The home and basic support you provide must be offered without any exchange of services in return (for example, working on the family farm). We must be very explicit about this due to laws on human trafficking and indentured servitude."[37]

Queer and trans migrants and allies have wrestled with these and other systemic inequalities when trying to create housing options. The Santa Fe Dreamers Project has undertaken large-scale efforts to get queer and trans migrants out of detention and into private homes while waiting for their asylum cases to be processed. Others like the Queer Detainee Empowerment Project have facilitated informal arrangements like finding sofas or beds where people can stay temporarily and connecting queer and trans migrants with housing services where they navigate high demand, limited options, and multiple barriers that are compounded by migrant status.[38]

Queer and trans migrants are sometimes directly at the forefront of the work to create housing options. Edafe Okporo, a gay man from Nigeria, founded and directed the RDJ Refugee Shelter in Harlem, New York, for homeless LGBTQ asylum seekers. Okporo understood these needs: upon landing at JFK Airport in New York in 2016, he requested asylum and was instead taken to a New Jersey detention center. His fictionalized account of these experiences centers a gay Nigerian asylum seeker who, while in detention, was referred to not by name but by the bed he was placed in: "Bed 26."[39] Also serving LGBTQ asylum seekers, the LGBT Asylum Task Force in Worcester, Massachusetts, has created an impressive program of housing and comprehensive services for LGBT asylum seekers that is currently directed by a self-identified gay man from Jamaica.[40] Anandrea Molina, who describes herself as an undocumented trans migrant from Tamaulipas, Mexico, opened Casa Anandrea in Houston, Texas, in May 2017.[41] She characterizes the shelter as "the city's only refuge specifically for undocumented trans, queer, and non-binary people."[42]

Shelters for LGBTQ migrants traveling from Central America and farther afield through Mexico to the United States border have also emerged in the last decade, some run by faith-based organizations. La 72 in Tenosique, Mexico, which is run by Franciscans, was the first shelter to explicitly seek to meet the needs of LGBTQ people on the move.[43] Other shelters have included Casa Frida, Casa De Las Muñecas Tiresias AC, Casa de Luz, and Jardín de las Mariposas.[44]

Shelters provide critical shelter, food, and other vital resources and assistance that help people on the move.[45] At the same time, they are embedded in what Wendy A. Vogt and others call "the migrant industry" that has vastly expanded in the face of punitive immigration policies that seek to exclude and criminalize migrants. That industry facilitates journeys but transforms migrants into commodities.[46] Shelters cannot avoid being embedded in the migrant industry; they are where migrants rest, eat, find smugglers, transfer money, and find illicit work and where outsiders find migrants to prey on. Shelters also participate in the logic of humanitarian governance that has been deeply critiqued for its implication in neoliberal logics and its role in producing not just deserving but also implicitly undeserving and disposable people.[47] Martha Balaguera argues that shelters are where migrants often learn the expectations of normative transness and queerness on which assistance depends.[48] Within this complex context, shelters nonetheless provide important assistance to queer and trans people on the move.

Shelters became even more critical after the Trump administration implemented the so-called Migrant Protection Protocols that indefinitely stranded tens of thousands of migrants in Mexico as they waited for their asylum claims to be heard. In 2020, as the COVID-19 pandemic worsened, the Trump administration issued an order allowing for the rapid expulsion of migrants, including asylum seekers, at the southern border based on public health concerns.[49] These policies continued under the Biden administration. Queer, trans, and all migrants affected by the policies have faced multiple harms and risks, such as sexual assault, kidnapping, trafficking, and murder.[50] Access to shelter helps to mitigate these risks.

Without minimizing the challenges and limitations, shelters, sponsorships, and other housing options significantly contribute to helping people on the move. Queer and trans migrants and allies who are building infrastructures continually negotiate the complexities of creating life-building possibilities from within multiple systems of oppression. An abolitionist approach requires serving people's immediate, urgent needs while building infrastructures that contribute to the demise of oppressive systems. There is no blueprint for the work, but extensive discussions about the importance of nonreformist, rather than reformist, changes offer helpful guidance. Wikipedia succinctly defines *nonreformist reform* as a reform that "is conceived, not in terms of what is possible within the framework of a given system and administration, but in view of what should be made possible in terms of human needs and demands."[51] Activist individuals and groups including Critical Resistance, Dean Spade, Peter Gelderloos, Ruth Wilson Gilmore, Mariame Kaba, and Harsha Walia have developed criteria for assessing whether a proposed change is nonreformist.[52] Future research and action must continue to address and support the complexities of queer and trans migrants and ally infrastructure-building efforts to create noncarceral futures.[53] The voices and experiences of deported queer and trans migrants must become a critical part of the work.

Beloved Home?

Housing is not necessarily home. Yet, housing is often an important part of creating a world where people may experience and feel at home in its broadest sense. The Trans Agenda for Liberation offers one vision of what it takes to create what they call "beloved home." The Trans Agenda for Liberation "is a community-led guide" toward creating "a future where we can all not only survive but thrive. This agenda addresses the urgent political, legal, and social violence enacted against our communities, while channeling trans imagination to bring our boldest visions to life."[54] The "Beloved Home" pillar describes the interlocking inequalities that must be addressed in order to realize home:

> A beloved home represents the physical structure of a shelter, a home, but also encompasses the deep connection with land, ancestors, family, community, and ability to thrive. . . .
>
> We purposefully bring together transgender, gender non-conforming, nonbinary, and two-spirit people working within the movements for Indigenous sovereignty, migrant justice, and climate justice in order to create a holistic approach to our relationship to the concept of home that is multilayered and addresses the complexities of living at the center of multiple systems of oppression. We center those of us who've been living in the shadows, fleeing for their lives, and searching for refuge without any recognition—in order to create a more expansive room, so that all of us can find a home within.[55]

"Beloved Home" situates the authors' lack of home in ongoing histories of settler colonialism, genocide, slavery, empire, and cisheteropatriarchy that fuel forced migration and structural inequalities within nation-states. It foregrounds coalitions among diverse communities, histories, and struggles, without erasing their differences, as a basis for transformation. "Beloved Home" prioritizes the perspectives and needs of those who are most harmed by the current system. Their approach "is not based on established identities but always prioritizes non-privileged political positionalities and their subjectification," which shift.[56] Moreover, "Beloved Home" and the Trans Agenda for Liberation as a whole do not rely on a simple reversal of hierarchies of oppression because they do not exclude more privileged people. Rather, they offer "a blueprint for liberation for all."[57]

"Beloved Home" does not guarantee a particular outcome. Rather, it offers one compelling diagnosis of the intersecting structures of violence and inequality that trans and queer migrants experience, centers those who are most harmed, and suggests concrete steps for transformation. Showcasing the critical analysis and complex work that trans and queer migrants and allies are engaged in, the statement asserts that a beloved home is possible.[58]

The possibility of creating conditions for beloved home to flourish for everyone offers a fitting place to end this book about queer and trans migrants of color and allies' struggles to abolish deportation. Deportation serves as an anchor for global apartheid, the criminalization and exploitation of displaced people, the negation of Indigenous sovereignties, nation-based citizenship grounded in violence, and deep inequalities among the citizenry. Authorizing violence toward migrants and those who are perceived as migrants, deportation thoroughly depends on and contributes to other systems of violence, including mass incarceration. Abolishing deportation would meaningfully challenge these multiple forms of violence while unfolding transformed futures "at the edge of the possible."[59] Infrastructures and intimacies, in their interaction with one another, are the grounds from which queer and trans migrants and allies' struggles for transformation continue to unfold.

1   Nathalie Peutz and Nicholas De Genova define *deportation* as "the compulsory removal of 'aliens' from the physical, social, and juridical space of the state." Peutz and De Genova, "Introduction," 1.
2   Goodman, *The Deportation Machine*.
3   Park, "Self-Deportation Nation," 1887.
4   Peutz and De Genova, "Introduction," 2. Moreover, Shahram Khosravi highlights that the terminology commonly associated with deportation—such as *return, home, homeland, country of origin,* and *reintegration*—"naturalises the nation state system," pathologizes movement, depoliticizes deportation, and moralizes. Khosravi, "Introduction," 10–11.
5   See, for example, Anderson, Gibney, and Paoletti, "Citizenship, Deportation and the Boundaries of Belonging."
6   De Genova, "Migrant 'Illegality' and Deportability in Everyday Life," 438.
7   Prevention Through Deterrence became the national Border Patrol strategy in 1994. In 1993, a study commissioned by the Office of National Drug Control Policy described how the southwest border was "being overrun" and how drug smuggling was a serious threat (Haddal, *Border Security*, 4). The study recommended that what was then the INS should switch its focus from apprehending people after entry to preventing their entry in the first place. Prevention strategies drew on Operation Gatekeeper in California and Operation Blockade (later renamed Operation Hold the Line) in Texas. The basic concept involved trying to make it impossible to cross at major urban centers by deploying hundreds of agents and surveillance technology and equipment. This meant that migrants were funneled into crossing through more hostile and difficult terrain, such as the Sonoran Desert. Policymakers understood that migrants would face increased injury and sometimes "mortal danger." These increased dangers, in turn, were expected to deter others from trying to cross, eventually reducing undocumented migration significantly. Prevention Through Deterrence strategies have been widely shown not only to fail in their objective of preventing unauthorized migration but also to increase injury or death and to make migrants who succeed in crossing even more exploitable. See Nuñez-Neto, *Border Security*.
8   Organizations like the Colibrí Center for Human Rights address the missing and disappeared. See Colibrí Center for Human Rights, "About Us."

9 Goodman, *The Deportation Machine*, 6.
10 Goodman, *The Deportation Machine*, 6.
11 Goodman, *The Deportation Machine*, 6.
12 Golash-Boza, *Deported*.
13 Goodman, *The Deportation Machine*, 1. Goodman explains that judicial deportations (now called "removals") have been the most visible means through which the state has expelled noncitizens. "But formal deportations represent only a small sliver of the total. More than 85 percent of all expulsions throughout US history have been via an administrative process euphemistically referred to as 'voluntary departure.'"
14 Goodman, *The Deportation Machine*, 4.
15 Goodman, *The Deportation Machine*, 7. Since 1996, with the introduction of expedited removal, reinstatement of removal, and stipulated removal, deportation processes and associated records have changed. "Migrants whom officials would have once expelled via voluntary departure now found themselves subject to formal deportation, bans on reentry ranging from five years to life, and possible felony criminal charges for returning to the United States." Goodman, *The Deportation Machine*, 177.
16 Material in this section includes wording and concepts from Chávez and Luibhéid, "Introduction," and Luibhéid, "Queer/Migration."
17 Somerville, "Queer," 203. See also Cohen, "Punks, Bulldaggers, and Welfare Queens."
18 Cohen, "Punks, Bulldaggers, and Welfare Queens," 458.
19 Clairborne, "Anyone Can Be an Ally."
20 Luibhéid, "Introduction," xi.
21 Casas-Cortes et al., "New Keywords," 63–64.
22 See Malkki, "Refugees and Exile."
23 People who have been granted refugee status by the UNHRC or its representatives are eligible for resettlement, including in the United States. People who arrive at US borders without holding refugee status, but who are seeking protection nonetheless, may apply for asylum, which is granted on the same basis as refugee status. People may also apply for asylum from within the United States. The refugee/asylum process depends on and reproduces a binary distinction between forced (political) and voluntary (economic) migration, even though such distinctions may not be clear-cut in migrants' lives.

INTRODUCTION

1 In "Op Ed," Alcaraz Ochoa describes himself as a "queer man born in Jalisco, Mexico." Elsewhere, he shares that his pronouns are he/they/él.
2 Some media accounts give his name as "Huertha," but most say "Huerta," so I use the latter.
3 Woodhouse, "Waging the Fight for Migrant Justice."
4 A handful of book-length works and special issues of journals address conjunctions between queer and transgender migrants and state deportation regimes: Lewis and Naples, "Queer Migration, Asylum, and Displacement"; Luibhéid and Chávez, *Queer and Trans Migrations*; Das Gupta, *All of Us or None*. See also Balaguera, "Trans-Migrations."

Articles about UndocuQueer, UndocuTrans, and DREAMer activism also variously address these conjunctions, although deportation is not usually the central analytic focus. Works include Batzke, "From Coming Out to Undocuqueer"; Cabas-Mijares and Grant, "No Longer Interested"; J. Cisneros, "Working with the Complexity"; Cisneros and Gutierrez, "'What Does It Mean to Be UndocuQueer?'"; Dahms, "Queering Citizenship"; Escudero, *Organizing While Undocumented*, chap. 3; Keogh Serrano, "Dreaming a Radical Citizenship"; M. L. Ramirez, "Beyond Identity"; E. Sandoval, "More Than Violence"; Sánchez Cruz, "Debility, Negative Affect, Mobility"; Seif, "'We Define Ourselves'"; Terriquez, "Intersectional Mobilization"; Unzueta Carrasco and Seif, "Disrupting the Dream"; White, "Documenting the Undocumented." UndocuQueer is also addressed in works about Salgado's art—for example, Hart, "The Artivism of Julio Salgado's *I Am Undocuqueer! Series*." Several dissertations also critically analyze UndocuQueer identities and activisms—for example, J. Cisneros, "Undocuqueer"; Corral, "Latiné Undocuqueer Students"; Galta, "Intersectional Subaltern Counterpublics"; Longoria, "Beyond Butterflies"; Padilla, "Queering Diasporic Activism"; Sandoval, "Undocuqueer Disidentifications"; Solórzano, "The Trail of Dreams."

The conjunction between queer/trans migrants and deportation is also addressed to varying degrees in scholarship about Julio Salgado's artwork, Jennicet Gutiérrez's interruption of a Pride event at the White House in 2015, activism to end trans detention and deportation, protests aimed at returning Pride parades to radical roots, and law review articles about the significance of recognizing same-sex marriage, which opened the door to legal immigration for some queer and trans couples.

Read against the grain, an extensive scholarship about the refugee/asylum system, the (im)possibilities for queer and trans people to meet its standards, and what's at stake also provides insight about queer and trans migrants' experiences of deportation and deportability. Books include Camminga, *Transgender Refugees and the Imagined South Africa*; Camminga and Marnell, *Queer and Trans African Mobilities*; Danisi et al., *Queering Asylum in Europe*; Giametta, *The Sexual Politics of Asylum*; Murray, *Real Queer?*; Raboin, *Discourses on LGBT Asylum in the UK*; Spijkerboer, *Fleeing Homophobia*; and numerous articles.

On methodological heteronormativity in scholarship about refugees and asylum seekers, see Carastathis and Tsilimpounidi, *Reproducing Refugees*.

The growing number of article- and book-length studies of queer and trans migrants' lives also implicitly, and sometimes explicitly, includes significant information about experiences of living in the constant shadow of deportability.

5 Global Detention Project, "United States Overview"; Detention Watch Network, "Immigration Detention 101."

6 Goldberg and Conron, *LGBT Adult Immigrants*.

7 In queer studies, critical discussions of carcerality observe that the rise of homonationalism and expanding rights for respectable, middle-class, gay, lesbian, and trans people coincide with the rise of mass incarceration and detention into which other LGBTQ folks are shoveled; the works participate in critiques of queer complicities with neoliberalism and respectability politics and the limits of visibility and rights as strategies for political change. See Agathangelou, Bassichis, and Spira, "Intimate Investments"; Lamble, "Queer Investments in Punitiveness."

8 This concept of a transnational circuit of displacement and confinement comes from Balaguera, "Trans-Migrations."

9 People often experience "a pernicious cascade of hardships and . . . a truly Kaf-kaesque multiplication of unfathomable punishments" in the countries to which they are deported, including being viewed as failed migrants, criminals, and cultur-ally contaminated; scapegoated for social problems; and targeted for harassment and violence by police, gangs, and communities. De Genova, "Afterword," 257.

10 This argument builds on B. Anderson, *Us and Them?*, but uses somewhat different categories.

11 In this book, I use *allies* as a general term to describe migrants and citizens who offer a variety of kinds of support, including, in some cases, acting as accomplices, cocon-spirators, or coliberators. See "A Note on Terminology" for further explanation.

12 *Beyond Walls and Cages* offers tools for further thinking prison abolition and border abolition struggles together in order to "build sturdier bridges between the anti-prison and immigrant justice movements," including by challenging "the idea that borders and prisons create safety, security, and order." Loyd, Mitchelson, and Burridge, "Introduction," 3. See also Escobar, *Captivity beyond Prisons*, and works by Alán Pálaez López. Queer and trans folks, allies, and organizations, many of whom are people of color and migrants, have been centrally involved in making the connections. For example, in "Queer Liberation: No Prisons, No Borders," Tourma-line, CeCe McDonald, Angélica Cházaro, and Dean Spade "examine the connec-tions being made in queer and trans anti-police, anti-prison and anti-deportation activism." The video includes art by Micah Bazant, Roan Boucher, Julio Salgado, Rommy Torrico, and Zuleica Zepeda. Spade, "Queer Liberation." See K. R. Chávez's *Queer Migration Politics* for a generative framework.

13 Paik, "Abolishing Police Includes Abolishing ICE." Recent books advocating abol-ishing nation-state migration controls include Bradley and de Noronha, *Against Borders*; Shah, *Unbuild Walls;* and Washington, *The Case for Open Borders.*

14 Bey and Goldberg, "Queer as in Abolition Now!," 159.

15 Davis et al., *Abolition. Feminism. Now,* 5.

16 Ben-Moshe, "Dis-epistemologies of Abolition," 348. Angela Y. Davis, Gina Dent, Erica R. Meiners, and Beth E. Richie similarly describe how abolition work does not offer prescriptions or quick fixes and instead demands collective engagements and experiments. Davis et al., *Abolition. Feminism. Now,* 5, 7.

17 Scholarship about the difference between reformist and nonreformist reforms includes Walia, "Dismantle and Transform"; Kaba, *We Do This 'Til We Free Us*; Abo-litionist Futures, "For Social and Transformative Justice"; and Detention Watch Net-work, *Ending Immigrant Detention,* which is "modeled after the Critical Resistance's 'Reformist Reforms versus Abolitionist Steps to End Imprisonment Chart'" (1).

18 Wilson, "The Infrastructure of Intimacy," 249, 274.

19 Oswin and Olund, "Guest Editorial," 60.

20 Darling, "Asylum and the Post-political," 84.

21 Brian Larkin explains, "Infrastructures are built networks that facilitate the flow of goods, people, or ideas and allow for their exchange over space. As physical forms, they shape the nature of a network, the speed and direction of its movement, its

temporalities, and its vulnerability to breakdown" (Larkin, "The Politics and Poetics of Infrastructure," 328). Infrastructure, however, extends beyond built environments like roads, border walls, fences, and detention cells: "Infrastructure is . . . an articulation of materialities with institutional actors, legal regimes, policies, and knowledge practices that is constantly in formation across space and time" (Appel, Anand, and Gupta, "Introduction," 12).

22 On migration and infrastructure generally, see Xiang and Lindquist, "Migration Infrastructure"; Lin et al., "Migration Infrastructure and the Production of Migrant Mobilities." See also Aizeki, Mahmoudi, and Schupfer, *Resisting Borders*; Chaar López, *The Cybernetic Border*. For a framework that connects migration infrastructure with vehicles of migration and geophysical environments, see Walters, Heller, and Pezzani, *Viapolitics*. My conceptualization of migration as an infrastructure of chokepoints differs from but is not incompatible with William Walters's conceptualization of deportation infrastructure as "the systematically interlinked technologies, actors and institutions that facilitate and condition the forced movement of persons who are subject to deportation measures, or the threat of deportation." Walters, "Aviation as Deportation Infrastructure," 2800.

23 Infrastructure "permit[s] states to separate politics from nature, the technical from the political, and the human from the nonhuman. Thus depoliticized, the management of infrastructure" became treated as a technical problem. This is despite the fact that infrastructure, which organizes the flow of resources and life possibilities, "differentiate[s] populations and subject[s] some to premature death." Appel, Anand, and Gupta, "Introduction," 4, 5.

24 Berlant, "The Commons," 394.

25 Activists have particularly challenged what they conceptualize as the "pipeline to deportation" (and the prison to deportation pipeline and the school to prison to deportation pipeline). For example, Detention Watch Network offers "ICE Death Watch: An Advocacy and Organizing Toolkit," which provides an overview of these issues, lists demands, provides talking points, and suggests tactics.

Some scholarly books also pay close attention to migration-control infrastructure and possibilities for contestation (e.g., Aizeki, Mahmoudi, and Schupfer, *Resisting Borders*; Chaar López, *The Cybernetic Border*). *Intimate Economies of Immigration Detention*, which does not adopt an explicitly infrastructural perspective, nonetheless "scrutinizes at close range the increasingly complex, tangled, and proximal relations between the multiple actors subject to and involved in operating and managing immigration detention" in a manner that deeply resonates with this book's analysis. See Conlon and Hiemstra, "Introduction," 5.

26 "The solution [to the presence of undocumented people] is to create 'virtual choke points'—events that are necessary for life in a modern society but are infrequent enough not to bog down everyone's daily business. . . . The objective is not mainly to identify illegal aliens for arrest (though that will always be a possibility) but rather to make it as difficult as possible for illegal aliens to live a normal life here." Krikorian, "Downsizing Illegal Immigration," 5.

27 I use *chokepoint* to refer to points of encounter with the state or its designated authorities. Migrants may seek out these points of encounter to do things like apply

for legal status, they may inadvertently encounter these points, or they may try to deliberately avoid these points. In recent decades, these points of encounter have multiplied as the policing of legal status has become diffused into more and more relationships, especially those related to paid employment and social reproduction. This multiplication expands deportability as an ever-present possibility into many new domains. Navigating these points demands resources, even for those whose status may seem secure, which further adds to exhaustion and wearing down.

28 For example, see the vast scholarship on undocumented status as constructed by law in changing ways and as a status that people may transit in and out of, including Luibhéid, *Pregnant on Arrival*; Menjívar and Kanstroom, *Constructing Immigrant "Illegality"*; and Ngai, *Impossible Subjects*.

29 See, for example, Vogt, *Lives in Transit*.

30 Vogt, *Lives in Transit*, 86.

31 Vogt, *Lives in Transit*, 104.

32 See, for example, Foucault, *The History of Sexuality*; Foucault, *Society Must Be Defended*.

33 Mbembe, "Necropolitics."

34 In *Cruel Optimism*, Lauren Berlant underscores the everydayness of being "let die" by highlighting that people die not just from emergencies and catastrophes but also from ongoing conditions of life that do not allow for flourishing but instead exhaust and wear them out. Jasbir K. Puar's *The Right to Maim* suggests that we need to further develop understanding of experiences of being situated in the space between "make live" and "let die" (11). See also Elizabeth A. Povinelli's *Geontologies*, which argues that biopolitics no longer captures the operations of power under late liberalism and that a framework of geontological power involving struggles over the boundaries between life and nonlife is more useful.

35 Inda, "The Value of Immigrant Life," 154.

36 Aradau and Tazzioli, "Biopolitics Multiple," 204. They're building on Puar, *The Right to Maim*.

37 Tazzioli, "Choking without Killing," 1.

38 Tazzioli, "Choking without Killing," 4.

39 Tazzioli, "Choking without Killing," 4.

40 See, for example, Shahksari, "The Queer Time of Death."

41 Tazzioli, "Choking without Killing," 5.

42 Aradau and Tazzioli, "Biopolitics Multiple," 219; Squire, "Governing Migration through Death."

43 Prevention Through Deterrence (PTD) became a core strategy after a study commissioned by the Office of National Drug Control Policy, in 1993, described the southwest border as "being overrun" and suggested that drug smuggling presented a serious threat (Haddal, *Border Security*, 4). The study recommended that the then-INS switch its focus from apprehending people after entry to preventing their entry in the first place. This was the core concept of "prevention through deterrence." Border Patrol was aware that the strategy put migrants at risk of serious injury or death; its 1994 Plan says frankly, "Illegal entrants crossing through remote, uninhabited expanses of land and sea along the border can find themselves in

mortal danger" (U.S. Border Patrol, *Border Patrol Strategic Plan 1994 and Beyond: National Strategy*, accessed February 22, 2024, https://www.hsdl.org/?abstract&did =721845, 2). Indeed, after PTD was implemented, the number of migrant deaths rose exponentially. Scholars have described how PTD involved deliberately driving migrants into environments that significantly heightened the risk of death. Yet Border Patrol avoids direct blame for the deaths even while its policies are a significant cause of death. As Jason De León summarizes, "Nature has been conscripted by the Border Patrol to act as an enforcer while simultaneously providing this federal agency with plausible deniability" (De León, *The Land of Open Graves*, 29–30). The bodies of those who have died crossing show that PTD may cause quite specific forms of death. For example, Raquel Rubio Goldsmith and colleagues found that after PTD was implemented, there was a significant shift in the manner of death, as a majority of migrants began to die from heat-related causes including dehydration and heat stroke (Rubio Goldsmith et al., "The 'Funnel Effect,'" 48). In these ways, PTD materialized chokepoints that contributed to rising numbers of deaths that included choking and dying from thirst

Alongside death, the terrain through which PTD routes migrants has produced thousands of disappearances without trace each year. It also routinely produces injury, on which Border Patrol counts: "Extreme heat and bitter cold, scarce and polluted water sources, treacherous topography, and near-total isolation from possible rescue are used as weapons of border enforcement" (La Coalicion de Derechos Humanos and No More Deaths, *Disappeared*, 7). Migrants are also injured by cacti, venomous animals, and reptiles. Tactics of patrolling the border and responding to sightings of migrants further contribute to death, disappearance, and injury. No More Deaths describes a common tactic used by Border Patrol: "Border Patrol agents chase border crossers through the remote terrain and utilize the landscape as a weapon to slow down, injure, and apprehend them" (*Disappeared*, 7). Chases cause people to scatter and become separated, often losing vital water and food supplies, and contribute to disappearance and death.

44 Tazzioli, "Choking without Killing," 4.
45 See, for example, Baker et al., "Three Words."
46 Appel, Anand, and Gupta, "Introduction," 22.
47 See Riley and Carpenter, "Decolonizing Indigenous Migration," 109.
48 John Torpey describes how "the monopolization of this authority by states emerged only gradually . . . and paralleled states' monopolization of the legitimate means of violence." Torpey, *The Invention of the Passport*, 5.
49 Hindess, "Citizenship in the International Management of Population."
50 Hindess, "Citizenship in the International Management of Population."
51 Luke de Noronha argues that this system reproduces "a racist world order." Noronha, "Hierarchies of Membership," 431.
52 Shachar, *The Birthright Lottery*, 8.
53 Walia, *Undoing Border Imperialism*, 52.
54 Spijkerboer, "The Global Mobility Infrastructure."
55 Nevins, *Dying to Live*, 199. See also Walia, *Undoing Border Imperialism*; Walia, *Border and Rule*.

Reflecting the global dynamics that generate but then criminalize migration across borders, the authors of the "Beloved Home" pillar of the *Transgender Agenda for Liberation* write, "Transgender, gender non-conforming, nonbinary people who flee from Africa, Asia, South Asia, the Middle East, Latin America, and the Caribbean are escaping hunger, poverty, crime, and war, coupled with transphobia, homophobia, religious persecution, and misogyny. As we migrate, we will experience more transphobia, homophobia, and misogyny, in addition to anti-Black racism, xenophobia, and Islamophobia. . . . And yet, if we leave our communities to seek a new home and find belonging, we are caged, criminalized, abused, and sadly in many cases killed." See Transgender Law Center, "Beloved Home."

56 Sharma explains, "It is important to note that like past forms of apartheid, global apartheid is not based on keeping differentiated people *apart* but instead, on organizing two (or more) separate legal regimes and practices for differentiated groups *within* the same space." Sharma, "Global Apartheid and Nation Statehood," 72.

57 Sharma, "Global Apartheid and Nation Statehood," 74.

58 Golash-Boza, *Deported*, 3.

59 Khosravi, "Introduction," 6.

60 Anderson, Gibney, and Paoletti, "Citizenship, Deportation and the Boundaries of Belonging," 548.

61 Legal status includes officially recognized nationality, which authorizes the right to cross the national border, vote, stand for public office, and engage in the duties associated with citizenship. Normative belonging includes recognition as a member of the polity, legitimacy to participate in public debates, and access to collective resources, among other aspects. Legal citizens who don't match up to or are seen as actively threatening the norms of belonging may be ignored, actively discriminated against, or treated as threats. Mackie, "Rethinking Sexual Citizenship."

62 Walia, *Border and Rule*, 36.

63 Rosenbloom, "The Citizenship Line," 1964.

64 American Immigration Lawyers Association, "Featured Issue."

65 Das Gupta, *All of Us or None*.

66 Gentry et al., *Out of Sight*, 50, 46. See also Miller, *Border Patrol Nation*, 115–50.

67 Gentry et al., *Out of Sight*, 48.

68 Gentry et al., *Out of Sight*, 54.

69 Hernández, *City of Inmates*, 64.

70 Fong Yue Ting v. United States, 149 U.S. 698 (1893).

71 Wong Wing v. United States, 163 U.S. 228 (1896).

72 Hernández, *City of Inmates*, 89. Helpful histories of deportation include Hester, *Deportation*; Kanstroom, *Deportation Nation*; Maloney, *National Insecurities*.

73 On postentry social control, see Kanstroom, *Deportation Nation*.

74 Murdza and Ewing, *The Legacy of Racism*, 4.

75 Hernández, *City of Inmates*, 91.

76 American Immigration Council, "How the United States Immigration System Works."

77 American Immigration Council, "How the United States Immigration System Works."

78 See Villa-Nicholas, *Data Borders*; Aizeki, Mahmoudi, and Schupfer, *Resisting Borders and Technologies of Violence*; Just Futures Law and Mijente, *The Data Broker

to *Deportation Pipeline Report*; Mijente, Just Futures Law, and No Border Wall Coalition, *The Deadly Digital Border Wall*. See also #NoTechForICE, "About."

79 Stumpf, "The Crimmigration Crisis."

80 Chacón, "Managing Migration through Crime," 137.

81 Criminalization confers a status that follows people for life, severely restricting their possibilities and justifying ever more punitive measures against them. For migrants, criminalization also affects their possibilities for claiming asylum or legally migrating in the future.

82 Macías-Rojas, *From Deportation to Prison*, 59.

83 This conjunction pushed Congress to expand the deportation of noncitizens who were "swept up in the drug war as a way to free up detention space and prison beds for Black and Latino/a youth." Macías-Rojas, *From Deportation to Prison*, 58.

84 Macías-Rojas, *From Deportation to Prison*, 59.

85 In 1996, Congress passed the Illegal Immigration Reform and Immigrant Responsibility Act and the Antiterrorism and Effective Death Penalty Act, both of which contributed to the criminalization of immigrants. The American Immigration Lawyers Association provides a summary of their provisions. American Immigration Lawyers Association, "Current Immigration Laws."

86 Stumpf, "The Crimmigration Crisis."

87 Chacón, "Managing Migration through Crime."

88 Macías-Rojas, *From Deportation to Prison*, 130.

89 Macías-Rojas, *From Deportation to Prison*, 130.

90 On the 287(g) Program, see American Immigration Council, "The 287(g) Program." On Secure Communities, see American Immigration Council, "Secure Communities." On CAP, see American Immigration Council, "The Criminal Alien Program (CAP)."

91 Walia, *Border and Rule*, 29.

92 *Merriam-Webster*, s.v. "attrition (*n.*)," accessed July 15, 2024, https://www.merriam -webster.com/dictionary/attrition. Krikorian claims credit for first articulating in print in 2005 the concept of "attrition through enforcement," but the logics he describes have been driving immigration policy, practice, and rationales for much longer. Krikorian's publication crystallized this approach, naming it, somewhat realigning various existing policies and practices to contribute to it, and advocating for new policies and resources to further serve attrition. His publication reflected the existence of a wider network of politicians, researchers, and pundits who systematically advocated for these logics and were very successful in getting them implemented into law. Many GOP and right-wing advocates suggest that by interfering in daily life, undocumented migrants will be forced to "self-deport." Waslin, *Discrediting "Self-Deportation,"* 5.

Attrition as a mode of state-induced "wearing or grinding down" names the effects of the massive state divestment from collective resources to capacitate lives, which occurs in tandem with expanding criminalization and new formations of capitalist exploitation. Critical ethnic, gender, and queer studies make clear that wearing-down processes do not fall evenly on everyone but instead reflect and reproduce racist, capitalist, settler colonialist, patriarchal, and heteronormative inequalities.

93 Waslin, *Discrediting "Self-Deportation,"* 2. Krikorian said as much (in "Downsizing Illegal Immigration"): "The objective is . . . to make it as difficult as possible for illegal aliens [*sic*] to live a normal life here."

94 For example, in their study of how the nonconsensual capture and sale of data related to everyday life needs contribute to deportation, Nina Wang and her colleagues argue that "ICE should stop exploiting [data related to] people's need for water, electricity, heat, phone or internet to target them for deportation." Wang et al., *American Dragnet*, 69.

95 Park, "Self-Deportation Nation," 1889. Park further historicizes deportation by describing that the Indian Removal Act (1830) made the threat of deportation/removal imminent, which caused some to voluntarily leave; for the rest, a deportation force was assembled. The act provided an opportunity to "experiment with direct mass removal" and consolidate an indirect removal policy at the same time ("Self-Deportation Nation," 1903). Park also explores how logics of attrition and self-deportation informed national debates over the abolition of slavery. Statesmen who could not contemplate a society where Black people were present and equal if slavery was abolished had long debated the possibility of mass deportation of free Black people. Ultimately, mass deportation was not undertaken, and instead, a system of racial apartheid was set in place that resecured the subordination of Black American labor and life. For valuable historical information about policies intended to generate self-deportation, see Seeley, *Race, Removal, and Right to Remain*.

96 These strategies were widely justified through false claims that these systems serve as a "giant magnet" that incentivizes undocumented migration and that migrants do not pay into these systems, even though many do.

97 This law circulated dehumanizing, racist, heterosexist images of migrant women supposedly having children as a deliberate strategy to get legal status and welfare access—even though undocumented parents must wait at least thirty-one years to get status through a US-born baby and migrants were already definitively cut off from welfare access. Templeton, "Baby-Baiting."

98 Mackey, "The Deep Comic Roots."

99 Right-wing groups are exploring possibilities for further weaponizing schooling as a tool of attrition, including by bringing a case that enables the Supreme Court to overturn *Plyler v. Doe*. They calculate that excluding children from K–12 schooling will further impel migrants to "self-deport." See Bazelon, "The Right-Wing Dream."

100 Places of worship are also designated as protected areas yet remain vulnerable to surveillance and enforcement.

101 Camacho, "Hailing the Twelve Million," 8. Following Shah, we could conceive of attrition as involving systemic efforts to estrange undocumented migrants from all possible intimacies and resources, and thereby from life and living, in order to render them maximally exploitable before driving them out.

102 Khosravi, "Introduction," 7; Bhatia and Canning, "Introduction," xix.

103 See, for example, Ewing and Cantor, *Deported with No Possessions*. People who, on crossing the border, are arrested and processed for deportation also experience that Border Patrol generally confiscates, destroys, or does not return their belongings, including identity documents, medications, medical devices, cell phones,

religious items, clothing, and items of personal importance. See ACLU et al., *From Hope to Heartbreak*.

104 Porotsky, "Rotten to the Core."

105 Porotsky, "Rotten to the Core," 354–55. Sophia Porotsky continues, "At the national level, Secretary of War James Calhoun established the Office of Indian Affairs in 1824 and tasked it with mapping and counting Native Americans. . . . The US government had two concerns: 1) security . . . and 2) the removal of Indigenous people to lands not then occupied by the United States" (355).

106 Porotsky, "Rotten to the Core," 360; Chacón, "The Security Myth," 148.

107 Nicholls, "Between Punishment and Discipline," 581.

108 Villa-Nicholas, *Data Borders*, 7.

109 Benjamin, "Foreword: Borders and Bits."

110 Porotsky, "Rotten to the Core," 375.

111 When Barack Obama came to power, he "turbocharged the Endgame approach" through the Secure Communities program (Porotsky, "Rotten to the Core," 381).

112 Sampaio, *Terrorizing Latina/o Immigrants*, 18, 10. Sampaio summarizes, "In combination, masculine protectionism and racialized demonization yielded particularly harsh consequences for immigrants who were unlawfully detained and deported. These discursive shifts also had perilous effects on US citizens" (18). See also L. Chávez, *The Latino Threat*; Licona, "The Non/Image of the Regime of Distortion."

113 Border Patrol's official narrative about these changes can be found in Schroeder, *Holding the Line*.

114 American Immigration Council, "The Cost of Immigration Enforcement and Border Security," 2.

115 American Immigration Council, "The Cost of Immigration Enforcement and Border Security," 2.

116 American Immigration Council, "The Cost of Immigration Enforcement and Border Security," 3.

117 A. Brady, "How the US Exported Its Border." See also Miller, *Empire of Borders*.

118 Oswin and Olund, "Guest Editorial," 60.

119 Karma Chávez offered this gloss. It was based on the definition given by the *Oxford English Dictionary*: "Intimacy (*n.*) The quality of being intimate. 1.a. The state of being personally intimate; intimate friendship or acquaintance; familiar intercourse; close familiarity. . . . 1.b. *euphemistic* for sexual intercourse. 1.c. Closeness of observation, knowledge, or the like. 2. Intimate or close connection or union. 3. Inner or inmost nature; an inward quality or feature." *Oxford English Dictionary*, s.v. "intimacy (*n.*)," March 2024, https://doi.org/10.1093/OED/3908729850. Karma suggested that the idea of "closeness of observation, knowledge, or the like" seems especially relevant when considering state migration-control processes. Thank you, Karma.

120 See, for example, Carter, *The Heart of Whiteness*.

121 Thus, Lisa Lowe argues that dominant conceptions of intimacy that are "figured as conjugal and familial relationships in the bourgeois home distinguished from the public realm of work, society, and politics" depended on and naturalized capitalist, colonialist, white supremacist, and patriarchal conditions of subordination that spanned the globe. Lowe, *The Intimacies of Four Continents*, 28.

122 Scholarship includes Douglass, *Narrative of the Life of Frederick Douglass*; Jacobs, *Incidents in the Life of a Slave Girl*; Hartman, *Scenes of Subjection*; Sharpe, *Monstrous Intimacies*.

123 Sharpe, *Monstrous Intimacies*.

124 Stoler, *Carnal Knowledge and Imperial Power*.

125 Luibhéid, "Sexualities, Intimacies, and the Citizen/Migrant Distinction."

126 Shah, *Stranger Intimacy*, 264. See also Canaday, *The Straight State*.

127 See, for example, Acosta, *Amigas y Amantes*; Bailey, *Butch Queens Up in Pumps*; Hartman, *Wayward Lives, Beautiful Experiments*; Manalansan, *Global Divas*; Weston, *Families We Choose*. For a critical discussion of how refugee law remains heteronormative even when now claiming to recognize LGBTQ families, see Ritholtz and Buxton, "Queer Kinship and the Rights of Refugee Families."

128 Eskridge, "Beyond Lesbian and Gay 'Families We Choose,'" 277.

129 Wilson, "The Infrastructure of Intimacy," 264.

130 Wilson, "The Infrastructure of Intimacy," 248.

131 Murphy, *The Economization of Life*, 141–42.

132 NACLA, "Civil Disobedience Against Deportation."

133 Studies repeatedly show the multiple, harmful impacts of these situations on the health, well-being, food and housing security, educational attainment, and opportunities of everyone in a household affected by deportation. See, for example, Abrego, *Sacrificing Families*; American Immigration Council, "U.S. Citizen Children Impacted by Immigration Enforcement"; Caldwell, *Deported Americans*; Dreby, *Everyday Illegal*; Yoshikawa, *Immigrants Raising Citizens*.

134 The impacts of deportation radically reconfigure and often sever intimacies, with devastating biopolitical and material effects. These terrible scenarios also play out for same-sex and trans couples with and without children, but systemic research about this has yet to be conducted.

135 Shah, *Stranger Intimacy*, 55; Warner, *Publics and Counterpublics*. Shah further argues, "Queer epistemologies destabilize assumptions that personhood and citizenship emanate from the 'domestic private' and conventional coupled intimacy" (273).

136 "Narrowing civic sociality politics to intimacies cultivated within families suppresses alternatives that emerge in meetings between strangers." These include alternatives that emerged among the transient queer South Asian migrant laborers who are at the center of Shah's study. Shah, *Stranger Intimacy*, 266.

137 Shah, *Stranger Intimacy*, 261.

138 Shah, *Stranger Intimacy*, 262, quoting Merriam-Webster's Online Dictionary, accessed March 21, 2011, www.merriam-webster.com/dictionary/estrange.

139 Siegfried, "Feeling Collective"; Spira, "Intimate Internationalisms."

140 Siegfried, "Feeling Collective," 26–27.

141 Woodhouse, "Waging the Fight for Migrant Justice."

142 In *Entry Denied*, I argue that state migration controls contribute to and operate through racialized, settler, capitalist, heteronormative logics that shape migrants' (im)possibilities for legal admission while coproducing citizenship norms. My *Pregnant on Arrival* centered the demonization of pregnant migrant women and theorized racialized, capitalist heteronormativity as a key nexus through which

migrants, citizens, and states struggle over where to draw the line between who's a documented migrant and who's not.

143 Haley, "Abolition," 13. Haley highlights that abolitionist critique builds on the "theoretical contribution of Black feminist history and theory, which has centered reproductive violence, gender violence, and the exploitation of socially reproductive labor as technologies of captivity and argued for necessary alternatives" and "posit[s] a future beyond gendered racial terror and racial capitalist modes of social reproduction" (14, 13).

144 Bey and Goldberg, "Queer as in Abolition Now!," 159.

145 Bey and Goldberg, "Queer as in Abolition Now!," 160.

146 See Migrant Rights Centre Ireland, "A Statement from the Leaders." An image of the photograph can be found in Escalante, "Ireland Waves 'Hello.'"

147 Scholars have extensively debated the ethics of interviewing people about traumatizing experiences when such interviews may be retraumatizing, unnecessary, and extractive. For example, Lynn Fujiwara describes realizing that her efforts to interview immigrant women who were facing benefit cutoffs were experienced as "invasive and threatening" and "ignited a terror," which led her to adopt other research methods (Fujiwara, *Mothers without Citizenship*, xxv). Such decisions require careful assessment of contexts and positionalities, and there is no hard and fast rule to follow. Some scholars have made important contributions by directly interviewing detained and deported migrants, but I decided not to interview.

148 M. J. Alexander, "Not Just (Any) Body Can Be a Citizen"; Manalansan, *Global Divas*.

149 Shaw and Verghese, *LGBTQI Refugees and Asylum Seekers*, 6–7. The Williams Institute has been a leader in producing valuable demographic information about queer and trans migrants in the United States. Sharita Gruberg at the Center for American Progress has also generated invaluable reports.

150 Participants at the webinar "Treatment of Black Immigrants in Immigration Detention," hosted by the American Immigration Council on November 18, 2021, highlighted the issues discussed here.

151 Historian Adam Goodman describes that many aspects of the migration-control infrastructure, including deportations, are intended to leave no official record:

> When I began working on this book a decade ago, the first person I went to see was Marian Smith, chief of the Historical Research Branch of the Department of Homeland Security's US Citizenship and Immigration Services. That morning, in her office in a generic building located north of Washington, DC's Union Station, Smith told me what a historian embarking on a new project hopes to never hear: despite the wealth of materials documenting the immigration service's history, there were no records on voluntary departures, much less on self-deportations. There was nothing for me to look at. "That was the whole point," she explained. The government's effort to streamline expulsions and cut enforcement expenses depended not only on reducing the use of detention and bypassing removal hearings, but also on minimizing the processing of apprehended immigrants—and the voluminous records that would generate. (Goodman, *The Deportation Machine*, 7)

152 Balaguera, "Trans-Asylum."

153 Davis et al., echoing numerous radical scholar/activists, call for centering the voices and priorities of those most harmed by the current system in *Abolition. Feminism. Now.*

In the "Beloved Home" pillar of the *Transgender Agenda for Liberation*, the authors describe how they are "rendered invisible in mainstream US immigration narratives as well as organizing and movement building strategies" and that this "translates to policy and litigation goals that cannot and do not reflect the experience of those most impacted," instead normalizing neocolonial relationships that fuel "forced migration and displacement." In response, the authors demand "not only a seat at the table, but [to] be positioned in key decision making roles and structures." They also demand that those with more institutional power and authority must redirect their focus and "anchor their work in Black liberation and engage in active solidarity with Black transgender, gender non-conforming, nonbinary, and queer migrants by prioritizing our survival, our presence, and leadership," as well as engaging climate change and Indigenous sovereignty. See Transgender Law Center, "Beloved Home."

Pascha Bueno Hansen explains that "more research" is not always needed; instead, communities already have knowledge, and scholars can contribute to communities by making space for and holding that knowledge at the center of what they are doing. Her remarks were offered as part of the "Transnational Feminisms Panel" at the National Women's Studies Association Annual Conference on November 21, 2021.

154 Ngai, *Impossible Subjects*, 58.

155 Speed, *Incarcerated Stories*, 12–13.

156 #Not1More Deportation, *Blue Ribbon Commission Report on Deportation Review.*

157 Ahmed, "Affective Economies."

1. PATHWAYS

1 Nathalie Peutz and Nicholas De Genova describe how modern deportation law emerged from a particular confluence: modern nation-states began monopolizing the control over deciding legitimate mobility and "the post-World War I enactment of the *citizen*, not the individual person, as the only formal bearer of inalienable rights" (Peutz and De Genova, "Introduction," 10). De Genova highlights that states do not have to engage in actual deportations in order to reproduce normative citizenship and sovereignty; the fact that migrants *could be deported* at any time keeps them highly vulnerable and exploitable and keeps the whole system in place (De Genova, "Migrant 'Illegality' and Deportability in Everyday Life"). Undocumented migrants are the obvious targets of the state's deportation powers, yet they are not the only targets; documented migrants may become deportable on various grounds, too. Moreover, the boundaries between these legal status categories are fluid and changeable.

2 Walters, "Deportation, Expulsion, and the International Police of Aliens," 97.

3 Walters, "Deportation, Expulsion, and the International Police of Aliens," 97.

4 Citizenship is a dense concept that has been theorized in different ways. For a helpful overview, see Berlant, "Citizenship." In recent decades, diverse constructs, including cosmopolitan, consumer, cultural, sexual, transgender, and ecological citizenship, have generated critical debate.

5 Somerville, *Queering the Color Line*. See also Carter, *The Heart of Whiteness*.

6 Gill-Peterson, *Histories of the Transgender Child*.

7 See, for example, Freeman, *Time Binds*; McClintock, "Family Feuds"; Povinelli, *The Empire of Love*. In "The Queer Temporalities of *Queer Temporalities*," Elizabeth Freeman reviews what thinking about time queerly allows us to address. See also the scholarship on reproductive futurism that departs from Lee Edelman's *No Future*.

8 Winterman, "Queueing"; Ingold, *Lines*.

9 Larson quoted in Conan, "'Dr. Queue' Helps You Avoid Rage."

10 "Why don't they just get in line?" is sometimes offered as an obvious solution (as if undocumented migrants had not thought of it). Or it is used as blame. For example, on February 6, 2018, White House chief of staff John Kelly suggested some undocumented youth were "too lazy to get off their asses" (in other reported versions of these comments, "too lazy to get off the couch") to apply for Deferred Action for Childhood Arrivals (DACA), a form of temporary status. See Valverde, "In Context." Those seeking refugee or asylum status are commonly accused of being "merely economic migrants" who are trying to "cut the lines" for regular admission.

11 Immigration Policy Center, "Why Don't They Just Get in Line?" The Immigration Policy Center became the American Immigration Council. In August 2016, they reissued the briefing as "Why Don't They Just Get in Line and Come Legally?" The 2021 version of this publication is now called "Why Don't Immigrants Apply for Citizenship?"

12 For petitions filed before March 15, 2022, the minimum investment required for an EB-5 investor visa is $1,000,000 "for standard investment" or $500,000 for "a commercial enterprise principally doing business in a targeted employment area or in a regional center-associated infrastructure project." These minimums have since risen. See US Citizenship and Immigration Services, "EB-5."

13 Lal, "About."

14 The American Immigration Council publication "Did My Family Really Come 'Legally'?" is a companion to the Immigration Policy Center's "Why Don't They Just Get in Line?" That second publication explains: "Many people assume that their family immigrated to the United States legally, or did it 'the right way.' In most cases, this statement does not reflect the fact that the U.S. immigration system was very different in the past and that their families might not have been allowed to enter had today's laws been in effect."

15 Landolt and Goldring, "Assembling Noncitizenship." Kellynn Wee, Charmian Goh, and Brenda S. A. Yeoh suggest that the metaphor of chutes and ladders "emphasizes that for migrants . . . gaining citizenship is not a straightforward linear movement through 'doors and tracks.'" These authors further suggest that "the chutes-and-ladders model shows us how varying degrees of precarity are actively produced by and grappled with by actors across a game board structured, as all

games are, by rules, regulations, and laws. The analogy also crackles with uncertainty, idiosyncrasy and risk." Wee, Goh, and Yeoh, "Chutes-and-Ladders," 2677.

16 Bier, "Why Legal Immigration Is Nearly Impossible," 6.

17 Making people governable entails objectifying populations as a flock to be governed, children to be coddled, human resources to be exploited, and so on (Rose, *Powers of Freedom*). Each objectification entails conceiving living people in specific ways, with characteristics that are to be instrumentalized, harnessed, and directed toward diverse ends. It requires the inculcation of particular kinds of capacities and dispositions, including, under liberalism, a specific relation of the self to the self that has historically been viewed as the marker of morality, reason, and capacity to participate in democracy. Aihwa Ong describes how governance is subjectifying in a dual sense: it is a process of being made and self-making (Ong, "Cultural Citizenship as Subject-Making," 263). And it is simultaneously individualizing and collectivizing. Finally, governance is spatializing—it requires conceptualizing populations as existing within specific spaces and, in the process of governing them, continually reimplanting that logic that materializes the space in particular ways. A major framework through which populations have been objectified for purposes of governance is that of "the citizen," with associated rights and obligations.

18 Foucault, *Discipline and Punish*.

19 Linton Weeks writes: "There is in the line a premise—and a promise. It's an inherently American notion that at some point, if you are polite and patient and play by the rules, you will move to the front of the line. And at last it will be your turn. And you will finally get the chance to do what you want to do." Weeks, "Pumps and Polls."

20 See Berlant, *Cruel Optimism*.

21 Ahmed, *The Promise of Happiness*.

22 Ong, "Cultural Citizenship as Subject-Making."

23 Ong, *Buddha Is Hiding*.

24 Carbado, "Racial Naturalization," 633.

25 Carbado, "Racial Naturalization," 633.

26 Reflecting anxiety about citizens' failure to live up to ideals, some states—including Arizona, Arkansas, Idaho, Kentucky, North Dakota, Oklahoma, Tennessee, and Wisconsin—now require high school students to pass the citizenship test in order to be eligible to graduate. See Shapiro and Brown, *The State of Civics Education*.

27 To be eligible for naturalized citizenship, one must be at least eighteen years old, be a lawful permanent resident, demonstrate continuous residence in the United States for at least five years (three years if married to a US citizen), and have lived for at least three months in the state or district where one claims residence. US Citizenship and Immigration Services, "Naturalization Eligibility Tool," accessed August 26, 2024, www.uscis.gov/naturalization-eligibility.

28 According to USCIS, "USCIS conducts an investigation of the applicant upon his or her filing for naturalization. The investigation consists of certain criminal background and security checks. The background and security checks include collecting fingerprints and requesting a 'name check' from the Federal Bureau of Investigations (FBI). In addition, USCIS conducts other inter-agency criminal

background and security checks on all applicants for naturalization. The background and security checks apply to most applicants and must be conducted and completed before the applicant is scheduled for his or her naturalization interview." Moreover, "The FBI's National Name Check Program (NNCP) includes a search against the FBI's Universal Index (UNI), which contains personnel, administrative, applicant, and criminal files compiled for law enforcement purposes. The FBI disseminates the information contained in the FBI's files to USCIS in response to the name check requests." See US Citizenship and Immigration Services, "Chapter 2."

29 US Citizenship and Immigration Services, "10 Steps to Naturalization." Note that in December 2020, the Trump administration introduced a new civics test; after Joe Biden became president, this version of the test was dropped. The Trump version had 128 potential questions (compared with 100 in the prior version); applicants were asked 20 (rather than 10) questions and had to get 12 (rather than 6) right. Critics described the new test as needlessly difficult, containing inaccuracies, and designed to discourage and thwart efforts at naturalization. See, for example, Lubet, "Trump's New Citizenship Test."

30 Before the ceremony, applicants submit form N-445, turn in their green card, and take the oath of allegiance; afterward, they receive a certificate of naturalization.

31 Turner, "Testing the Liberal Subject," 339.

32 Turner, "Testing the Liberal Subject," 335.

33 Turner, "Testing the Liberal Subject," 341. In the citizenship education classes that I observed and then taught, learning entailed not just practicing reading, writing, and speaking in English, and the details of civics and history, but also learning to respond to questions about one's N-400. Effectively, students come to view and explain their life histories through the lens of official forms—which meant not just being objectified as governable subjects but also learning to objectify themselves.

34 Turner, "Testing the Liberal Subject," 340.

35 Scholarship that critically examines connections among morality, Protestantism, capitalism, white heterosexuality, and US nation-making is vast. See, for example, Jakobsen, "Perverse Justice."

36 See, for example, Luibhéid, *Pregnant on Arrival*; Tormey, "'Everyone with Eyes Can See the Problem'"; Ferguson, *Aberrations in Black*.

37 Ahmed, *The Promise of Happiness*. Thus, migrants rather than citizens are expected to engage in movement and change that makes them more proximate to "Americans." This also reflects a relation of power.

38 Conversion, of course, implies processes of currency exchange (and has strong religious overtones, too).

39 Turner, "Testing the Liberal Subject," 344.

40 Turner, "Testing the Liberal Subject," 344.

41 Ahmed, *The Promise of Happiness*, 56.

42 Ahmed, *The Promise of Happiness*, 58. Although the process is fairly standardized, there are faster and slower tracks for becoming eligible to naturalize. This difference reveals who is desired, privileged, and seen as representing the nation's future. Serving in the military or being the spouse of a citizen are among the grounds that

offer a faster track to or waiver of some of the requirements of naturalized citizenship. Unlike in some other countries, capital investment is not a more direct route to citizenship—but it is one of the migrant-selection lines that tends to move the fastest.

Everything I have described can also be framed in terms of debates about assimilation. For a critical appraisal, see C. S. Ramírez, *Assimilation.*

43 While the migrant-becoming-citizen is clearly a target of the process, so too are citizens, as the process becomes spectacularized, including through showing naturalization ceremonies on the nightly news.

44 In some cases, seeking citizenship has become a path to deportation, as LPRs find themselves caught out by new rules and regulations.

45 This general model informed proposals before S.744, too, and the proposal introduced by Democrats in 2021.

46 Their presence became treated as an index that the immigration system was "broken" and needed fixing. The framework of a "broken system" was widely used to argue for immigration reform (though disputed by critical analysts who suggest the system is doing exactly what is expected of it).

47 Nicholls, "Between Punishment and Discipline," 584.

48 Nicholls, "Between Punishment and Discipline," 585.

49 Ahmad, "Beyond Earned Citizenship," 269.

50 Nicholls "Between Punishment and Discipline," 580.

51 Nicholls, "Between Punishment and Discipline," 590. Reflecting these logics, Marco Rubio, one of the Gang of Eight, argued that the pathway proposal would resecuritize the nation and state by bringing undocumented migrants "out of the shadows," ensuring they were individually registered, inscribed into the vast documentary apparatus of the state, and thereby rendered knowable, countable, and trackable. Each would be evaluated in terms of whether they had been or might in the future become a criminal or security threat. Furthermore, Rubio argued, dispelling the shadows within which undocumented people lived would make visible criminals and terrorists who were hiding out among the undocumented, so they could be dealt with. Rubio, "Frequently Asked Questions."

52 American Immigration Lawyers Association, "Talking Points."

53 American Immigration Lawyers Association, "Talking Points."

54 According to Rubio, the dangers of the current status quo/situation are that "we have 11 million undocumented immigrants here and don't know who they are, what activities they're engaged in, or anything else about them." Later he says, "Today's situation is a de facto amnesty that allows these very individuals [criminals, drug traffickers, human traffickers, gang members, or even terrorists] to game our system and avoid capture, deportation and incarceration. These are exactly the kind of people we need to deport immediately, and it's why the process of identifying who is here and figuring out what they have been doing is so crucial." Rubio, "Frequently Asked Questions."

55 Ahmad, "Beyond Earned Citizenship," 289.

56 Ahmad, "Beyond Earned Citizenship," 261.

57 Landolt and Goldring explain that "conditionality denotes the material and discursive conditions that must be met to acquire and exercise the formal or substantive right to remain present within a national territory and/or to access entitlements

and social goods, including the labor market" ("Assembling Noncitizenship," 857). The regulatory and policy framework sets baseline conditions for migrants; frontline workers interpret regulations narrowly or generously; other social and institutional actors help move people in various directions in relation to the conditions; and migrants learn and strategize about how best to address the conditions. Wee, Goh, and Yeoh introduce the idea of compounded conditionality: "An interrelated number of conditions must be simultaneously met, many of which are outside of a worker's control. A worker's security is contingent on meeting a full set of interrelated conditions. Failure to meet one condition, for whatever reason, quickly compounds the possibility of failing to meet others." "Chutes-and-Ladders," 2677.

58 Note, DREAMers and those who worked in agriculture were eligible for a somewhat more accelerated process.

59 These later requirements usually attach to naturalization, not to seeking LPR status.

60 Schey, "Analysis of Senate Bill 744's Pathway."

61 In their analysis of requirements for earned legalization in five major bills proposed by Congress between 2006 and 2011, the Migration Policy Institute found that language requirements, depending on how they are structured, could rule out between 3.3 million to 5.8 million unauthorized adults, especially given the lack of available ESL courses and people's difficulty finding money and time for these. See Rosenblum, Capps, and Lin, *Earned Legalization*, 1.

62 Ahmad, "Beyond Earned Citizenship," 273.

63 Ahmad, "Beyond Earned Citizenship," 280, 281. On similarities to and differences from welfare reform, see especially 284–85.

64 White House, "Fact Sheet."

65 Caputo, "Undocumented Immigrants Face Major Hurdles," cited by Rubio, "Myth vs. Fact."

66 Rubio, "Myth vs. Fact."

67 Ahmed captures the moral logics at work in these conditions: "The promise of happiness takes the form: 'if you have this or that, or if you do this or that, then happiness is what follows.' . . . [This is also] the basic formula for religion and morality." She continues: "The promising nature of happiness suggests happiness lies ahead of us, at least if we do the right thing." Ahmed, *The Promise of Happiness*, 29.

68 Demands for displays of remorse and rituals of atonement have been pronounced throughout debates over regularization, and these demands are directed at both migrants and citizens. Dominant discourse suggests that undocumented migrants have wronged US citizens by being present without permission and that they need to "set things right." Furthermore, the capacity to atone for wrongdoing is deemed to be an important quality in a reflexive citizen. Thus, Rubio presents the strictness of the regularization process and its protracted nature as an opportunity for migrants to be made, and publicly demonstrate that they are, remorseful. Mandatory fines are part of atonement, too. Overall, the regularization process is framed as a mechanism to, in Ahmed's words, "turn" migrants away from lawbreaking and toward following the rules (that have been set by citizens and their political representatives).

The *Christian Science Monitor* suggests the atonement process is also an opportunity to make citizens recommit to rules that they, too, have been breaking: "The terms of forgiveness on a mass scale are meant not only to help offenders become honest and law-abiding residents but also help restore the consensus that rules are worth following. Enforcement of any laws can only go so far. Society also needs shared values—such as a desire for secure borders—along with having a majority of residents who will feel the pangs of conscience if they break the law." Editorial Board, "Immigration Reform as a Path to Conscience."

69 "Earned citizenship promises to redeem those moral failings through a neoliberal program of moral worthiness: fines, work, self-reliance, education, and assimilation." Ahmad, "Beyond Earned Citizenship," 289.

70 Carens, "The Case for Open Borders."

71 Schey, "Analysis of Senate Bill 744's Pathway," 10. Peter Schey, like others, offered alternatives, which were not taken up.

72 Ahmad argues that the protracted process, during which migrants are excluded from social benefits and forced to work continually or maintain income that reaches a certain threshold, serves to "effectively redefine the substantive content of citizenship itself." Moreover, it is a "key technology to ensure . . . that citizenship is meaningfully differentiated from mere lawful residence." Ahmad, "Beyond Earned Citizenship," 284.

73 Schey, "Analysis of Senate Bill 744's Pathway," 14.

74 Schey, "Analysis of Senate Bill 744's Pathway," 9.

75 #Not1More Deportation, *Blue Ribbon Commission Report on Deportation Review.*

76 Marquez-Benitez and Pallares, "Not One More," 22.

77 Franco used this self-description at the 2016 Creating Change Conference where she received an award for Leadership on Immigration (Mijente, "'Movement Spaces Must Be Sanctuaries'"). At Franco's acceptance speech, she named LGBTQ organizations that "took a leap of faith" in helping her found the Not1More campaign: the Transgender Law Center, Familia, GetEQUAL, and Southerners on New Ground. They gave support in a context where trying to stop deportation "was not popular. Leaders in our own movement told us that comprehensive immigration reform was the only way. Stopping deportations was not on the cards, except perhaps for DREAMers. But we tried anyway. See, movements in this country have come alive because so many people can't wait anymore." Franco notes that "some of you might have heard about the Not1More Deportation campaign through Jennicet Gutiérrez, an undocumented trans woman of color who spoke out at a White House fandango where she was told by a gay leader, 'This is not for you,' even though she stood there from a lineage of all our community, who made a way when there was no way."

Franco's work in directing Not1More was also recognized by the National Organizing Institute in 2014, which deemed it the Campaign of the Year.

According to Robert Winn, other queer migrants, including Tania Unzueta Carrasco, played important roles in the Not1More campaign. See Winn, *Out of the Closets,* 24. After the Not1More campaign, both Franco and Carrasco helped to cofound Mijente.

78 Morrison, "Obama Wants to Make Deportations More Humane."

79 #Not1More Deportation, *Blue Ribbon Commission Report on Deportation Review.*

80 #Not1More Deportation, *Blue Ribbon Commission Report on Deportation Review.*

81 #Not1More Deportation, *Blue Ribbon Commission Report on Deportation Review.*

82 De Genova, "Migrant 'Illegality' and Deportability in Everyday Life," 420.

83 These include the Humanizing Deportation digital storytelling project that has become an extraordinary archive of deported migrants' accounts. Robert McKee Irwin, the project's coordinator explains, "We neither interview nor film migrants; instead, we offer them a platform to tell their own stories, from their own perspectives, in their own words, with their own visual design, and featuring their own arguments." Irwin and his collaborators emphasize the importance of deeply listening to what people say, without expectations or preset theories, as a route for transformation and new knowledge. Irwin, "The Humanizing Deportation Project," 4.

84 Abrego and Negrón-Gonzales, "Introduction," 11.

85 Wikipedia, s.v. "Blue-ribbon committee," accessed June 15, 2018, https://en.wikipedia.org/wiki/Blue-ribbon_panel.

86 #Not1More Deportation, *Blue Ribbon Commission Report on Deportation Review.*

87 #Not1More Deportation, *Blue Ribbon Commission Report on Deportation Review.* This paragraph concerns recommendation 14.

88 In making these recommendations, the report displays expert knowledge of the mechanics of the migration system and the laws, policies, and debates that ensure migration control works as an infrastructure of chokepoints.

89 #Not1More Deportation, *Blue Ribbon Commission Report on Deportation Review.* For the presentation of recommendations in a press conference, see NDLONvideos, "Blue Ribbon Commission Presents Recommendations for the President."

90 Their temporal horizon is very different from that of s.744, which proposed conditions that were difficult to meet, would generate exploitability and subordination, and wanted to impose these conditions for an extremely prolonged time period. The protracted time period seemed designed to ensure as few people as possible could complete the process. See the massive scholarship on time as a mode of discipline and exploitation of migrants, including Andersson, "Time and the Migrant Other"; Baas and Yeoh, "Introduction"; Bhatia and Canning, *Stealing Time*; Coutin, "Being En Route"; Griffiths, Rogers, and Anderson, "Migration, Time, and Temporalities."

As Haley describes, abolition requires "immediacy rather than gradualism." Haley, "Abolition," 9.

91 In January 2021, on his first day in office, President Biden introduced the US Citizenship Act of 2021. The act's key components were "providing work-related reforms for both immigrants with legal statuses and undocumented immigrants; modernizing border security measures; and addressing root causes of migration to the U.S. from the south" (Ishak, "How Congress Killed Immigration Reform"). The act's centerpiece involved a pathway to citizenship for undocumented people who were living in the United States. The proposed pathway included many of the elements evident in s.744: registering oneself, passing criminal and background

checks, and filing one's taxes. Those who successfully navigated these steps gained temporary legal status, with an opportunity to seek Legal Permanent Resident status after five years and citizenship after three further years, conditional on continuing to meet all requirements and passing an English-language and civics test. The act envisioned a shorter timeline, and a more generous approach to eligibility, than s.744. In addition, holders of DACA status and Temporary Protected Status (TPS), as well as farmworkers, were eligible to immediately seek LPR status. Democrats calculated that to win support, the act needed to be divided into smaller bills that carved out paths for DREAMers and DACA holders, groups with TPS, farmworkers, essential workers, each with varying conditionalities and timeframes. These bills were the American Dream and Promise Act, the Farm Workforce Modernization Act, and the Citizenship for Essential Workers Act, none of which passed. Next, Democrats sought to incorporate some of these provisions into the 2021 Build Back Better Act, in a severely watered-down form that would not benefit undocumented people, but the parliamentarian objected.

92 The *Report* can be considered as what Engin F. Isin describes as an "act of citizenship." Acts of citizenship involve moments when people, regardless of their formal legal status, come together to publicly assert a demand; doing so has the potential to remake the meanings and boundaries of legal statuses and what belonging as a citizen could mean. See Isin, "Theorizing Acts of Citizenship"; Isin, "Citizenship in Flux."

93 Here I am extrapolating rather than quoting directly from the introduction, which says: "We thus envision a dual mandate for queer methods: to outline the conditions for queer worldmaking and to clarify, but not overdetermine, the conditions that 'make life livable,' to borrow a lovely phrase from an interview with the gender theorist Judith Butler." Ghaziani and Brim, "Queer Methods," 7.

94 Walters, "Deportation, Expulsion, and the International Police of Aliens"; Anderson, Gibney, and Paoletti, "Citizenship, Deportation and the Boundaries of Belonging."

2. LOVE, MARRIAGE, AND DEPORTATION

Warmest thanks to the following people who generously allowed me to interview them for this chapter (listed affiliations reflect their positions when I interviewed them in 2016): Yesenia Acosta, attorney, Law Offices of Scott Warmuth; Pamela Denzer, director of client programs, Immigration Equality; Sharita Gruberg, assistant director, LGBT Research and Communications, Center for American Progress; Jamila Hammami, executive director, Queer Detainee Empowerment Project; Jason Ortega, Equal Justice Works Fellow, Los Angeles LGBT Center; and Marco Antonio Quiroga, director of public policy, True Colors Fund.

1 See American Immigration Council, "How the United States Immigration System Works."

2 This situation for citizens is exacerbated by the fact that people may lose certain state supports when they marry. On the issue of marriage equality for disabled people and discussions about the Marriage Equality for Disabled Adults Act that was introduced into Congress on January 1, 2022, see Evans, "Marriage Equality."

3 Adams v. Howerton, 673 F.2d 1036 (9th Cir. 1982). *Limited Partnership*, a documentary about their experiences directed by Thomas G. Miller, was released in 2014. On January 5, 2016, US Citizenship and Immigration Services finally approved Adams's 1975 petition on behalf of his husband. Adams had passed away by then, but Sullivan received his green card in April 2016 (Masters, "United States Government Says").

4 Hasso, "Bargaining with the Devil," 108.

5 Hasso, "Bargaining with the Devil," 108, 109.

6 D'Aoust, "Love as a Project of (Im)Mobility," 322.

7 Foucault, *The History of Sexuality*, 103.

8 Freeman, "Marriage," 162.

9 Povinelli, *The Empire of Love*, 3.

10 Freeman, "Marriage," 162.

11 Thus, romance is "an ideology that tells us stories that keep gender and racial hierarchies in place." The ideology also "teaches us that certain people (mostly white, mostly straight, mostly well-off, and mostly normatively gendered) deserve happily ever after as well as full citizenship and extra rights and privileges from the state" while others do not. Essig, *Love Inc.*, 5.

12 Cott, *Public Vows*, 136. See Luibhéid, *Entry Denied*.

13 Marriage continued to be defined through contrast with sex work. In 1910, in the context of a widespread panic over "white slavery" and presumed sex trafficking, immigration law was altered to allow for deportation for infractions that occurred after entry—a significant expansion of the logics and practices of deportation (Hester, *Deportation*, 106). During this period, officials also sought to prevent women deemed "immoral" from avoiding deportation by marrying a US citizen man. In 1917, Congress revised naturalization law as it applied to white, foreign-born women married to US citizens: "The marriage to an American citizen of a female of the sexually immoral classes the exclusion or deportation of which is prescribed by this act shall not invest such female with United States citizenship if the marriage of such alien shall be solemnized after her arrest or after the commission of acts which make her liable to deportation" (111). This is an early instance of government attention to the connections among stigmatized sexual behavior, patriarchal marriage, and deportation or deportability.

14 Cott, *Public Vows*; M. Gardner, *The Qualities of a Citizen*; Ngai, *Impossible Subjects*.

15 Cott, *Public Vows*, 155.

16 D'Aoust, "Love as a Project of (Im)Mobility," 326–27.

17 White, "Ambivalent Homonationalisms," 39. White describes how demands to produce intelligible intimacy involve "epistemological violence," but couples acquiesce because these "highly contingent representations of intimacy in effect function like a pass in a global apartheid system . . . facilitating the movement of some embodied-subjects-in-relation and not others" (39, 51).

18 D'Aoust, "Love as a Project of (Im)Mobility," 330.

19 These outcomes reflect that, as D'Aoust describes, love is an object and anchor for governance "in the hopes of producing certain desired effects and averting certain undesired events" ("Love as a Project of (Im)Mobility," 325). D'Aoust also briefly addresses deportation.

20 Immigrant Legal Resource Center, "Introduction to Conditional Permanent Residence," 2.

21 Congressional Research Service, "Immigration Provisions of the Violence Against Women Act (VAWA)," N86.

22 For example, see Schaeffer-Grabiel, *Love and Empire*; Lee, *Fictive Kinship*; Villalon, *Violence against Latina Immigrants*; Longo, "Keeping It in 'the Family.'" Non-US examples include Friedman, *Exceptional States*. See also D'Aoust, *Transnational Marriage and Partner Migration*. Note that scholars also address migrants' resistance and subversion.

23 For historical information, see Bredbenner, *A Nationality of Her Own*; Luibhéid, *Entry Denied*; Maloney, *National Insecurities*.

24 Margaret Franz analyzes how these discourses work through racial and gender logics to demonize classes of migrants while legitimizing whiteness and patriarchy as patriotism. See Franz, "Will to Love, Will to Fear"; N. Cisneros, "'Alien' Sexuality."

25 Tomchin, "Bodies and Bureaucracy"; Josephson, *On Transits and Transitions*.

26 Matter of Lovo, 23 I&N Dec. 746 (BIA 2005).

27 Puhl, "Family-Based Petitions for Same-Sex Couples," 5. Em Puhl further explains:

> Before 2013, when marriage equality was achieved at the federal level, the primary question was whether a couple's marriage was considered a "heterosexual" one, or whether one person in the couple was legally recognized as being "female" and the other person as "male." This issue hinged upon the laws regarding biological sex designation and gender identity in the state of birth, residence, and marriage. It was of particular concern for marriages where at least one person in the couple identified as transgender. The question of whether or not a marriage was considered "heterosexual" hinged upon whether a person relied on their sex designation or gender marker under the law *before* or *after* a gender confirming treatment.

28 Josephson, *On Transits and Transitions*, 81.

29 Puhl, "Family-Based Petitions for Same-Sex Couples." Toby Beauchamp analyzes how people who do not match expected gender norms are often accused of deception or fraud, which is taken to justify additional surveillance measures. He astutely notes, "The perception of fraud clings more tightly to some than to others" (Beauchamp, *Going Stealth*, 10). Effectively, *Lovo-Lara* established the terms under which certain marriages involving trans people were not defined as fraudulent.

30 Josephson, *On Transits and Transitions*, 86.

31 Josephson, *On Transits and Transitions*, 87.

32 Tomchin, "Bodies and Bureaucracy," 833–34.

33 In addition to the culture industry, politicians across the political spectrum tell us that romantic love and marriage are the answer to nearly every problem. Laurie Essig ironically notes: "Poverty? Marriage will fix it. The U.S. has been running a marriage campaign in poor neighborhoods for over a decade. The campaign, known as the Healthy Marriage Initiative, tells poor primarily black and Latino Americans . . . the answer to being poor is to get hitched. Despite all evidence that poverty is caused by a lack of money and the lack of opportunity to earn money, about $300 million annually

is spent to place billboards in poor neighborhoods showing the ideal family—mom, dad, two kids—and the words 'Marriage makes you richer.'" Essig, *Love Inc.*, 8.

34 Congressional Research Service, "Immigration Provisions of the Violence Against Women Act (VAWA)," 17, N86.

35 See Constable, "The Commodification of Intimacy."

36 Overall, the demand for migrants to demonstrate that their marriages are based on love has become tied to discourses and practices of preventing crime and exploitation. The USCIS materials also warn citizens of stiff penalties for knowingly participating in "sham" marriages. See US Citizenship and Immigration Services, "Marriage Fraud Is a Federal Crime."

37 See, for example, Hill, *Trafficking Rhetoric*; Oliver, *Carceral Humanism*.

38 J. Williams, "Protection as Subjection," 420. On the relevance of these arguments for trafficking scholarship, see Doonan, "A House Divided." On the problematic intersection of humanitarianism and borders, see Walters, "Foucault and Frontiers"; Fassin, *Humanitarian Reason*.

39 See, for example, Krajeski, "The Hypocrisy of Trump's Anti-trafficking Argument"; S. Anderson, "A Wall and Trump Immigration Policies"; Vongkiatkajorn, "The Trump Administration Just Made It Easier." Scholarship suggests that decriminalizing migration, rather than demanding performances of liberal love and stepping up deportation, would more effectively reduce crime, exploitation, and trafficking.

40 Chauncey, *Why Marriage?*, 96.

41 Chauncey, *Why Marriage?*, 105–7.

42 As one of this book's reviewers highlighted, the most well-funded and widely publicized strands of the marriage equality movement tended to ignore trans people and issues altogether.

43 Kandaswamy, "State Austerity and the Racial Politics of Same-Sex Marriage," 714. Kandaswamy notes that these liberal inclusion narratives ignore and erase the important role of marriage as an institution that upholds, reproduces, and naturalizes multiple inequalities.

44 Duggan defines *homonormativity* as "a politics that does not contest dominant heteronormative assumptions and institutions but upholds and sustains them, while promising the possibility of a demobilized gay constituency and a privatized, depoliticized gay culture anchored in domesticity and consumption." Duggan, *The Twilight of Equality?*, 50.

45 A. H. Johnson, "Transnormativity."

46 Puar, "Homonationalism as Assemblage."

47 Haritaworn, Kuntsman, and Posocco, *Queer Necropolitics*.

48 Beam, "What's Love Got to Do with It?," 54. Beam describes how many queer-identified people did not feel compelled by this vision but deployed it as a strategy to gain straight support (55).

49 Human Rights Watch and Immigration Equality, *Family, Unvalued*, 7, 8–9.

50 Conceptually, *Family, Unvalued* centers same-sex couples but includes accounts by several trans people about struggles they faced because their relationships were not recognized by the immigration service. Amber's struggles included being detained, strip-searched, placed in an all-male holding facility, enduring constant threats,

then being placed in solitary confinement, being denied appropriate medical care, being denied her mail, and losing her housing and job while she was detained—while living in fear of being sent back to the Bahamas, where she'd likely face imprisonment based on that country's antisodomy laws (Human Rights Watch and Immigration Equality, *Family, Unvalued*, 85). The report also acknowledges that poverty dispro-portionately affects trans communities (94). And it highlights the HIV ban.

51 United States v. Windsor, 570 U.S. 744 (2013).

52 ABC News, "First Green Card Approved for Same-Sex Couple."

53 US Citizenship and Immigration Services, "Same-Sex Marriages."

54 US Citizenship and Immigration Services, "Same-Sex Marriages."

55 Obergefell v. Hodges, 576 U.S. 644 (2015). Before this ruling, some migrants in couple relationships had to travel to states that allowed same-sex marriage when they wanted to get married, but such travel put undocumented migrants at risk. Marco Quiroga, interview with author, March 9, 2016.

56 President Obama (@POTUS), "Today is a big step in our march toward equality. Gay and lesbian couples now have the right to marry, just like anyone else. #LoveWins," Twitter, June 26, 2015, https://x.com/POTUS44/status/614435467120001024.

57 Until this law, only some trans marriages were recognized under immigration law, as described above.

58 Illustrating the difficulties of getting basic information from US immigration authorities, in 2017, I submitted a Freedom of Information Act request to USCIS asking for statistical information about the numbers of people who had received green cards based on a same-sex marriage since 2013, when DOMA was repealed. Although USCIS provides statistics about the total numbers of people who receive green cards each year through marriage, they replied that they were unable to tell me how many of these involved same-sex marriages specifically. According to them, they do not collect such information.

Based on the American Community Survey, Nathan I. Hoffmann and Kris-topher Velasco estimate that "the number of same-sex couples that included immigrants in the US" increased from 61,000 in 2013 to 107,000 by 2019 ("Sexual-ity, Migration, and LGB Policy," 20). The authors' analysis focused on "four types of couples: (1) two-immigrant couples who came to the US together; (2) two-immigrant couples that formed once in the US; (3) mixed-status couples where an immigrant migrated with or to be with their US-born partner; and (4) mixed status couples that formed in the US" (8–9). However, "one-immigrant couples seem to be driving the results" (23).

Note that the data do not necessarily mean that all the migrants in these couples received green cards through marriage; they could have received green cards through other paths such as employment, investment, or the refugee/asylum system.

Hoffmann and Velasco found, "Compared to immigrants in different-sex couples, those in same-sex couples came from richer, more democratic countries that are less represented among immigrants in the US. They also tend to be more highly educated, work in more prestigious occupations, and have higher incomes" ("Sexuality, Migration, and LGB Policy," 1). This difference seems to affirm the analyses that suggested opening the door to legal status based on same-sex marriage would likely benefit more privileged people while leaving others out in the cold. Hoffmann and Velasco echo this point: while the repeal of DOMA opened up marriage as a pathway to getting legal immigration status, "the inequities in the immigration system likely mean that known patterns of discrimination and bias are being reproduced in this new population" (22).

59 Wright, "Longtime Gay Activist Is 1st to Marry." In 1994, Swann won a lawsuit against the navy over discrimination based on sexual orientation and HIV status. He also helped erect the nation's first memorial for gay military veterans, near Palm Springs, California.

60 Solis, "Immigration Arrest Moves Gay Wedding." Sara Ahmed critically explores how marriage and happiness become linked in normalizing ways. She describes that marriage is promoted as promising happiness to which one is expected to aspire and that since happiness per se is viewed as a good and a means to facilitate subjective well-being, these discourses contribute to the promotion of "certain types of families" and "make certain forms of personhood valuable." Ahmed, *The Promise of Happiness*, 11.

61 Massey, Durand, and Malone, *Beyond Smoke and Mirrors*; Zavella, *I'm Neither Here nor There*.

62 Solis, "Immigration Arrest Moves Gay Wedding."

63 "Guillermo, who has been here since he was seven years old, has not had a pathway to citizenship and he should have had one. I'm opposed to building a fence and I think we should fix our immigration laws and give people a path to citizenship," Swann said. "I just believe we should have compassion for people. They're coming to this country for a better life." Wright, "Longtime Gay Activist Is 1st to Marry."

64 The DACA program was created by President Obama in 2012. It allowed young people who had been brought to the United States as children, and who were undocumented, to receive permission to remain and work in the United States. However, DACA status had to be regularly renewed and offered no pathway to more permanent legal status. The Trump administration made numerous efforts to undermine or entirely end the program. For further information, see National Immigration Law Center, "DACA."

65 Solis, "Immigration Arrest Moves Gay Wedding."

66 Solis, "Immigration Arrest Moves Gay Wedding"; Nolasco, "What Tom and Guillermo's Detention Center Wedding Reveals."

67 Solis, "Immigration Arrest Moves Gay Wedding."

68 Solis, "Immigration Arrest Moves Gay Wedding."

69 Nolasco, "What Tom and Guillermo's Detention Center Wedding Reveals." In August 2018, a bill was sent to California governor Jerry Brown that would bar ICE from conducting arrests at courthouses. See *Los Angeles Times*, "California Would Bar Immigration Arrests."

Thus, while agreements may exist on paper, the agreements are not necessarily followed. Hernández's arrest also shows that individual ICE agents may take actions or make decisions that run counter to official agreements, that they may do so with or without support of other authorities within the system, and that their power is not easily checked.

Note that courthouses do not fall under ICE and Customs and Border Protection's Protected Areas (formerly Sensitive Locations) Policy. See US Immigration and Customs Enforcement, "Protected Areas Enforcement Actions."

70 See the Morton Memorandum, which outlines deportation priorities that were in effect at that time: Memorandum from John Morton to All ICE Employees, March 2, 2011, available at US Immigration and Customs Enforcement, https://www.ice.gov/doclib/news/releases/2011/110302washingtondc.pdf.

71 Solis, "Should Feds Close Private Immigration Detention Centers?" Because he was in detention, Hernández missed a follow-up court hearing, and the judge issued a bench warrant for his arrest. Hernández's lawyer and Swann told the authorities that Hernández was in federal detention, but sheriff's deputies showed up several times at Swann's Rancho Mirage, California, home to look for him anyway. This included on March 2, when Swann was speaking with a reporter: "About a dozen deputies wearing bullet-proof vests searched every room of the house for a person who was in federal custody more than 100 miles away. That was their third visit, Swann said." Solis, "Immigration Arrest Moves Gay Wedding."

72 Solis, "Immigration Arrest Moves Gay Wedding." I reference María and organizations that supported this couple's struggle since networks of support are crucial to the outcome of individual cases.

73 Jordan, "Policy Ends Deportation of Troops' Families."

74 Swann's disabled status, however, was likely to be used against him by USCIS.

75 Media noted, "The couple has not retained a lawyer for the deportation case— Swann says lawyers have asked for $4,000 which he cannot afford—but they are hopeful their marriage will help. Detainees can fight a deportation case if their 're-moval would result in exceptional and extremely unusual hardships to your United States citizen or lawful permanent resident spouse, parent, or child, and you are deserving of a favorable exercise of discretion on your application,' according to the executive office for Immigration Review." Solis, "Immigration Arrest Moves Gay Wedding."

76 Solis, "Immigration Arrest Moves Gay Wedding."

77 Wright, "Longtime Gay Activist Is 1st to Marry."

78 Solis, "Gay Couple Wedding First in a US Immigration Detention Center."

79 Author interview with Sharita Gruberg (Center for American Progress) about how same-sex marriage became incorporated into the immigration system, March 7, 2016.

80 See US Citizenship and Immigration Services, "Fraud Referral Sheet." The worksheet provides a "general behavioral fraud indicators guide" and an "I-130 family-based petition fraud indicators guide" that would be relevant to Swann and Hernández. See also Sinha and Plambeck, "Green Card Marriage Interview." For the ICE handout "Marriage Fraud Is a Federal Crime" (emphasizing that marriage fraud is not a victimless crime and will be prosecuted), see US Citizenship and Immigration Services, "Marriage Fraud Is a Federal Crime." Those suspected of fraud are sent for a Stokes interview. Bernstein, "Do You Take This Immigrant?" See also Chetrit, "Surviving an Immigration Marriage Fraud Investigation."

81 I value their case precisely because they do not easily fit into dominant norms and demand critical reflection about the norms. As Sara L. Friedman argues, the norms

create "a narrow vision of domestic relations that often fails to capture the complexities of cross-border unions." Efforts to police migrants around these norms "may produce the very kinds of irregular or unconventional intimacy they aim to prevent." Friedman, "Regulating Cross-Border Marriage," 206, 207.

82 White, "Ambivalent Homonationalisms."

83 Solis, "Rancho Mirage Man Celebrates Gratitude."

84 Ortega, "ICE libera a inmigrante."

85 Ortega, "ICE libera a inmigrante."

86 Melanie Griffiths notes, "Far from being absolute, the line separating migrants from citizens is fluid and contested. Although in theory immigration systems help demarcate such binaries, in practice immigration policies operate across the division, with even 'good' citizens at risk of having their insider status queried through intimate ties to an undesirable foreigner. Family migration, mixed-immigration status families and family-based challenges to deportation especially illuminate the intertwined nature of these categories and the 'failed citizen' and deportable migrant's shared vulnerability to queried belonging, character and worthiness." Griffiths, "'My Passport Is Just My Way out of Here,'" 31.

87 Hasso, "Bargaining with the Devil," 108, 109.

88 Whether marriage can trump deportation logics varies depending on the specific circumstances of the couple and the immigration rules and practices in place at the time.

89 Rueb, "Is Trump Pushing Immigrants."

90 Rueb, "Is Trump Pushing Immigrants." Notably, this logic takes us a long way away from mainstream and governmental discourses of true love.

91 "Enhancing Public Safety in the Interior of the United States," Exec. Order No. 13768 (Jan. 25, 2017), https://trumpwhitehouse.archives.gov/presidential -actions/executive-order-enhancing-public-safety-interior-united-states/. Lazaro Zamora explains: "The Trump policy is governed by the overarching principle that no group of immigrants will be exempted or excluded from enforcement through prosecutorial discretion. . . . Unlike the priorities put in place in 2014 [under Obama], there is no inherent hierarchy in the list of priorities listed in Trump's [executive] order—all are listed as equally important for removal. . . . The memos also give much wider latitude to ICE agents with little guidance or oversight. . . . Prosecutorial discretion in the context of Trump's policy is strictly framed as a disclaimer that the listed priorities do not constrain ICE agents' ability to otherwise apprehend, detain, or remove any unauthorized immigrant." Zamora, "Comparing Trump and Obama's Deportation Priorities."

92 The attack on married couples was part of a broader effort by the Trump administration to severely reduce or entirely end family-based migration. At the southern border, from 2017 to 2019, his administration deliberately separated adults from children in an effort to terrorize them and deter their arrival. The administration also launched an attack on so-called chain migration—in other words, migration based on family ties. Characterizing family migration as chain migration drew directly from the white supremacist, anti-immigrant language and policy advocacy of the Far Right, such as the Federation for American Immigration Reform and NumbersUSA.

93 Yee, "A Marriage Used to Prevent Deportation."

94 Note, some migrants were unaware that a deportation order had been issued against them because issuing a deportation order was often a routine administrative matter, not a reflection that someone was a serious threat, and migrants did not necessarily receive notice of such orders.

95 According to a lawsuit filed against the Trump administration, these were the steps in the process: "The process requires first filling out a form I-130, which establishes a qualifying relationship to a United States citizen. . . . After the form I-130 is approved, the individual must file a form I-212, which requests a waiver of admissibility, and . . . can be conditionally approved while the individual remains in the United States. Id. Once the I-212 is conditionally approved, the individual must complete Form I-601A, an application for a provisional unlawful presence waiver. . . . Once the waiver is approved, the individual departs from the United States to obtain the visa through the consular processing procedure, thereby executing the prior removal order." Alyse Sanchez et al. v. Kevin McAleenan et al., Case No. GLH-19-1728 (D. Md. Feb. 7, 2020), 3–4, available at ACLU Maryland, https://www.aclu-md.org/sites/default/files/field_documents/sanchez_-_28_-_pi _opinion.pdf.

96 Calderon v. Nielson, Case No. 1:18-cv-10225-MLW, Document 27 (D. Md. April 10, 2018), available at ACLU Maryland, https://www.aclum.org/sites/default/files/wp -content/uploads/2018/04/Calderon-v-Nielsen-Class-action.pdf.

97 *Calderon v. Nielson.*

98 *Calderon v. Nielson*, 2. See also Jawetz, "Bait and Switch": "This deportation-only approach is reflected in the Trump administration's actions over the past three years to undermine the provisional waiver process by using it as a tool to entice people to come forward and then to arrest, detain, and ultimately deport them from the country."

99 *Calderon v. Nielson*, 23.

100 This lawsuit focused on practices in Massachusetts. In August 2019, the ACLU filed a similar lawsuit in the District of Maryland, accusing DHS of using "bait and switch" tactics to entice migrants to seek status and then deporting them. In February 2020, the judge sided with the plaintiffs and "barred the agency from deporting Maryland residents who have started the process to obtain legal immigration status based on their marriage to a U.S. citizen." See E. Williams, "Feds Blocked from Using Marriage Interviews."

101 In August 2018, the ACLU filed supplementary materials in support of their claim. They had interviewed Rebecca Adducci, the interim field office director of the Boston Enforcement and Removal Operations (ERO), who was brought in abruptly after an initial hearing on this case in May. Adducci said that she was unaware of the provisional hardship waiver process, and even though she now knew, she believed ERO officials are nonetheless required to detain and deport migrants even when they have waivers, based on the Trump executive order from 2017 and John Kelly's implementation memo. See Calderon v. Nielson, Case No. 1:18-cv-10225-MLW, Document 137 (D. Md. August 13, 2018), available

at ACLU Maryland, https://www.aclum.org/sites/default/files/field_documents
/20180813_calderon_petitionernoticeoffiling.pdf.

102 See, for example, Da Silva, "ICE Releases U.S. Army Chaplain's Husband"; Cunningham, "Chaplain Launches 'Operation Save Sergio.'" Note that many of these
cases involve complexities beyond marriage; for example, in the second case,
Nuñez had also gone through a "credible fear" process because he feared persecution if he was returned to Mexico.

103 Gammage, "Seeking Legal Status in America." Migrants were targeted, but their
citizen partners were also clearly viewed as risky subjects who needed to be pressured to conform to dominant norms. For example, as the COVID-19 pandemic
ravaged the United States, Congress passed a massive relief act that provided
payments of $1,200 to adults earning below $75,000, with an additional $500 for
every qualifying child. Yet married couples comprising a citizen spouse married
to an undocumented migrant were excluded if they filed their taxes jointly, as were
their children. The only exception was when one member of the couple had served
in the military. Strikingly, if the couple did not file taxes jointly, or the undocumented
spouse did not pay or file taxes at all, then the citizen members of the family did
indeed receive the payment. These rules suggested that undocumented migrants who
were following the law by paying tax on their earnings, and couples that filed jointly
because this showed the bona fides of their marriage (which in turn would help the
migrant to legalize), were being singled out. Lawsuits filed in federal court on behalf
of the citizen spouses and citizen children challenged their treatment as a violation of
equal protection and due process. A *New York Times* article about this issue included
the experiences of a male couple where one spouse was a citizen and the other was
undocumented. Dickerson, "Married to an Undocumented Immigrant?"

104 See also Horton and Heyman, *Paper Trails*. Valles's suggested publicity for the
play reads: "With a single phrase, you can give up your country. With a single
signature, you can tear a family apart. With a single word, you can learn to
transform. In their first full-length solo show, *(Un)Documents*, award-winning
actor and poet Jesús I. Valles journeys across both sides of a river with two names,
moving between languages to find their place as a child, a lover, a teacher, and a
sibling in a nation that demands sacrifice at the altar of citizenship. In doing so,
they create a new kind of documentation written with anger, fierce love, and the
knowledge that what makes us human can never be captured on a government
questionnaire." "About (Un)Documents," draft viii, on file with author.

105 Valles quoted in K. Gardner, "Jesús I. Valles' '(Un)Documents' Opens Tonight."

106 At a discussion titled "Home/Land" that was part of OUTsider's Conference on the
Couch organized by Laura Gutiérrez in Austin, Texas, on February 23, 2019, Valles
invoked bell hooks when calling for love that rejects possessive individualism or
control of another in favor of collective action grounded in ethical principles that
identify with the priorities of the most marginalized. See hooks, *All about Love*.
See also Berlant, "A Properly Political Concept of Love"; Lugones, "Playfulness,
World-Travelling, and Loving Perception"; C. Sandoval, *Methodology of the Oppressed*; Simpson, *Islands of Decolonial Love*.

107 Valles, in "(Un)Documents," connects their call for transformative love with a call for kinds of writing that differ from that of the state and corporations:

> when we are dead, we will leave behind our bills, our mountains of leases, loan applications, past due notices, our names on envelopes
> and i'd like to imagine we'd leave our love letters, the notes we passed our longings and poems and prayers and things we scrawled on the wall and those are documents, too, proof we were here once and why.

108 Recognition of same-sex and trans marriage constitutes a reformist reform rather than a nonreformist reform that contributes to abolishing the system.

109 Here I am referencing White, "Ambivalent Homonationalisms," 51. White is paraphrasing Gayatri Chakravorty Spivak.

110 Gehi and Arkles, "The Tacit Targeting of Trans Immigrants," 58.

3. DRIVING WHILE UNDOCUMENTED

1 Vargas, "My Life as an Undocumented Immigrant." Vargas is the author of *Dear America: Notes of an Undocumented Citizen* and founder of Define American, a "culture change organization that uses the power of narrative to humanize conversations about immigrants." Define American, "About."

2 Effective 2021, driver's licenses became available to all Oregon residents regardless of legal status.

3 Li, "Speeding Tickets, Minor Infractions." The report she references is Transactional Records Access Clearinghouse, *Secure Communities and ICE Deportation*. Similarly, Walter A. Ewing, Daniel E. Martínez, and Rubén G. Rumbaut found that in 2013, 45 percent of the 438,421 migrants who were "removed" were classified as "known criminal aliens." Among this group, 31 percent were removed for immigration offenses (illegal entry or reentry), 15.4 percent were removed for "dangerous drugs" (including possessing marijuana), and 15 percent were removed for traffic offenses. Ewing, Martínez, and Rumbaut, *The Criminalization of Immigration*, 10, 11.

4 Transactional Records Access Clearinghouse, *Secure Communities and ICE Deportation*, 2.

5 Ewing, Martínez, and Rumbaut, *The Criminalization of Immigration*, 10.

6 Stumpf, "The Crimmigration Crisis."

7 Chacón, "Managing Migration through Crime," 137.

8 Research consistently shows that LGBTQ folks disproportionately experience being targeted by police and frequently experience harassment, violence, and injustice during interactions with police and the criminal injustice system. Trans women of color are especially liable to be targeted, harassed, criminalized, and harmed. As Andrea Ritchie explains, policing violently sustains the racialized gender binary in US society, and "often acts of police violence are informed by racialized and gendered narratives framing women of color and transgender people of color as inherently devious, mercurially violent, superhumanly strong, and most of all, deserving of annihilation or disappearance," including through being locked up. Ritchie, *Invisible No More*, 138; see also Hereth, "I Don't Think the Police Think

We're Human"; James et al., *The Report of the 2015 U.S. Transgender Survey*; Luhur, Meyer, and Wilson, *Policing LGBQ People*.

9   Rosenfeld, *The Social Construction of Crime*, 5.

10 Rosenfeld, *The Social Construction of Crime*, 5.

11 Marginalized citizens have richly engaged automobility as a means to express resistance and offer alternative cultural logics. See, for example, Gilroy, "Driving While Black"; Clarsen, "Revisiting 'Driving While Black.'" Nonetheless, "across the span of 100 years, the growth of citizen automobility has brought with it an unwelcome passenger: a constantly expanding pile of thousands of local, state and federal laws focused on policing people in their vehicles." Jallow, "What Would Happen."

12 See, for example, M. Alexander, *The New Jim Crow*, chaps. 2 and 3; Baumgartner et al., "Racial Disparities in Traffic Stop Outcomes."

13 Seo, *Policing the Open Road*, 5, 266. See also Sterling and Joffe-Block, *Driving While Brown*; Sorin, *Driving While Black*. On police violence against Black women and women of color during traffic stops, see Ritchie, *Invisible No More*.

14 In *The New Jim Crow*, Michelle Alexander describes how the Supreme Court "eviscerat[ed] Fourth amendment protections against unreasonable searches and seizures by police" (78); "pretext stops, like consent searches, have received the Supreme Court's unequivocal blessing" (85), and the Supreme Court ruled that "no one needs to be informed of their rights during a stop or search, and police may use minor traffic stops as well as the myth of 'consent' to stop and search anyone they choose for imaginary drug crimes, whether or not any evidence of illegal drug activity actually exists. . . . But there's more. Even if motorists, after being detained and interrogated, have the nerve to refuse consent to a search, the police can arrest them anyway" (87).

15 This issue received national attention in the course of investigating the death of unarmed Black teenager Michael Brown in Ferguson, Missouri, in 2014. See W. Johnson, "The Economics of Ferguson"; Rakia, "It's Not Just Ferguson"; US Department of Justice, "Justice Department Announces Findings."

16 Arizona SB 1070, Support Our Law Enforcement and Safe Neighbors Act, April 23, 2010.

17 Arias, "Immigrant's Nightmare Began with Traffic Stop."

18 Arias, "Immigrant's Nightmare Began with Traffic Stop."

19 On March 4, 2014, the *Arizona Daily Star* printed a diagram titled "How a Traffic Stop Can Lead to an Immigration Check" (https://bloximages.chicago2.vip .townnews.com/tucson.com/content/tncms/assets/v3/editorial/6/bd/6bdc1b06 -a3c7-11e3-8692-0019bb2963f4/531615a974825.pdf.pdf, accessed December 2, 2019). The diagram describes the expected process. First, an officer asks for a driver's license and proof of insurance and registration. When the driver can show all three documents, "the officer can cite and release the driver, issue a warning, or do nothing." However, when the driver cannot show a license because the license is suspended or the driver has never been issued a license, "the officer can always ask questions. . . . The officer can use the answers to develop a reasonable suspicion a person is in the country illegally. . . . Under SB 1070's Section 2(B), if it's practical and doesn't hinder an investigation, the officer is required to do an immigration

check on the driver after developing reasonable suspicion. But the officer cannot extend the stop only to do the check. . . . The officer must release the driver if immigration officials don't arrive by the time the officer issues a citation or otherwise resolves the initial reason for the stop." The diagram also lists "factors officers consider in developing reasonable suspicion of unlawful status": "lack of ID/false ID/foreign ID; evasiveness or preparing to flee; voluntary statements; location; vehicles traveling in tandem; an officer's prior knowledge; inconsistent information; demeanor (i.e. nervousness); foreign vehicle registration; overcrowded or heavy-riding vehicle; passengers trying to hide; inability to provide address; unfamiliarity with the people with them; and dress (e.g. multiple layers or clothing soiled from travel in the desert)." This list merits thorough discussion.

20 Gamboa, "A Traffic Violation."

21 Critics of ICE describe the numerical targets as quotas. The agency denies that it has arrest quotas and instead insists raids simply entail fulfilling the mission of enforcing immigration laws and ensuring national security, border security, and public safety.

22 For example, in an MPI report, Capps et al. found that in Gwinnett County, Georgia, in 2010, "local police . . . arrested large numbers of unauthorized immigrants based on traffic violations, particularly driving without a license. When the Obama administration narrowed priorities to exclude most traffic crimes, these arrests declined, but by the time of MPI visited in 2017, such arrests were common again" (Capps et al., *Revving Up the Deportation Machinery*, 10). Thus, the authors stress, "the fortunes of an unauthorized immigrant are quite different in Texas, Tennessee, and Georgia, where the mere act of driving can result in arrest and deportation, than in California, Chicago, and New York, where immigrants can be arrested for a variety of crimes and still not be taken into ICE custody" (2). The authors highlight that making everyone eligible for a license regardless of legal status and decriminalizing minor drug offenses and other misdemeanors are also having an impact (14).

23 See the introduction for a discussion of attrition through enforcement.

24 In "Affect/Emotion," Ahmed discusses why she prefers the term *emotion* rather than the term *affect*. Schmitz and Ahmed, "Affect/Emotion," 97.

25 Ahmed, *The Cultural Politics of Emotion*; Ahmed, "Affective Economies."

26 Scholarship increasingly explores affect and emotions in relation to migration processes in general and deportation experiences specifically. In "Aspiration, Desire, and Drivers of Migration," Jørgen Carling and Francis Collins provide an overview of the affective turn in migration studies. Heike Drotbohm and Ines Hasselberg describe intersections among deportation, anxiety, and justice ("Introduction"). Susan Bibler Coutin reviews scholarship about the interconnections between deportation and fear, including in the context of expanding state securitization logics ("Deportation Studies"). Joanna Dreby explores how children of undocumented migrants live with and are affected by pervasive fear that their parents or other relatives and friends may be deported (*Everyday Illegal*). Scholars describe how the cultivation of citizens' fears is used to expand and normalize enforcement and deportation. A growing number of studies show how the prospect or actual experience of deportation causes fear, stress, anxiety, and trauma for migrants, which intertwines with material experiences of deprivation, incapacitation, and blockage. Scholars show

that Latinx populations in the United States, regardless of their citizenship or legal status, experience heightened fear, stress, and nonbelonging as a result of pervasive racializing immigration-enforcement strategies that are intended to generate deportation while affecting their everyday lives. Some scholarship shows that as youth moved from undocumented to DACAmented, they experienced lessening fear, hopelessness, and unbelonging; as the limits of DACAmentation became clearer, and as the Supreme Court became poised to abolish this program, these feelings returned. See Abrego, "Legal Consciousness of Undocumented Latinos"; Gonzales, Terriquez, and Ruszczyk, "Becoming DACAmented."

27 De Genova, "Migrant 'Illegality' and Deportability in Everyday Life," 438.

28 De Genova, "Migrant 'Illegality' and Deportability in Everyday Life," 439.

29 Unzueta Carrasco and Seif, "Disrupting the Dream," 284.

30 See, for example, Goodman, *The Deportation Machine*. White nationalists like Donald Trump rely on stoking white citizens' fears of migrants to achieve their goals. Eric Levitz's article "White House Opens New Office Devoted to Encouraging Fear of Immigrants" offers just one example among a flood of such efforts. The new office, VOICES, promised services to victims of crimes that were committed by immigrants.

31 Homan quoted in Sacchetti, "ICE Chief Tells Lawmakers."

32 Homan quoted in Kopan, "ICE Director."

33 See, for example, De Genova, "Migrant 'Illegality' and Deportability in Everyday Life"; Inda, *Targeting Immigrants*; Luibhéid, *Pregnant on Arrival*; Menjívar and Kanstroom, *Constructing Immigrant "Illegality."* The argument that undocumented status does not reflect millions of individual acts of wrong is discussed by Ahmad, "Beyond Earned Citizenship," 289.

34 This participates in a racialized, gendered, colonialist history concerning who is deemed human and a history of how having the "right" feelings (or not) becomes central to such judgments. See Schuller, *The Biopolitics of Feeling*; Rowe and Royster, "Loving Transgressions."

35 Beltrán, *Cruelty as Citizenship*, 10.

36 Beltrán, *Cruelty as Citizenship*, 19.

37 Beltrán, *Cruelty as Citizenship*, 23.

38 Beltrán's analysis resonates with the report by Aizeki et al., *Cruel by Design*. The report argues that the US migration-control system as a whole is "cruel by design" and must be ended. Jenn Budd, a former Border Patrol agent and suicide survivor, attributes the Border Patrol crisis of employee suicide to "the culture of cruelty the agency fosters." She describes how the Border Patrol's culture of cruelty demands very harsh treatment of migrants while "excoriating" any agent who becomes traumatized by the violence inflicted on migrants or by abusive workplace conditions they personally experience (Budd, "Opinion"). In regard to inducing fear through a cruel system, Marcella Alsan and Crystal S. Yang show that the fear of deportation that was induced by the rollout of the Secure Communities program resulted in significant declines in SNAP and SSI enrollment among Latinx citizens, especially in mixed-status households. Notably, these are conceived as "safety net" programs that are vital to everyday sustenance. Alsan and Yang, "Fear and the Safety Net."

39 Adair, "Licensing Citizenship."

40 Adair, "Licensing Citizenship," 575.

41 Adair, "Licensing Citizenship," 575.

42 Driving without a license because one does not have a license is usually a misdemeanor the first time; driving without a license because one had a license but it was suspended or revoked is generally more serious. The laws and consequences vary by state.

43 Sen, "Driver's Licenses and Undocumented Immigrants."

44 National Commission on Terrorist Attacks upon the United States, *The 9/11 Commission Report*, 384. Janice Kephart, a key figure at the right-wing Center for Immigration Studies, was the counsel for the 9/11 Commission on the border security team. See *Border Security and Enforcement: The 9/11 Commission Staff Report on Training for Border Inspectors, Document Integrity, and Defects, in the U.S. Visa Program before the U.S. Senate Judiciary Subcommittee on Immigration, Border Security, and Citizenship and U.S. Senate Judiciary Subcommittee on Terrorism, Technology, and Homeland Security*, 108th Cong. 1st Sess. (2005) (testimony of Janice L. Kephart), https://www.judiciary.senate.gov/imo/media/doc/Kephart%20 Testimony%20031405.pdf. The commission recommended: "The federal government should set standards for the issuance of birth certificates and sources of identification, such as drivers licenses. . . . At many entry points to vulnerable facilities, including gates for boarding aircraft, sources of identification are the last opportunity to ensure that people are who they say they are and to check whether they are terrorists." National Commission on Terrorist Attacks upon the United States, *The 9/11 Commission Report*, 390.

45 For state-by-state information, see National Immigration Law Center, "Driver's Licenses."

46 The National Immigration Law Center's website has extensive information related to histories of debates about allowing undocumented migrants to access driver's licenses, as well as various state and local campaigns over this issue. See National Immigration Law Center, "Driver's Licenses."

47 See, for example, Beauchamp, *Going Stealth*, 40–48.

48 Newton, "Immigration Politics by Proxy," 2100.

49 Driver's licenses that are not REAL ID compliant generally say so. To acquire the license, people must provide personal information and pass a driving test. Immigration and Customs Enforcement has been accessing much of the personal information provided by those seeking these licenses. The benefits of the license, however, include that holders cannot be charged with driving without a license, and the document is usable for many everyday purposes (although not air travel or entering federal facilities).

50 There is extensive scholarly discussion about these different models of citizenship and of the critical role of undocumented migrants in refashioning what citizenship can or should mean. See, for example, Swerts and Nicholls, "Undocumented Immigrant Activism and the Political"; de Graauw, "City Government Activists and the Rights of Undocumented Activists."

51 To gain traction, such appeals are mostly framed in the language of security and safety; thus, they do not radically reconfigure the terms of debate about nations, citizens, and migration control.

52 Ansley, "Constructing Citizenship without a License," 171.

53 Ansley, "Constructing Citizenship without a License," 171.

54 The video, which is no longer available, is called "LGBT Communities in Support of Measure 88 for Safe Roads in Oregon." I found the video on the website for GLAAD under the section "Covering LGBTQ Immigration Issues" and within that, "Spotlight: Covering LGBT Immigrants: Sample Stories." The information and video were included in the section called "Driving" (GLAAD, "Covering LGBTQ Immigration Issues"). I could not find the video under a general search of YouTube videos. Note that Causa has closed its doors since the video was made. Janet Arelis Quezada, "In Oregon, LGBT Lives Are at a Crossroads," is the source for my characterization of video participants as both immigrant and not. The video does not say, nor does Quezada, that all participants in the video are Latinx, but based on the stories they tell and the fact this is a Causa project, it seems likely that at least a majority, and possibly all, are Latinx people. All of the following quotations are from the video, unless otherwise specified.

55 Another way to grasp the harm comes from the lawsuit filed against Governor Jan Brewer of Arizona after she refused to allow DACA recipients to acquire driver's licenses, even though this was precisely one of the limited rights conferred by DACA status. The Arizona Dream Act Coalition, with assistance from the ACLU and other partners, sued for their right to acquire driver's licenses and eventually won. The brief filed with the Ninth Circuit Court of Appeals documents the harm that the youth experienced as a result of being denied driver's licenses. Overall, they experienced "harms related to employment, family relations, and everyday activities" (iii). Specific harms included "limitations on Plaintiffs' professional opportunities, restrictions on their ability to accomplish simple errands, and an inability to visit family and friends" (46). The plaintiffs also described "limit[ed] freedom to engage in everyday life activities, and . . . dependency on others to accomplish basic tasks" (47). They experienced "lost job opportunities and restrictions on career advancement" because of their inability to get a driver's license (49). "Several Plaintiffs testified that Arizona's policy hampers their ability to conduct everyday activities, including social visits with family and friends or errands such as grocery shopping. They either drive less because of their inability to obtain a license, or rely on friends and family who are not always available to drive them" (49–50). "One plaintiff even testified that the lack of state issued identification prevented her from completing basic errands, such as returning merchandise, and disqualified her from viewing an apartment for rent" (50). Moreover, the youth experienced "Stigmatic, Psychological Harms," including being treated in a discriminatory manner and as if inferior (51–52). They also experienced "harm stemming from the threat of potential prosecution for driving without a license" (53). Four of the five plaintiffs engaged in driving without a license, and three described their fear of being stopped and ticketed for doing so; one feared his car might be impounded. Fear caused them to curtail

their driving when possible (56). Finally, denial of driver's licenses prevented them from engaging in activities that were central to their organization's mission: promoting the educational success of immigrant youth, increasing civic and community engagement, and advocating for national immigration reform, including the Dream Act (58–59). Lacking driver's licenses, they were unable to attend events, mobilize volunteers, and work with partner organizations across the state (61). Moreover, the organization's resources were diverted to supporting this lawsuit against discrimination rather than fulfilling its stated mission. See Arizona Dream Act Coalition et al. v. Janice K. Brewer et al., No. 2:12-CV-02546-DGC (D. Ariz. August 21, 2014).

56 Abrego, "Renewed Optimism and Spatial Mobility," 192.

57 Pallares and Gomberg-Muñoz, "Politics of Motion," 6.

58 Writings on "undocumented and unafraid" include Galindo, "Undocumented and Unafraid"; Gálvez, "Unafraid and Unapologetic, Still"; Muñoz, *Identity, Social Activism, and the Pursuit of Higher Education*; Muñoz, "Unpacking Legality through La Facultad"; Negrón-Gonzales, "Undocumented, Unafraid, and Unapologetic"; Nicholls, *The DREAMers*, chap. 5; Oliviero, "Challenging 'Americans Are Dreamers, Too'"; Seif, "Unapologetic and Unafraid"; Wong et al., *Undocumented and Unafraid*.

59 The full title is the Development, Relief, and Education for Alien Minors (DREAM) Act, S.1291, 107th Cong. (2001). As of 2024, at least twenty versions of the bill had been introduced and failed (American Immigration Council, "The DREAM Act"). In "Disrupting the Dream," Unzueta Carrasco and Seif suggest that activism around the DREAM Act partly reflects the fact that the 1.5 generation experienced undocumented status in a distinct manner. Unlike their parents, they were raised in the United States and had access to K–12 public education, yet, unlike their citizen peers, they faced blocked opportunities at every stage, which intensified once they finished high school. Genevieve Negrón-Gonzales suggests that the 1.5 generation experienced a deep disjuncture between their "subjective and juridical identities." "Undocumented, Unafraid, and Unapologetic," 272.

60 Osmani R. Alcaraz Ochoa's "A Letter to the DREAM Movement" expresses discomfort and disagreement with this framing.

61 K. R. Chávez, *Queer Migration Politics*; Unzueta Carrasco and Seif, "Disrupting the Dream." See also Hogan, *On the Freedom Side*, chap. 4.

62 The four students were Lizbeth Mateo, Mohammad Abdollahi, Yahaira Carrillo, and Tania Unzueta Carrasco; the high school counselor, a legal resident, was Osmani R. Alcaraz Ochoa. All except Unzueta Carrasco were arrested on misdemeanor trespassing charges and later released.

63 Unzueta Carrasco and Seif, "Disrupting the Dream," 281. As Karma R. Chávez argues in *Queer Migration Politics*, the strategy of coming out as undocumented risked mirroring the limitations of coming out as LGBTQ, which had shifted from being a collective, transformative action to a process that largely sought mainstream inclusion for sufficiently respectable, propertied, gender-normative queers.

64 Pallares and Gomberg-Muñoz note,

> When the DREAM Act failed to pass the Senate in 2010, a cadre of youth activists diverged from the mainstream model to forge new space in the

immigrant rights movement that challenged distinctions between worthy and unworthy immigrants. . . . Youth rejected their portrayal as exceptional individuals and, instead, employed relational strategies that discursively emphasized familial and community connections, invoking the bravery and resilience of their parents and refusing to censure their migration decisions. . . . Youth activists also began collaborating with working undocumented adults on "coming out" events and civil disobedience actions, drawing on leftist critiques of neoliberal globalization to point to the role of undocumented labor in the US economy. ("Politics of Motion," 7)

65 Unzueta Carrasco and Seif, "Disrupting the Dream," 281. Increasingly, youth organizers identified with belonging to a broad, undocumented community to whom they felt responsibility; this identification shaped "the way undocumented youth organize, who we perceive being accountable to, and for whom we mobilize" (290).

66 Unzueta Carrasco and Seif, "Disrupting the Dream," 290.

67 Unzueta Carrasco and Seif, "Disrupting the Dream," 296.

68 Lal, "How Queer Undocumented Youth Built the Immigrant Rights Movement." There are competing accounts of how the term *UndocuQueer* emerged; Lal's is one of the most cited. Published works on UndocuQueer activisms are listed in the introduction, note 4.

69 Seif, "'Layers of Humanity,'" 304–5.

70 UndocuTrans highlighted the needs and priorities of undocumented trans people, which were often rendered invisible within queer communities and migrant rights struggles. See X. O. Vargas, "What It Means to Be UndocuTrans."

71 Some scholars discuss the UndocuBus in their work. See, for example, Schreiber, *The Undocumented Everyday*, chap. 6. Irene Mata, in "Invoking History," offers an account of the UndocuBus that explicitly centers queer people.

72 The experience of living and traveling on the bus, and the communities created and engaged along the journey, involved complex intimacies, too.

73 No Papers, No Fear: Ride for Justice, accessed September 10, 2024, http://nopapers nofear.org.

74 See, for example, Vallejo, "Undocubus Connects Immigrants."

75 "We have overcome our fears and are ready to set a new example of courage. We hope that this country and its elected officials will be brave enough to follow." No Papers, No Fear.

76 No Papers, No Fear.

77 Franco quoted in Winn, *Out of the Closets*, 22. Winn also lists "Kemi Bello, an undocumented Nigerian writer, and others, including Puente member Gerardo Torres," among the self-identified LGBTQ people who rode the bus (22).

78 Knefel, "No Papers, No Fear."

79 US Commission on Civil Rights, *Civil Rights Implications of State Immigration Laws*, 8.

80 US Commission on Civil Rights, *Civil Rights Implications of State Immigration Laws*, 10.

81 Torres, "Fearless and Speaking for Ourselves." This post includes the video.

82 US Commission on Civil Rights, *Civil Rights Implications of State Immigration Laws*, 27–29, 30–31.

83 Torres, "Fearless and Speaking for Ourselves."

84 US Commission on Civil Rights, *Civil Rights Implications of State Immigration Laws*, 35.

85 US Commission on Civil Rights, *Civil Rights Implications of State Immigration Laws*, 189.

86 Torres, "Fearless and Speaking for Ourselves."

87 Carpio, Barnd, and Barraclough, "Introduction to the Special Issue," 186.

88 Efforts to use driving regulations to dispossess migrants and marginal citizens continue unabated. In 2023, Florida's anti-immigrant law, SB 1718, included vaguely worded and potentially far-reaching provisions that criminalize transporting anyone who entered the United States without federal inspection. A lawsuit filed by the Farmworker Association of Florida, Inc., describes some of the potential consequences of this law for citizens and migrants of all statuses. Farmworker Association of Florida Inc. et al. v. Ashley Moody et al., No. 23-CV-22655 (D. Fla. July 17, 2023), https://www.americanimmigrationcouncil.org/sites/default/files/litigation_documents/challenging_florida_unconstitutional_anti_immigrant_law_complaint.pdf.

89 For example, see Beltrán, *Cruelty as Citizenship*; Franz, "Will to Love, Will to Fear."

90 Not just the architects of attrition through enforcement but many everyday citizens believe that undocumented migrants *should* continually experience and be debilitated by fear, including when driving.

91 This framing shows that different migrants ended up with undocumented status in different ways, depending on their standing in relation to multiple axes of power.

4. CITIES AS CHOKEPOINTS AND RESISTANCE

Epigraph: Orange County Immigrant Youth United, "Immigrant and LGBTQ Leaders to Launch Hunger Strike."

1 This information is taken from Cambron, "Activists Begin Hunger Strike."

2 The introduction explains that immigration enforcement is a federal matter in which cities and states have become critical players in terms of facilitating, or in some cases resisting, the federal agenda. Vast scholarship on and struggles over sanctuary cities reinforce this point. For a discussion of how sanctuary city policies and practices may contribute to antiprison and antiborder abolitionist thought and action, see Jeffries and Ridgley, "Building the Sanctuary City."

3 Balaguera, "Trans-Migrations."

4 Camacho, "Ciudadana X," 276; De Genova, *Working the Boundaries*; Heyman, "Ports of Entry as Nodes."

5 Balaguera reminds us that traffickers, NGOs, and others, not just the state, confine migrants. On value in addition to labor being extracted from confined migrant bodies, see Coddington, Conlon, and Martin, "Destitution Economies"; Conlon and Hiemstra, *Intimate Economies*.

6 See, for example, Boehm, *Returned*; Golash-Boza, *Deported*; Zilberg, *Spaces of Detention*. Note, not all detained migrants are deported.

7   Camacho, "Ciudadana X," 286.

8   Detention Watch Network explains that mandatory detention exploded after the passage of two 1996 immigration laws: the Antiterrorism and Effective Death Penalty Act and the Illegal Immigration Reform and Immigrant Responsibility Act. Detention Watch Network, "Mandatory Detention."

9   Detention Watch Network, "Mandatory Detention Fact Sheet."

10 Detention Watch Network, "Mandatory Detention Fact Sheet."

11 In "Hailing the Twelve Million," Camacho describes how these circumstances keep migrants in conditions of "absolute alienage" (10). Walter A. Ewing, Daniel E. Martínez, and Rubén G. Rumbaut describe how "whole new classes of 'felonies' have been created which apply only to immigrants." Ewing, Martínez, and Rumbaut, *The Criminalization of Immigration*, 1.

12 Menjívar, "Document Overseers," 157–58.

13 All these factors are part of the infrastructure of enforcement that creates, transforms, or abolishes intimacies.

14 ACLU, Human Rights Watch, and National Immigrant Justice Center, *Justice-Free Zones*, 14.

15 Detention Watch Network and the Center for Constitutional Rights, *Banking on Detention*, 2. See also Detention Watch Network and the Center for Constitutional Rights, *Banking on Detention, 2016 Update*.

16 "In 2009, 49 percent of immigration detention beds were run by private prison companies. By 2015, private prison companies ran 62 percent of detention beds; private prison corporations ran 73 percent of detention beds by 2016. At the same time, the overall revenues of private prison companies have risen as well. . . . As of January 2020, 81 percent of people detained in ICE custody were held in facilities owned or managed by private prison corporations." ACLU, Human Rights Watch, and National Immigrant Justice Center, *Justice-Free Zones*, 17.

17 Kate Coddington, Deirdre Conlon, and Lauren L. Martin note that "there is a burgeoning interdisciplinary field interrogating the economies of migration control and a litany of neologisms describing these economies," including the migration industry, the immigration industrial complex, the illegality industry, and the detention rights industry. "Each implies a different conceptualization of economy" ("Destitution Economies," 1428). Deirdre Conlon and Nancy Hiemstra explain that privatization has been key to the massive expansion of detention ("Introduction," 2–3), but their book's framework seeks to go "beyond macro-economic considerations . . . to consider intimate economies that enmesh with and exacerbate the impacts of detention" (8).

18 Mass incarceration also often involves guarantees to pay private contractors for a minimum number of bed spaces, regardless of whether they are filled. Thanks to one of the book's reviewers for pointing out this important connection.

19 The executive order was Enhancing Public Safety in the Interior of the United States, Exec. Order No. 13768, 82 C.F.R. 8799 (Jan. 25, 2017). See also the anti-immigrant executive orders Border Security and Immigration Enforcement Improvements, Exec. Order No. 13767, 82 C.F.R. 8793 (Jan. 25, 2017); Protecting the Nation from Foreign Terrorist Entry into the United States, Exec. Order No. 13769, 82 C.F.R. 8977 (January 27, 2017).

20 ACLU, Human Rights Watch, and National Immigrant Justice Center, *Justice-Free Zones*, 5.

21 "DHS has circumvented the appropriations process by transferring $200 million from various other DHS agencies, including nearly $10 million from FEMA. . . . In addition to seeking appropriations for adult detention, the Trump administration has also sought out more space in which to detain growing numbers of unaccompanied children." Chishti and Pierce, "Trump Administration's New Indefinite Family Detention Policy."

22 National Immigrant Justice Center, "Cut the Contracts"; US Gov't Accountability Off., GAO-21-149, Immigration Detention: Actions Needed to Improve Planning, Documentation, and Oversight of Detention Facility Contracts (2021). In "ICE Lies: Public Deception, Private Profit," Detention Watch Network and the National Immigrant Justice Center argue that ICE consistently misrepresents "its so-called operational need for detention space," provides "inflated detention cost estimates," prioritizes "the demands of prison contractors over responsible stewardship," and "disregards congressional oversight." This consistent pattern of behavior "contributes to failure of accountability for its ongoing rights violations" (1).

23 Detention Watch Network and the Center for Constitutional Rights, *Banking on Detention*, 7. Even when ICE goes through the theater of a "risk classification assessment" for an individual that results in a recommendation for release, they overwhelmingly detain anyway. Gruberg, "No Way Out."

24 American Immigration Council, "Alternatives to Detention."

25 Sullivan, "Biden to Ask Congress."

26 Sullivan, "Biden to Ask Congress."

27 Kight, "The For-Profit Detention Circle."

28 Villa-Nicholas, *Data Borders*, 57.

29 Panjwani and Lucal, *Tracked and Trapped*. See also Just Futures Law and Mijente, *ICE Digital Prisons*.

30 Kilgore, "'E-Carceration' Is the Newest Surveillance Trend."

31 Kight, "The For-Profit Detention Circle."

32 Thompson, "Shackled."

33 Gill, "Health and Intimacies in Immigration Detention."

34 Coddington, Conlon, and Martin, "Destitution Economies"; Conlon and Hiemstra, *Intimate Economies of Immigration Detention*.

35 Gill, "Health and Intimacies in Immigration Detention," 172.

36 Gill, "Health and Intimacies in Immigration Detention," 172.

37 Solitary confinement has been widely condemned because of its extremely severe impacts and is especially atrocious in the case of people suffering physical and mental distress. See, for example, James and Vanko, "The Impacts of Solitary Confinement."

38 Luan, "Profiting from Enforcement." See also ACLU, Detention Watch Network, and National Immigrant Justice Center, *Fatal Neglect*.

39 Shoichet, "The Death Toll in ICE Custody." Immigration and Customs Enforcement is required to issue detainee death reports; see US Immigration and Customs Enforcement, "Detainee Death Reporting." Note that ICE's reports are not considered

comprehensive. The American Immigration Lawyers Association tracks numbers of detainee deaths reported by ICE. See American Immigration Lawyers Association, "Deaths at Adult Detention Centers."

40 See Human Rights Watch et al., *Code Red*. On the inappropriate use of solitary confinement and inadequate or no mental-health provisions, see ACLU, Human Rights Watch, and National Immigrant Justice Center, *Justice-Free Zones*, 31. *Code Red* notes, "The fact that the same types of healthcare and oversight failures are present in so many [detention facilities] point to larger, systemic deficits in immigration detention facility health care. The lapses occur in both publicly and privately run facilities, and are not being addressed by existing oversight and monitoring systems" (2). *Justice-Free Zones* notes that "ICE's oversight and transparency practices on fatalities appear to have gotten worse" since 2018 when ICE replaced Detainee Death Reviews with Detainee Death Reports, which are significantly less detailed. "The newer 'reports' do not include a complete accounting of relevant facts leading up to the death, any analysis or assessment of the care provided, or a comparison of the care provided to the governing standards in place at the relevant facility. They do not in any case provide recommendations for addressing failures. Even more worrying, it is not clear whether ICE continues to investigate failures that may have led to a death or might lead to another death in the future" (32). *Justice-Free Zones* notes that many deaths appear to be linked to subpar medical care and lack of oversight and that there is a lack of transparency in regard to people who are "released" from ICE custody only to immediately enter hospital facilities where they die (31–32). This includes Johana Medina Leon, a transgender migrant woman whose health rapidly deteriorated during her detention at the Otero detention center. When she was found unconscious in her cell, she was "released" and placed in hospital, where she died of pneumonia (33). *Justice-Free Zones* also states that a third of the deaths in custody between January 2017 and March 2020 (thirteen of thirty-eight) were suicides, which are growing in a context of inadequate mental-health services and inappropriate use of isolation and, we may reasonably suspect, despair at the horrific conditions that offer little hope for successfully challenging a deportation order or gaining asylum, no matter how compelling one's circumstances (34).

41 Speri, "Detained, Then Violated."

42 Speri, "Detained, Then Violated."

43 The Prison Rape Elimination Act (PREA) was passed by Congress in 2003 to supposedly protect against sexual assault in jails and prisons. However, DHS did not finalize regulations for implementing PREA in migrant detention facilities until 2014, and even then, they insisted that the standards applied only when the agency entered into a new contract or renewed or modified an existing contract. Even when PREA is included in a facility's contract, the requirements are rarely followed. The 2011 detention standards also included provisions for the prevention of sexual assault and for the protection of transgender detainees in particular, but these are also largely ignored.

The Prison Rape Elimination Act exemplifies how urgently needed changes may become addressed through laws that entrench or even extend the violence of the system. Lena Palacios notes that PREA's enforcement provisions are "virtually non-existent" and that PREA's mandate has been "turned on its head," as the law frequently gets used to shield "the perpetrators of state sanctioned sexual violence." This includes interpreting PREA "to limit incarcerated people's access to the courts by first requiring that they exhaust all steps of an institution's internal grievance system . . . [which] further exacerbates the already serious barriers faced by survivors who want to bring their claims to court." In addition, "PREA has provided an excuse for correctional staff to force unwanted penetrative exams on prisoners and to place more prisoners in solitary confinement." Palacios notes, "Transgender and gender non-conforming prisoners, in particular, have experienced unanticipated negative impacts from PREA, including being punished through new policies purportedly created to comply with PREA that punish consensual sex and forbid gender non-conforming behavior." Palacios, "The Prison Rape Elimination Act."

44 Hiemstra and Conlon, "Captive Consumers and Coerced Labourers." Lawsuits have been filed against private detention companies accusing them of "forced labor" that violates the Trafficking Victims Protection Act.

45 Hiemstra and Conlon, "Captive Consumers and Coerced Labourers."

46 "One human rights organisation employee we interviewed estimated that one 187-bed facility may save between five and six million dollars per year through detainee labour." Hiemstra and Conlon, "Captive Consumers and Coerced Labourers," 134.

47 Shadel, "Inside America's Mass Detention." In a study of the experiences of thirty detained Latinx transgender migrants, five reported a desire to self-deport, even though they had fled violence and life-threatening conditions in their home countries. "For these participants, their experiences in detention were worse than the violence and mistreatment they had experienced in their home countries" (Minero et al., "Latinx Trans Immigrants' Survival," 48). One explained that conditions were so hard that her alternatives seemed to be to kill herself or self-deport.

48 Speed, *Incarcerated Stories*, 81.

49 Speed, *Incarcerated Stories*, 80, 81.

50 Damian Vergara Bracamontes describes how "the space of detention isolates and disembeds migrants from their various forms of social support, both familial and communal." Bracamontes, "Migrant Insubordination," 4.

51 On family separation, see Dickerson, "The Secret History." John Kelly, Trump's first secretary of Homeland Security, said that when it comes to immigration control, "a big name of the game is deterrence" and separating families "could be a tough deterrent." He "disputed the notion that such action was cruel." Cummings, "John Kelly Defends Separating Families." For further discussion, see Licona and Luibhéid, "The Regime of Destruction." On detained migrant parents losing their children through the child protective service system, see Rodriguez, *Fragile Families*.

52 M. P. Brady, *Scales of Captivity*, 1.

53 M. P. Brady, *Scales of Captivity*, 1.

54 For the rules for visiting the Eloy Detention Center in Arizona—the nearest detention center from where I live—which I visited with Adela Licona, see US Immigration and Customs Enforcement, "Eloy Detention Center."

55 Ryo and Peacock, *The Landscape of Immigration Detention*, 18.

56 National Immigrant Justice Center, "Cut the Contracts."

57 National Immigrant Justice Center, "Cut the Contracts," 5.

58 Washington, "ICE Wants to Destroy Its Records."

59 T. Johnson, "ICE Has Been Granted the Same Level of Secrecy."

60 See, for example, Cullen, "ICE Releases Its Most Comprehensive Immigration Detention Data Yet"; Martínez, Cantor, and Ewing, *No Action Taken*; National Immigrant Justice Center, *Freedom of Information Act Litigation*; National Immigrant Justice Center, *Lives in Peril*; Office of Inspector General, *ICE's Monitoring of Detention Facilities*.

61 Bracamontes explains:

> [Queer migrant kinship] is not defined by familial or emotional ties, even as they can contribute to this formation. Instead, queer migrant kinship is rooted in practices. Second, while queer people of color are often the protagonist of these formations . . . [this] is not a defining factor to make it queer. Queer tactics are not only enacted by LGBT people but also by those marked as nonnormative because of oppressive regimes. This is true for cisgender and heterosexual migrants who are often portrayed as nonnormative. . . . Third, queer migrant kinship honors the historical legacies and contributions of queer people of color to expand the boundaries of what can constitute kinship. ("Migrant Insubordination," 7–8)

62 On the importance of the 1980s in the history of migrant detention, see Loyd and Mountz, *Boats, Borders, and Bases*. On HIV, migrant detention, and resistance, see K. R. Chávez, *The Borders of AIDS*. On the Mariel boatlift and the development of gay Cuban Miami, see Peña, *Oye Loca!* On queer and trans detention and protest, see Shull, "QTGNC Stories from US Immigration Detention."

63 Bracamontes, "Migrant Insubordination," 20–21. He explains succinctly, "Networks of support are seen as a threat that enables the reproduction of migrant communities that ICE seeks to remove" (20).

64 Bracamontes, "Migrant Insubordination," 22.

65 Amnesty International, *USA*, 53. See also Balaguera, "Trans-Migrations."

66 United We Dream, *No More Closets*, 2. Here, United We Dream (UWD) uses the category "LGBTQ" and explains that "for purposes of the survey, UWD defines an LGBTQ immigrant as an individual that self-identifies as lesbian, gay, bisexual, transgender or queer and is either foreign-born or U.S.-born citizen with foreign-born parents" (1). Of their respondents, 24.52 percent were US-born with foreign-born parents.

One particularly interesting finding: "The survey indicated that the LGBTQ immigrant community cannot be split into a binary of documented and undocumented. Indeed, in carrying out the survey, many individuals reported confusion about the question or did not know their current immigration status" (8).

67 In addition, ten interviewees became detained when they sought asylum at the border, and nine were "apprehended while migrating." Minero et al., "Latinx Trans Immigrants' Survival," 11.

68 Minero et al., "Latinx Trans Immigrants' Survival," 44.

69 Minero et al., "Latinx Trans Immigrants' Survival," 44.

70 Much has been written on Arellano's experiences, including Human Rights Watch, *Chronic Indifference.*

71 National Immigrant Justice Center, "Mass Civil Rights Complaint."

72 Gruberg, *Dignity Denied*, 4.

73 Immigration and Customs Enforcement has a patchwork of standards that are supposed to govern detention conditions. These include the 2000 National Detention Standards, and the 2008 and 2011 Performance-Based National Detention Standards. It is often difficult to determine which standards apply. They are often not included in contracts, and even when included, they are rarely enforced.

   "In 2012, ICE created policies and procedures to address sexual assault in immigration detention facilities, including mandatory training for staff on ICE's zero-tolerance policy for sexual assault and abuse as well as on 'communicating effectively and professionally with lesbian, gay, bisexual, and transgender individuals.'" Gruberg, *Dignity Denied*, 9. See also note 43 concerning the Prison Rape Elimination Act.

   Performance-Based National Detention Standards 2011 includes provisions regarding trans people (62–63) and provides instructions for pat downs, strip searches, and body cavity searches (120, 122, 123). See US Immigration and Customs Enforcement, *Performance-Based National Detention Standards 2011.*

74 According to Sharita Gruberg, the facility was established in response to the National Immigrant Justice Center complaint. Gruberg, *Dignity Denied*, 10.

75 Gruberg, *Dignity Denied*, 10.

76 Balaguera, "Trans-Asylum," 1805.

77 State regimes also differentiate gender from sexuality in ways that migrants often do not.

78 Balaguera, "Trans-Asylum," 1794. See also Sarı, "Lesbian Refugees in Transit."

79 Balaguera importantly describes ways that immigrant detention gave heightened meaning to gender and sexuality labels among the women she interviewed. "Trans-Asylum," 1804.

80 Family detention centers have also been hyped as "models" by the government and widely condemned by others. For a short overview, see Detention Watch Network, "Family Detention."

81 In 2014, transgender women were moved to a distinct module within the jail, while gay and bisexual men remained in a different module that was also in the jail. Stahl, "Transgender Prisoners Suffer Abuse."

82 Balaguera, "Trans-Asylum," 1806.

83 Winn, *Out of the Closets*; United We Dream, "#BreakTheCage."

84 Black Alliance for Just Immigration et al., *Uncovering the Truth*, 9.

85 US Gov't Accountability Off., GAO-14-38, Immigration Detention: Additional Actions Could Strengthen DHS Efforts to Address Sexual Abuse (2013), 60. Note that the report was based on a very small number of substantiated cases—fifteen, of which three were cases involving transgender women. This report and its findings are still widely cited, including in 2021.

86 Minero et al., "Latinx Trans Immigrants' Survival," 46.

87 Minero et al., "Latinx Trans Immigrants' Survival," 46.

88 Stahl, "Transgender Prisoners Suffer Abuse."

89 Advocates for Informed Choice et al. to President Obama, December 16, 2014, available at Transgender Law Center, https://transgenderlawcenter.org/press-release-release-lgbtq-people-from-immigration-and-customs-enforcement-ice-detention-facilities/. The letter argues: "DHS and the Department of Justice have repeatedly recognized the vulnerability of LGBTQ people, both in the context of country of origin and in detention centers, but DHS/ICE has failed to protect us. In a November 20 memo, DHS has already recognized that detention resources should not be used for certain vulnerable populations, and any other population whose detention is not in the public interest. In the case of LGBTQ immigrants, the agency cannot continue to maintain inhumane detention conditions and waste millions of dollars detaining a vulnerable population that is overwhelmingly eligible for relief." The letter highlights the experiences of Johanna, a transgender woman from El Salvador who endured continual wrenching displacement and brutal confinement, including within the US detention system, until finally being granted a withholding of deportation. The letter argues that "her ordeal exemplifies that of many LGBTQ people fleeing to the U.S. from violence in Central America and around the globe."

The study by Minero and her colleagues also documents these abusive conditions. The overarching themes that emerged from the interviews were "(a) debilitating conditions in *la hielera* [i.e., the icebox, where captured people are held before being transferred to detention], (b) abusive and dehumanizing treatment by detention authorities, (c) denied access to basic human needs and medical care, and (d) solitary confinement as torture" (Minero et al., "Latinx Trans Immigrants' Survival," 44). Abusive and dehumanizing treatment included intimidation, forced labor, linguistic discrimination, and retaliation for reporting authorities' extrajudicial treatment. The interviewees also endured transphobic treatment, including being housed by their sex assigned at birth and offered solitary as a supposed alternative. Denial of access to basic needs and medical care included being denied access to food, hygiene products, medical care, and transition-related care. The authors also describe medical exploitation, such as excessive blood draws. Solitary confinement as torture included being placed in solitary because they were trans, as punishment, after being sexually assaulted, or after experiencing significant mental distress and instability. "Participants reported that 'queer and same-sex' appearing behavior and affection was punished while in detention. One participant recalled that more 'feminine-appearing gay men' were put in solitary after being harassed" (46). The authors include "Patricia, a 22 year old female person from Honduras, who reported being placed in solitary confinement, while nude, after having been raped by a cisgender man who was put into her detention cell. . . . Instead of holding him accountable, they told her they would be putting her in solitary 'for her own wellbeing' for the remainder of her time in detention" (47).

90 US Rep. Mike Honda et al. to Secretary of Homeland Security Jeh Johnson, March 23, 2016, available at Scribd, https://www.scribd.com/doc/306165410

/Honda-Hirono-and-Grijalva-Letter-to-DHS-Secretary-to-Protect-LGBT
-Immigrant-Detainees.

91 The Transgender Care Memorandum can be found at Thomas Homan to Assistant Directors et al., June 19, 2015, available at Immigration and Customs
Enforcement, https://www.ice.gov/sites/default/files/documents/Document/2015
/TransgenderCareMemorandum.pdf. Immigration and Customs Enforcement describes these guidelines as addressing data systems, identification, processing, and
detention placements. Thomas Homan, who at that time was the executive director
of ICE's Office of Enforcement and Removal, argued that the memo showed "ICE's
commitment to provide a safe, secure, and respectful environment for all those in
our custody, including those individuals who identify as transgender." See US Immigration and Customs Enforcement, "ICE Issues New Guidance."

92 Kwong, "Santa Ana Distances Itself."

93 Gilmore, *Golden Gulag*. Federal and state funding for cities began falling drastically, and social and educational supports were cut, while "get tough on crime"
logics expanded criminalization, the prison-industrial complex, and migrant
detention.

94 Santa Ana first detained ten migrants in 1996. In 2006, Santa Ana entered an
agreement to house up to two hundred detainees, and in April 2012, the LGBT pod
opened. See Kwong, "Santa Ana Distances Itself"; Elmahrek, "Santa Ana Backs
Away."

95 Elmahrek, "Santa Ana Backs Away."

96 Their demands can be found at Cambron, "Activists Begin Hunger Strike."

97 Hunger striking, a tactic with a long history that involves putting bodies on the
line, has been employed in detention facilities by migrants who have no other
recourse available to protest a brutal system. "Freedom for Immigrants . . . has
counted 1,600 individuals participating in hunger strikes [in migrant-detention fa-
cilities] just since 2015" (Washington, "The Epidemic of Hunger Strikes"). In *Behind
Closed Doors*, the ACLU and Physicians for Human Rights found that, rather than
addressing the inhumane and life-threatening conditions that cause detainees to
hunger strike, ICE responds with cruelty and coercion, including forced feeding,
solitary confinement, retaliatory deportation and transfer, and the use of force.
They have also restricted access to water, denied basic privileges, and threatened
prosecution. Physicians and nurses played a role in these responses, including
using forced feeding, forced hydration, forced urinary catheterization, involuntary
blood draws, and the use of force. When the COVID-19 pandemic raged in 2020,
detained people went on hunger strike to try to force ICE to provide basic sanitary
supplies like soap, to implement basic sanitation and safety procedures, and for the
ability to practice social distancing. However, ICE responded with pepper spray,
rubber bullets, physical force, and facility-wide lockdowns (9). The report describes
"an architecture of abuse" that organizes these responses, and it calls for the need
to end migrant detention (9).

98 Orange County Immigrant Youth United, RAIZ, and Familia: Trans Queer Liberation Movement, "Press Conference."

99 Whitlock and Heitzeg, *Carceral Con*, 8.

100 Kaba, "Toward the Horizon of Abolition," 96.

101 For example, see Critical Resistance, "Reformist Reforms vs. Abolitionist Steps"; Engler and Engler, "Making Our Demands Both Practical and Visionary"; Spade, "Facing the Limits of Law Reform"; Walia, "Dismantle and Transform."

102 Kice quoted in Vasquez, "Hunger Strikers to ICE."

103 Vasquez, "Hunger Strikers to ICE."

104 Human Rights Watch, *"Do You See How Much I'm Suffering Here?"*; Vasquez, "Hunger Strikers to ICE."

105 Benavides quoted in Kwong, "Santa Ana Distances Itself."

106 Stahl importantly notes that there is "a tension between harm reduction efforts and abolition . . . that persists to this day." Stahl, "Transgender Prisoners Suffer Abuse."

107 Testimony was available from other sources, too. For example, on the #Not1More page dedicated to closing the Santa Ana pod, Jessica Latona wrote, "I was locked up in Santa Ana city jail for six months, and it was like hell. I didn't have any proper resources, like health, that they claim are accessible inside. And that's the reason I am not afraid to speak publicly in support of my trans community and I will continue to do so until I die." #Not1More, "Tell Santa Ana."

108 Moreover, hunger strikers and protesters were concerned not just about trans and queer migrants but about all migrants caught up in the detention system. Balaguera notes that all trans people are punished in detention, but certain embodiments face more punishments than others, and certain placements offer the possibility of less (but never no) punishment. Balaguera, "Trans-Asylum," 1804.

109 Vasquez, "Hunger Strikers to ICE."

110 Vasquez, "Hunger Strikers to ICE."

111 Vasquez, "Hunger Strikers to ICE."

112 Vasquez, "Hunger Strikers to ICE."

113 Noyola, "The Movement for LGBTQ Rights and Immigrant Rights."

114 Gutiérrez quoted in Stahl, "Transgender Prisoners Suffer Abuse."

115 Gutierrez quoted in Stahl, "Transgender Prisoners Suffer Abuse."

116 This action showed that defiance of neoliberal economics comes with a cost: "Scaling back the city's contract with ICE . . . means shutting down one housing module and a $663,743 loss in annual revenue" (Carcamo, "Santa Ana Declares Itself a Sanctuary City"). They reduced the total number of available beds (which includes the trans and queer pod) from 200 to 128.

117 Stahl, "Transgender Prisoners Suffer Abuse."

118 The ordinance proclaimed that the City of Santa Ana will not comply with any immigration detainer requests, assist ICE with any joint operations, notify ICE of release dates, arrest a person solely based on violating immigration law, dedicate resources to enforce immigration law, maintain or request sensitive information, or enforce any program of registration based on ethnic, national, or religious background. Jennie Cottle connects these outcomes to the earlier mobilizations. Cottle, "Debate."

119 Enhancing Public Safety in the Interior of the United States, Exec. Order No. 13768, 82 C.F.R. 8799 (Jan. 25, 2017), para. 3, https://www.whitehouse.gov

/presidential-actions/executive-order-enhancing-public-safety-interior-united
-states/.

120 As of 2021, CoreCivic owns and operates 56 percent of all privately owned prison
beds in the United States, including beds used to detain migrants. In 2021, ICE
was CoreCivic's "largest single client" and ICE contracts generated over 30 percent
of CoreCivic's revenue. Investigate, "CoreCivic Inc."

121 Shull, "QTGNC Stories from US Immigration Detention," 182.

122 Balaguera, "Trans-Asylum," 1803.

123 Balaguera, "Trans-Asylum," 1803.

124 Hernández's cause of death was disputed. Officials initially said she died of complications associated with pneumonia, dehydration, and HIV. The Transgender
Law Center disputed that finding and also argued that her death was preventable. In addition, the Transgender Law Center described that her body showed
the marks of what looked like beatings that occurred while she was handcuffed
(Lawler, "What Happened to Roxana [*sic*] Hernández"; Shakur, "Roxsana Hernández"). In April 2019, the New Mexico Office of the Medical Examiner released an
updated autopsy report, classifying her cause of death as multicentric Castleman
disease due to AIDS and her manner of death as natural. The report did not agree
that she had been beaten while handcuffed; instead, it noted, "Ms. Hernandez had
extensive fractures of the ribs and sternum (breastbone) consistent with a series of
at least 10 cardiac arrests with successful rounds of cardiopulmonary resuscitation
(CPR) by medical personnel working to save her life. During the period when Ms.
Hernandez was being resuscitated, her platelet count (blood elements responsible
for clotting) was extremely low which would amplify the bleeding associated
with physically forceful CPR" (Sanchez, "Updated"). The Transgender Law Center
reiterated that this finding did not address culpability stemming from the fact that
Hernández's death was preventable. That an ill transgender migrant from Honduras
was routed into detention in the first place, that CBP uses "iceboxes," while failing to
provide medical care or adequate food and water, and the conditions under which
she was transported to Cibola and then the hospital all demand to be addressed.

125 Trans Queer Pueblo, "We received an urgent letter from trans women and non-
binary people who are detained at Cibola Correctional Center in New Mexico,"
Facebook, July 2, 2019, https://www.facebook.com/transqueerpueblo/videos/we
-received-an-urgent-letter-from-trans-women-and-non-binary-people-who-are
-deta/436718207180095/; Gómez, "Migrants Held in ICE's Only Transgender
Unit"; Walker, "Trans Detainees Say They Were Coerced."

126 Critchfield, "Migrants Inside ICE's Only Transgender Unit."

127 Huag, "Over 100 LGBTQ+ Activists." According to Huag, "#EndTransDetention
began as a partnership in 2016 between the LGBTQ+ migrant justice organizations
Familia: TQLM, Mijente, the Black LGBTQIA+ Migrant Project, and the Transgender Law Center."

128 Center for Victims of Torture et al. to Hon. Alejandro Mayorkas and
Mr. Tae D. Johnson, June 16, 2021, available at Immigration Equality, https://
immigrationequality.org/wp-content/uploads/2021/06/Ltr-to-DHS-and-ICE-re
-Abuse-of-Trans-and-HIV-Positive-People.pdf.

The conclusion subtitle is taken from Davis et al., *Abolition. Feminism. Now.*, 16.

1 Haley, "Abolition," 12.

2 Thus, there are harder and easier places to cross a border, judges who are more or less receptive to asylum claims, and so on.

3 "Abolish ICE" entered the mainstream in 2018, marked by the publication of Sean McElwee's "It's Time to Abolish ICE" in the *Nation*. Candidates for political office, including Alexandra Ocasio-Cortez, came into power partly by engaging this call. Mark Pocan (D-WI) introduced a bill to abolish ICE in the House of Representatives.

The documentary *Ghosts of Adelanto and the Rise of Abolish ICE* (previously called *Abolish ICE and All Border Prisons*) "tells the history of the Abolish ICE movement and centers the voices of feminist abolitionists and queer undocumented activists" ("Abolish ICE and All Border-Prisons: Screening & Panel," abstract, American Studies Association 2023 Annual Conference program, accessed October 11, 2024, https://convention2.allacademic.com/one/theasa/theasa23/index.php). The film is directed by Mayon Denton and Setsu Shigematsu and centers the life of Cinthya Martinez, who also contributed to writing the script. The 2023 ASA annual conference, where I saw the film, also hosted a panel of speakers including Martinez, the filmmakers, "undocuqueer activists Berto Hernandez and Mitzie Perez with California Immigrant Youth Justice Alliance and attorney Layla Razavi, Executive Director of Freedom for Immigrants, one of the few abolitionist immigrant rights non-profits."

The DeFundHate campaign ended in spring 2024. Its website includes a helpful report, *Insights from Closure of the Defund Hate Campaign* (2024), available at https://defundhatenow.org/wp-content/uploads/2024/05/DH_Report_Eng.pdf. For a helpful discussion of #FreeThemAll, see Kumpf and Webb, "Why We Support the Call."

4 See, for example, Mao et al., *Automating Deportation*; Just Futures Law and Mijente, *The Data Broker to Deportation Pipeline Report*; and Mijente's NoTech-ForICE campaign at https://notechforice.com.

5 For example, Mijente organized a campaign to shape the priorities that would be listed under the Biden administration's new prosecutorial discretion memo. The memo sets the framework within which enforcement activities are to be conducted. Although the final memo, in Mijente's view, "falls short of centering a protection-based framework," it nonetheless reflects the impact of grassroots immigrants' rights organizing (e.g., removing criminal convictions as an automatic basis for deportation). In collaboration with Just Futures Law, Mijente then created a *Deportation Defense Campaign Toolkit* based on the memo. See Mijente, "Deportation Defense under the Biden Administration." Thus, the memo, at one level a simple sheet of paper, sets the parameters for enforcement activities—and for defenses against deportations, too. The campaign to shape the memo allowed Mijente to further "grow the network of people who are ready and willing to organize and protect our communities from deportation." Mijente, "Deportation Defense Toolkit."

6 Information about Vargas's experiences is drawn from these accounts: Foley and Liebelson, "Dreamer Arrested"; Fowler, "Exclusive"; Hauser, "Woman Detained";

UnidosUS, "ICE Intimidates Latino Community"; Kessler, "Dreamer in Process of DACA Renewal"; Kocher and Stuesse, "Undocumented Activism and Minor Politics"; Simón, "The Sustained Efforts of Activists"; Villarreal, "Dreamer Faces Deportation"; Petition for Writ of Habeas Corpus, Daniela Vargas v. US Department of Homeland Security et al., No. 1:17-CV-00356 (W. D. La. March 6, 2017).

7   Petition for Writ of Habeas Corpus, *Vargas v. US Department of Homeland Security et al.*, 8.

8   "They rushed around the vehicle and opened Dany's side of her door and they were just like, 'You know who we are, you know who we're here for,' Sanders said. The agents drove off with her in handcuffs." Associated Press, "'All-American' Argentine Faces Deportation."

9   For details of the campaign, see Kocher and Stuesse, "Undocumented Activism and Minor Politics," 339. These authors describe how Vargas's case immediately gained national attention as a "bellwether for how the administration would treat the precarious class of DACA recipients nationwide" and because her arrest appeared to be in retaliation for speaking out against ICE enforcement actions (340). According to Angela Stuesse, Vargas seemed to be the first in a chain of immigrant rights defenders who were targeted for arrest and deportation by the Trump administration. Stuesse, "Vengeance Drives Trump Immigration Policy."

10 "She looked out the window the entire drive, telling herself, 'I just want to see the trees, I just want to see the road, I just want to see people before I can't do that again.'" Fowler, "Exclusive."

11 Or cars or other private property. The laws give some grounds for contesting police actions.

12 United We Dream, "Know Your Rights." Austin Kocher and Angela Stuesse reference United We Dream's materials since United We Dream took up Vargas's case, including organizing a petition that garnered more than fifty thousand signatures. Kocher and Stuesse, "Undocumented Activism and Minor Politics."

13 Transgender Law Center, "ICE Raids."

14 Transgender Law Center, "ICE Raids."

15 Instead, the Transgender Law Center suggests, people should assert their right to remain silent, deny consent to entry or a search, and ask to speak with a lawyer or loved one.

16 US Immigration and Customs Enforcement, "Protected Areas Enforcement Actions."

17 Walsh, "Watchful Citizens." James P. Walsh describes citizen involvement in immigration enforcement through "anonymous tip lines, voluntary immigration posses, border vigilantes, local immigration ordinances, and other practices that compel, encourage and include societal participation" (237).

18 Boyce, "The Neoliberal Underpinnings," 197.

19 Her experiences evoke Angela Davis's insight that "walls turned sideways are bridges," which reminds us that infrastructures of punishment, confinement, and expulsion can be repurposed for other uses. Davis, *An Autobiography*, 347.

20 Stoler, *Carnal Knowledge and Imperial Power*.

21 Davis et al., *Abolition. Feminism. Now.*, 51.

22 Davis et al., *Abolition. Feminism. Now.*, 15.

23 In 2020, the American Immigration Council and the Women's Refugee Commission released *Community Support for Migrants Navigating the U.S. Immigration System*, based on a survey of 224 community organizations. The survey showed extensive support for providing assistance to migrants navigating the US immigration system rather than spending money on detention and deterrence. The organizations do not address the idea of entirely ending the migration-control system, which would further reshape the availability of resources to be reallocated.

24 National Immigrant Justice Center, "Defund Hate."

25 McKeithen, "Queer Ecologies of Home," 124.

26 As Zaire Dinzey-Flores explains, "The physical, proverbial 'roof over the head' is also metaphorical. A shelter is deemed to provide more than a place for lodging and dwelling; it provides security, safety, dignity, supports identity, and is a place for belonging, a home, a *casa*, and an *hogar*. The range of significations for a casa-hogar/housing-home is vast—personal, collective, social, material" (Dinzey-Flores, "Housing," 86). For critical discussions of queer and trans migrants and housing/homes, see Borges, "Home and Homing as Resistance"; Gopinath, *Impossible Desires*; Wimark, "Housing Policy with Violent Outcomes"; Wimark, "Homemaking and Perpetual Liminality."

27 Power and Mee, "Housing."

28 The National Immigrant Justice Center's blog, *Rethink Immigration*, provides an example of ways that lack of housing may contribute to becoming detainable and deportable. The blog entry centers on Melissa (pseudonym), who found herself in detention awaiting deportation to Mexico. The author writes, "Melissa's immigration troubles began when she had a non-violent misdemeanor arrest as a teenager" that led to her being turned over to immigration authorities. She was released into her mother's custody, and all her case documents—including the notice of her immigration hearing—were sent to her mother's address. Unfortunately, "like many LGBT teens, Melissa had a strained relationship with her family and mostly relied on her friends for housing. She never received the documents from her family." Thus, she did not attend the hearing, and a judge ordered her deported. At the age of twenty, after a traffic stop, Melissa ended up in immigration custody again, where ICE tried to put the deportation order into effect.

Melissa had been living with her US citizen girlfriend, Alicia (pseudonym), and was the sole income provider while Alicia finished college. When Melissa became detained, Alicia had to drop out. She started working two jobs, which enabled her to pay for a lawyer for Melissa and cover the costs of expensive phone calls to the detention center but didn't leave enough for the rent. Alicia moved into a homeless shelter. Legal assistance, however, resulted in Melissa's deportation order being rescinded, and she was released on bond ($1,500) while exploring options for getting more permanent legal status. While the blog entry highlights the need for detained people to have access to legal assistance, it also reveals a lot about the ways that homelessness intersects with queer and trans migrants' struggles to avoid being detained and deported—and shows that citizen or LPR partners, family, and loved ones may also be rendered homeless through deportations. The vast scholarship on struggles and deprivations facing mixed-status families also underlines that migrant deportations deeply affect citizens' lives. See Georgevich, "Rethink Immigration."

29 Bonds, "Race and Ethnicity I," 577.

30 Bonds, "Race and Ethnicity I," 577.

31 See Oswin, "The Modern Model Family Home"; Shah, *Contagious Divides*.

32 Chakravartty and Ferreira da Silva, "Accumulation, Dispossession, and Debt."

33 There has been extensive analysis of the structural inequalities that leave LGBTQ youth particularly vulnerable to homelessness; the ways that migrant status further exacerbates housing precarity have received limited attention. Reports by the TransLatin@ Coalition offer a valuable exception. They consistently document that migratory status, intersecting with "gender identity . . . race, and language [that] are said to defy the norm" (Padrón and Salcedo, *TransVisible*, 2), renders trans Latin@ immigrants invisible, devalued, disrespected, and socially vulnerable, including in terms of accessing safe and affordable housing, which consistently emerges as one of their biggest needs and offers a critical anchor for other measures of well-being, including employment, health, and safety. See TransLatin@ Coalition, "Research."

Audre Lorde's well-known essay "The Master's Tools Will Never Dismantle the Master's House" reminds us that masters generally have houses and other properties. Questions about whose labor builds these houses, using which materials, and who gets to claim legal ownership of houses are inextricable from centuries of violence, dispossession, and inequality. In regard to possibilities for transforming this history, Hortense Spillers reflects:

> I have always sort of disagreed with that essay ["The Master's Tools"] by Audre Lorde, whom I really honour. . . . I have often thought it would be wonderful to have a conversation with her about that particular metaphor because I have always thought, well, the master's house, can they dismantle it with the master's tools? In some ways I have thought that it is the only tool that can dismantle the master's house, that they are not his tools in particular: anyway, in that they are no more the master's tools than they are mine and that I must particularly go after the master's house with his tools. (Spillers quoted in Emejulu, "The Master's Tools")

34 Even while there are somewhat more avenues to try to get asylum seekers out of detention and into housing while they wait for their cases to be processed, possibilities for seeking and being deemed by the state as eligible for asylum continue to narrow.

35 For discussion of these issues in the Canadian context, see Macklin et al., "Kindred Spirits?"

36 Williams and Massaro, "Managing Capacity, Shifting Burdens."

37 Freedom for Immigrants, "Sponsoring an Asylum Seeker," 2.

38 For example, the Queer Detainee Empowerment Project offers housing assistance. For a broad overview of the extent to which queer and trans migrants find their needs addressed, see Gruberg, *Serving LGBTQ Immigrants*.

39 Okporo, *Bed 26*. Okporo has since released *Asylum: A Memoir*. Okporo was recently described in *Penta* as an "author, activist and businessman" (Kaminer, "20 Minutes With"). His home page gives a sense of the scope of his activities: Edafe Okporo, accessed July 1, 2023, https://www.edafeokporo.com.

40 As of this writing, the director is Alford Green. See DiNatale, "Worcester-Based Ministry"; Mudambi, "Last Call with Al Green."

41 Zavaleta, "Houston Shelter for Undocumented Trans People."

42 Molina quoted in Zavaleta, "Houston Shelter for Undocumented Trans People."

43 Olayo-Méndez, "La 72."

44 Casa De Luz, which opened in 2019 in Tijuana, caters to trans women, gay men, and single women with children. Pixley, "Where LGBTQ Migrants Find the True Meaning of Shelter."

45 Bennet, "Queer Central Americans."

46 The migration industry involves not just labor brokers, smugglers, traffickers, and cartels but also state and local officials, local communities, transportation industries, money transfer and banking industries, and much more. Wendy A. Vogt's ethnography of Central Americans in transit through Mexico shows that "migrants may be valued as cargo to smuggle, bodies to prostitute, labor to exploit, organs to traffic, or lives to exchange for cash." Vogt, *Lives in Transit*, 86.

47 Didier Fassin's *Humanitarian Reason* provides an important ground for extensive conversations about humanitarianism as governance.

48 Balaguera, "Trans-Asylum."

49 The expulsions are called Title 42 expulsions because Title 42 of section 265 of public health law provided legal justification. See American Immigration Council, *A Guide to Title 42 Expulsions*.

50 Human Rights Watch, *"Every Day I Live in Fear"*; Human Rights Watch, "LGBT Asylum Seekers in Danger at the Border."

51 See Wikipedia, s.v. "Non-reformist reform," updated June 19, 2022, https://en .wikipedia.org/wiki/Non-reformist_reform.

52 Critical Resistance, "Reformist Reforms vs. Abolitionist Steps"; Gelderloos, *How Nonviolence Protects the State*; Gilmore, *Golden Gulag*; Kaba, *We Do This 'Til We Free Us*; Spade, "Facing the Limits of Law Reform"; Walia, "Dismantle and Transform."

53 Extensive discussions about how to ensure that proposed changes are nonreformist offer vital, helpful guidance.

54 Transgender Law Center, "Trans Agenda for Liberation." The agenda "centers the lives and voices of trans people of color, who have too often had to advance our collective liberation from the margins. Trans justice is migrant justice, disability justice, racial justice, environmental justice, reproductive justice, economic justice, and gender justice. An agenda for trans liberation is a blueprint for liberation for all."

55 Transgender Law Center, "Beloved Home." In regard to environmental justice and liberation, the Shut Down Adelanto Coalition highlights the environmental devastation wrought by carceral spaces like the Adelanto detention center. See Shut Down Adelanto, "About Us"; Shut Down Adelanto, "Adelanto Toxic Tour"; Chai, "Decarceration as Environmental Justice."

56 Schwiertz, "Transformations of the Undocumented Youth Movement," 622.

57 Transgender Law Center, "Trans Agenda for Liberation."

58 For further discussion of "Beloved Home," see Luibhéid, "National Citizenship, Migrant Deportation."

59 Davis et al., *Abolition. Feminism. Now.*, 16.

ABC News. "First Green Card Approved for Same-Sex Couple." July 1, 2013. https://abcnews.go.com/ABC_Univision/News/traian-popov-julian-marsh-sex-couple-receive-green/story?id=19542531.

Abolitionist Futures. "For Social and Transformative Justice." Accessed September 10, 2024. https://abolitionistfutures.com.

Abrego, Leisy J. "Legal Consciousness of Undocumented Latinos: Fear and Stigma as Barriers to Claims-Making for First- and 1.5-Generation Immigrants." *Law and Society Review* 45, no. 2 (2011): 337–69.

Abrego, Leisy J. "Renewed Optimism and Spatial Mobility: Legal Consciousness of Latino Deferred Action for Childhood Arrivals Recipients and Their Families in Los Angeles." *Ethnicities* 18, no. 2 (2018): 192–207.

Abrego, Leisy J. *Sacrificing Families: Navigating Laws, Labor, and Love across Borders.* Stanford, CA: Stanford University Press, 2014.

Abrego, Leisy J., and Genevieve Negrón-Gonzales. "Introduction." In *We Are Not Dreamers: Undocumented Scholars Theorize Undocumented Life in the United States*, edited by Leisy Abrego and Genevieve Negrón-Gonzales, 1–22. Durham, NC: Duke University Press, 2020.

ACLU, Detention Watch Network, and National Immigrant Justice Center. *Fatal Neglect: How ICE Ignores Deaths in Detention.* February 2016. https://www.aclu.org/sites/default/files/field_document/fatal_neglect_acludwnnijc.pdf.

ACLU, Human Rights Watch, and National Immigrant Justice Center. *Justice-Free Zones: US Immigration Detention under the Trump Administration.* April 2020. https://www.hrw.org/sites/default/files/supporting_resources/justice_free_zones_immigrant_detention.pdf.

ACLU, Kino Border Initiative, ProtectAZ Health, Sikh Coalition, and ACLU affiliates in Arizona, New Mexico, San Diego and Imperial Counties, and Texas. *From Hope to Heartbreak: The Disturbing Reality of Border Patrol's Confiscation of Migrants' Belongings.* February 12, 2024. https://www.aclu.org/publications/from-hope-to-heartbreak-the-disturbing-reality-of-border-patrols-confiscation-of-migrants-belongings.

ACLU and Physicians for Human Rights. *Behind Closed Doors: Abuse and Retaliation against Hunger Strikers in U.S. Immigration Detention.* 2021. https://phr.org/wp-content/uploads/2021/06/ACLU-PHR-Behind-Closed-Doors.pdf.

Acosta, Katie. *Amigas y Amantes: Sexually Nonconforming Latinas Negotiate Family.* New Brunswick, NJ: Rutgers University Press, 2013.

Adair, Cassius. "Licensing Citizenship: Anti-Blackness, Identification Documents, and Transgender Studies." *American Quarterly* 71, no. 2 (2019): 569–94.

Agathangelou, Anna M., M. Daniel Bassichis, and Tamara L. Spira. "Intimate Investments: Homonormativity, Global Lockdown, and the Seductions of Empire." *Radical History Review*, no. 100 (Winter 2008): 120–43.

Ahmad, Muneer I. "Beyond Earned Citizenship." *Harvard Civil Rights–Civil Liberties Law Review* 52, no. 2 (2017): 257–304.

Ahmed, Sara. "Affective Economies." *Social Text* 22, no. 2 (79) (2004): 117–39.

Ahmed, Sara. *The Cultural Politics of Emotion*. New York: Routledge, 2004.

Ahmed, Sara. *The Promise of Happiness*. Durham, NC: Duke University Press, 2010.

Aizeki, Mizue, Matt Mahmoudi, and Coline Schupfer, eds. *Resisting Borders and Technologies of Violence*. Chicago: Haymarket Books, 2024.

Aizeki, Mizue, Ghita Schwarz, Jane Shim, and Samah Sisay. *Cruel by Design: Voices of Resistance from Immigration Detention*. Immigrant Defense Project and the Center for Constitutional Rights, February 2022.

Alcaraz Ochoa, Osmani R. "A Letter to the DREAM Movement." *NACLA Report on the Americas* 44, no. 6 (2011): 18–19.

Alcaraz Ochoa, Osmani R. "Op-Ed: Why You Should Help Me Get LGBT People out of Detention." *Advocate*, October 14, 2014. https://www.advocate.com/commentary/2014/10/14/op-ed-why-you-should-help-me-get-lgbt-people-out-detention.

Alexander, M. Jacqui. "Not Just (Any) Body Can Be a Citizen: The Politics of Law, Sexuality and Postcoloniality in Trinidad and Tobago and the Bahamas." *Feminist Review* 48, no. 1 (1994): 5–23.

Alexander, Michelle. *The New Jim Crow: Mass Incarceration in the Age of Colorblindness*. New York: New Press, 2020.

Alsan, Marcella, and Crystal Yang. "Fear and the Safety Net: Evidence from Secure Communities." Working paper 24731, National Bureau of Economic Research, Cambridge, MA, July 2019. https://www.nber.org/papers/w24731.

American Immigration Council. "Alternatives to Immigration Detention: An Overview." July 11, 2023. https://www.americanimmigrationcouncil.org/research/alternatives-immigration-detention-overview.

American Immigration Council. "The Cost of Immigration Enforcement and Border Security." January 20, 2021. https://www.americanimmigrationcouncil.org/sites/default/files/research/the_cost_of_immigration_enforcement_and_border_security.pdf.

American Immigration Council. "The Criminal Alien Program (CAP): Immigration Enforcement in Prisons and Jails." August 1, 2013. https://www.americanimmigrationcouncil.org/research/criminal-alien-program-cap-immigration-enforcement-prisons-and-jails.

American Immigration Council. "Did My Family Really Come 'Legally'? Today's Immigration Laws Created a New Reality." August 10, 2016. https://www.americanimmigrationcouncil.org/sites/default/files/research/did_my_family_really_come_legally.pdf.

American Immigration Council. "The DREAM Act: An Overview." May 8, 2024. https://www.americanimmigrationcouncil.org/research/dream-act-overview.

American Immigration Council. *A Guide to Title 42 Expulsions at the Border.* May 25, 2022. https://www.americanimmigrationcouncil.org/research/guide-title-42 -expulsions-border.

American Immigration Council. "How the United States Immigration System Works." June 24, 2024. https://www.americanimmigrationcouncil.org/research/how-united -states-immigration-system-works.

American Immigration Council. "Secure Communities: A Fact Sheet." November 29, 2011. https://www.americanimmigrationcouncil.org/research/secure-communities -fact-sheet.

American Immigration Council. "The 287(g) Program: An Overview." July 8, 2021. https://www.americanimmigrationcouncil.org/research/287g-program-immigration.

American Immigration Council. "U.S. Citizen Children Impacted by Immigration Enforcement." June 24, 2021. https://www.americanimmigrationcouncil.org/research /us-citizen-children-impacted-immigration-enforcement.

American Immigration Council. "Why Don't Immigrants Apply for Citizenship? There Is No Line for Many Undocumented Immigrants." October 7, 2021. https://www .americanimmigrationcouncil.org/research/why-don't-they-just-get-line.

American Immigration Council and Women's Refugee Commission. *Community Support for Migrants Navigating the U.S. Immigration System.* February 2021. https:// www.americanimmigrationcouncil.org/sites/default/files/research/community _support_for_migrants_navigating_the_us_immigration_system_0.pdf.

American Immigration Lawyers Association. "Current Immigration Laws." September 21, 2001. https://www.aila.org/infonet/current-immigration-laws.

American Immigration Lawyers Association. "Deaths at Adult Detention Centers." September 12, 2024. https://www.aila.org/library/deaths-at-adult-detention-centers.

American Immigration Lawyers Association. "Featured Issue: Denaturalization Efforts by USCIS." August 27, 2021. https://www.aila.org/infonet/featured-issue -denaturalization-efforts-by-uscis.

American Immigration Lawyers Association. "Talking Points: Earned Legalization Is Not an Amnesty." Accessed June 22, 2014. http://www.aila.org/content/default.aspx ?bc=6755%7C37861%7C25667%7C38281%7C18779.

Amnesty International. *USA: "You Don't Have Any Rights Here": Illegal Pushbacks, Arbitrary Detention and Ill-Treatment of Asylum-Seekers in the United States.* October 11, 2018. https://www.amnesty.org/en/documents/amr51/9101/2018/en/.

Anderson, Bridget. *Us and Them? The Dangerous Politics of Immigration Control.* Oxford: Oxford University Press, 2013.

Anderson, Bridget, Matthew J. Gibney, and Emanuela Paoletti. "Citizenship, Deportation and the Boundaries of Belonging." *Citizenship Studies* 15, no. 5 (2011): 547–63.

Anderson, Stuart. "A Wall and Trump Immigration Policies Benefit Drug Cartels." *Forbes*, February 7, 2019.

Andersson, Ruben. "Time and the Migrant Other: European Border Controls and the Temporal Economics of Illegality." *American Anthropologist* 116, no. 4 (2014): 795–809.

Ansley, Fran. "Constructing Citizenship without a License: The Struggle of Undocumented Immigrants in the USA for Livelihoods and Recognition." *Studies in Social Justice* 4, no. 2 (2010): 165–78.

Appel, Hannah, Nikhil Anand, and Akhil Gupta. "Introduction: Temporality, Politics, and the Promise of Infrastructure." In *The Promise of Infrastructure*, edited by Nikhil Anand, Akhil Gupta, and Hannah Appel, 1–38. Durham, NC: Duke University Press, 2018.

Aradau, Claudia, and Martina Tazzioli. "Biopolitics Multiple: Migration, Extraction, Subtraction." *Millennium: Journal of International Studies* 48, no. 2 (2020): 198–220.

Arias, Eddy. "Immigrant's Nightmare Began with Traffic Stop." *Houston Chronicle*, December 22, 2015.

Associated Press. "'All-American' Argentine Faces Deportation without Hearing." *VOA*, March 3, 2017. https://www.voanews.com/a/all-american-argentine-faces -deportation-without-hearing/3748806.html.

Baas, Michiel, and Brenda Yeoh. "Introduction: Migration Studies and Critical Temporalities." *Current Sociology* 67, no. 2 (2019): 161–68.

Bailey, Marlon. *Butch Queens Up in Pumps*. Ann Arbor: University of Michigan Press, 2013.

Baker, Mike, Jennifer Valentino-DeVries, Manny Fernandez, and Michael LaForgia. "Three Words. 70 Cases. The Tragic History of 'I Can't Breathe.'" *New York Times*, June 29, 2020.

Balaguera, Martha. "Trans-Asylum: Sanctioning Vulnerability and Gender Identity across the Frontier." *Ethnic and Racial Studies* 46, no. 9 (2023): 1791–811.

Balaguera, Martha. "Trans-Migrations: Agency and Confinement at the Limits of Sovereignty." *Signs: Journal of Women in Culture and Society* 43, no. 3 (2018): 641–64.

Batzke, Ina. "From Coming Out to Undocuqueer: Intersections between Illegality and Queerness and the U.S. Undocumented Youth Movement." In *Global Youth Migration and Gendered Modalities*, edited by Glenda Tibe Bonaficio, 125–42. Bristol, UK: Bristol University Press, 2019.

Baumgartner, Frank, Leah Christiani, Derek A. Epps, Kevin Roach, and Kelsey Shoub. "Racial Disparities in Traffic Stop Outcomes." *Duke Forum for Law and Social Change* 9, nos. 1–2 (2017): 21–53.

Bazelon, Emily. "The Right-Wing Dream of 'Self-Deportation.'" *New York Times*, July 27, 2024.

Beam, Mryl. "What's Love Got to Do with It? Queer Politics and the 'Love Pivot.'" In *Queer Activism after Marriage Equality*, edited by Joseph Nicholas DeFilippis, Michael W. Yarbrough, and Angela Jones, 53–60. New York: Routledge, 2018.

Beauchamp, Toby. *Going Stealth: Transgender Politics and U.S. Surveillance Practices*. Durham, NC: Duke University Press, 2019.

Beltrán, Cristina. *Cruelty as Citizenship: How Migrant Suffering Sustains White Democracy*. Minneapolis: University of Minnesota Press, 2020.

Benjamin, Ruja. "Foreword: Borders and Bits: From Obvious to Invidious Violence." In *Resisting Borders and Technologies of Violence*, edited by Mizue Aizeki, Matt Mahmoudi, and Coline Schupfer, ix–xiv. Chicago: Haymarket Books, 2024.

Ben-Moshe, Liat. "Dis-epistemologies of Abolition." *Critical Criminology* 26 (2018): 341–55.

Bennet, Isadora. "Queer Central Americans Imagining Livable Lives." Master's thesis, Uppsala University, 2020.

Berlant, Lauren. "Citizenship." In *Keywords for American Cultural Studies*, 2nd ed., edited by Bruce Burgett and Glenn Hendler, 41–45. New York: New York University Press, 2014.

Berlant, Lauren. "The Commons: Infrastructures for Troubling Times." *Environment and Planning D: Society and Space* 34, no. 3 (2016): 393–419.

Berlant, Lauren. *Cruel Optimism*. Durham, NC: Duke University Press, 2011.

Berlant, Lauren. "A Properly Political Concept of Love: Three Approaches in Ten Pages." *Cultural Anthropology* 26, no. 4 (2011): 683–91.

Bernstein, Nina. "Do You Take This Immigrant?" *New York Times*, June 11, 2010. https://www.nytimes.com/2010/06/13/nyregion/13fraud.html.

Bey, Marquis, and Jesse A. Goldberg. "Queer as in Abolition Now!" *GLQ: A Journal of Lesbian and Gay Studies* 28, no. 2 (2022): 159–63.

Bhatia, Monish, and Victoria Canning. "Introduction: Contested Temporalities, Time and State Violence." In *Stealing Time: Migration, Temporalities and State Violence*, edited by Monish Bhatia and Victoria Canning, xv–xxv. Basingstoke, UK: Palgrave Macmillan, 2021.

Bhatia, Monish, and Victoria Canning, eds. *Stealing Time: Migration, Temporalities and State Violence*. Basingstoke, UK: Palgrave Macmillan, 2021.

Bier, David J. "Why Legal Immigration Is Nearly Impossible: U.S. Legal Immigration Rules Explained." Policy analysis no. 950, Cato Institute, Washington, DC, June 13, 2023. https://www.cato.org/sites/cato.org/files/2023-06/policy-analysis-950-updated.pdf.

Black Alliance for Just Immigration, Black LGBTQIA+ Migrant Project, UndocuBlack Network, and Freedom for Immigrants. *Uncovering the Truth: Violence and Abuse against Black Migrants in Immigration Detention*. October 2022. https://baji.org/wp-content/uploads/2022/10/Uncovering-the-Truth.pdf.

Boehm, Deborah. *Returned: Coming and Going in an Age of Deportation*. Oakland: University of California Press, 2016.

Bonds, Anne. "Race and Ethnicity I: Property, Race, and the Carceral State." *Progress in Human Geography* 43, no. 3 (2019): 574–83.

Borges, Sandibel. "Home and Homing as Resistance: Survival of LGBTQ Latinx Migrants." *Women's Studies Quarterly* 46, nos. 3–4 (2018): 69–84.

Boyce, Geoffrey Alan. "The Neoliberal Underpinnings of Prevention Through Deterrence and the United States Government's Case against Geographer Scott Warren." *Journal of Latin American Geography* 18, no. 3 (2019): 192–201.

Bracamontes, Damian Vergara. "Migrant Insubordination: Politicizing Detention through Queer Migrant Kinship." *Ethnic Studies Review* 45, no. 1 (2022): 3–22.

Bradley, Grace Marie, and Luke de Noronha. *Against Borders: The Case for Abolition*. London: Verso, 2022.

Brady, Aaron. "How the US Exported Its Border around the World." *Nation*, August 20, 2019. https://www.thenation.com/article/archive/todd-miller-new-book-empire-of-borders-interview/.

Brady, Mary Pat. *Scales of Captivity: Racial Capitalism and the Latinx Child*. Durham, NC: Duke University Press, 2022.

Bredbenner, Candice Lewis. *A Nationality of Her Own: Women, Marriage and the Law of Citizenship*. Berkeley: University of California Press, 1998.

Budd, Jenn. "Opinion: Migrant Deaths and Agent Suicides Plague U.S. Border Patrol." *Times of San Diego*, July 29, 2024.

Cabas-Mijares, Rachel, and Rachel Grant. "No Longer Interested in Convincing You of My Humanity: Undocuqueer Visualities Reclaim the Right to Exist." *Visual Communication Quarterly* 27, no. 4 (2020): 196–209.

Caldwell, Beth. *Deported Americans: Life after Deportation in Mexico*. Durham, NC: Duke University Press, 2019.

Camacho, Alicia Schmidt. "Ciudadana X: Gender Violence and the Denationalization of Women's Rights in Ciudad Juárez, Mexico." In *Terrorizing Women: Feminicide in the Américas*, edited by Rosa-Linda Fregoso and Cynthia Bejarano, 275–89. Durham, NC: Duke University Press, 2010.

Camacho, Alicia Schmidt. "Hailing the Twelve Million: U.S. Immigration Policy, Deportation, and the Imaginary of Lawful Violence." *Social Text* 28, no. 4 (105) (2010): 1–24.

Cambron, Rossana. "Activists Begin Hunger Strike, Call for Halt to Detention of Transgender Immigrants." *People's World*, May 19, 2016. https://peoplesworld.org/article/activists-begin-hunger-strike-call-for-halt-to-detention-of-transgender-immigrants/.

Camminga, B. *Transgender Refugees and the Imagined South Africa: Bodies over Borders and Borders over Bodies*. London: Palgrave Macmillan, 2019.

Camminga, B, and John Marnell, eds. *Queer and Trans African Mobilities: Migration, Asylum and Diaspora*. London: Zed Books, 2022.

Canaday, Margot. *The Straight State*. Princeton, NJ: Princeton University Press, 2009.

Capps, Randy, Muzzafar Chishti, Doris Meissner, and Michelle Mittlestadt. *Revving Up the Deportation Machinery: Enforcement and Pushback under Trump*. Washington, DC: Migration Policy Institute, May 2019.

Caputo, Marc. "Undocumented Immigrants Face Major Hurdles, More Than Decade Long Wait for U.S. Citizenship." *Miami Herald*, April 13, 2013.

Carastathis, Anna, and Myrto Tsilimpounidi. *Reproducing Refugees: Photographia of a Crisis*. Lanham, MD: Rowman and Littlefield, 2020.

Carbado, Devon W. "Racial Naturalization." *American Quarterly* 57, no. 3 (September 2005): 633–58.

Carcamo, Cindy. "Santa Ana Declares Itself a Sanctuary City in Defiance of Trump." *Los Angeles Times*, December 6, 2016. https://www.latimes.com/local/california/la-me-santa-ana-sanctuary-city-20161206-story.html.

Carens, Joseph H. "The Case for Open Borders." *OpenDemocracy*, June 5, 2015. https://www.opendemocracy.net/en/beyond-trafficking-and-slavery/case-for-open-borders/.

Carling, Jørgen, and Francis Collins. "Aspiration, Desire, and Drivers of Migration." *Journal of Ethnic and Migration Studies* 44, no. 6 (2018): 909–26.

Carpio, Genevieve, Natchee Blu Barnd, and Laura Barraclough. "Introduction to the Special Issue: Mobilizing Indigeneity and Race within and against Settler Colonialism." *Mobilities* 17, no. 2 (2022): 179–95.

Carter, Julian B. *The Heart of Whiteness: Normal Sexuality and Race in America, 1880–1940*. Durham, NC: Duke University Press, 2007.

Casas-Cortes, Maribel, Sebastian Cobarrubias, Nicholas De Genova, Glenda Garelli, Giorgio Grappi, Charles Heller, Sabine Hess, et al. "New Keywords: Migration and Borders." *Cultural Studies* 29, no. 1 (2014): 55–87.

Center for American Progress. "Crossing the Border: How Disability Civil Rights Protections Can Include Disabled Asylum Seekers." August 24, 2022. https://www .americanprogress.org/article/crossing-the-border-how-disability-civil-rights -protections-can-include-disabled-asylum-seekers/.

Chaar López, Iván. *The Cybernetic Border: Drones, Technology, and Intrusion.* Durham, NC: Duke University Press, 2024.

Chacón, Jennifer M. "Managing Migration through Crime." *Columbia Law Review* 109 (2009): 135–48.

Chacón, Jennifer M. "The Security Myth: Punishing Immigrants in the Name of National Security." In *Immigration, Integration, and Security: America and Europe in Comparative Perspective*, edited by Ariane Chebel d'Appollonia and Simon Reich, 145–63. Pittsburgh: University of Pittsburgh Press, 2008.

Chai, Nona. "Decarceration as Environmental Justice: Securing a Just Transition for Adelanto." Just Transition Alliance, June 29, 2023. https://jtalliance.org/2023 /06/29/decarceration-as-environmental-justice-securing-a-just-transition-for -adelanto/.

Chakravartty, Paula, and Denise Ferreira da Silva. "Accumulation, Dispossession, and Debt: The Racial Logic of Global Capitalism—an Introduction." *American Quarterly* 64, no. 3 (2012): 361–85.

Chauncey, George. *Why Marriage? The History Shaping Today's Debate over Marriage Equality.* New York: Basic Books, 2005.

Chávez, Karma R. *The Borders of AIDS: Race, Quarantine, and Resistance.* Seattle: University of Washington Press, 2021.

Chávez, Karma R. *Queer Migration Politics: Activist Rhetoric and Coalitional Possibilities.* Urbana: University of Illinois Press, 2013.

Chávez, Karma R., and Eithne Luibhéid. "Introduction." In *Queer and Trans Migrations: Dynamics of Illegalization, Detention, and Deportation*, edited by Eithne Luibhéid and Karma R. Chávez, 1–15. Urbana: University of Illinois Press, 2020.

Chávez, Leo. *The Latino Threat: Constructing Immigrants, Citizens, and the Nation.* Stanford, CA: Stanford University Press, 2008.

Chetrit, Samantha L. "Surviving an Immigration Marriage Fraud Investigation: All You Need Is Love, Luck, and Tight Privacy Controls." *Brooklyn Law Review* 77 (2012): 709–43.

Chishti, Muzaffer, and Sarah Pierce. "Trump Administration's New Indefinite Family Detention Policy: Deterrence Not Guaranteed." *Migration Information Source*, September 26, 2018. https://www.migrationpolicy.org/article/trump-administration -new-indefinite-family-detention-policy.

Cisneros, Jesus. "Undocuqueer: Interacting and Working within the Intersections of LGBTQ and Undocumented." PhD diss., Arizona State University, 2015.

Cisneros, Jesus. "Working with the Complexity and Refusing to Simplify: Undocuqueer Meaning Making at the Intersection of LGBTQ and Immigrant Rights Discourses." *Journal of Homosexuality* 65, no. 11 (2018): 1415–34.

Cisneros, Jesus, and Julia Gutierrez. "'What Does It Mean to Be UndocuQueer?': Exploring (Il)Legibility within the Intersections of Gender, Sexuality, and Immigration Status." *QED: A Journal of GLBTQ Worldmaking* 5, no. 1 (2018): 84–102.

Cisneros, Natalie. "'Alien' Sexuality: Race, Maternity, and Citizenship." *Hypatia* 28, no. 2 (2013): 290–306.

Clairborne, Maiysha. "Anyone Can Be an Ally, but Are You Willing to Be a Co-liberator?" March 8, 2023. https://drmaiysha.com/blog-2/anyone-can-be-an-ally.html.

Clarsen, Georgine. "Revisiting 'Driving While Black': Racialized Automobilities in a Settler Colonial Context." *Mobility in History* 8, no. 1 (2017): 51–60.

Coddington, Kate, Deirdre Conlon, and Lauren L. Martin. "Destitution Economies: Circuits of Value in Asylum, Refugee, and Migration Control." *Annals of the American Association of Geographers* 110, no. 5 (2020): 1425–44.

Cohen, Cathy J. "Punks, Bulldaggers, and Welfare Queens: The Radical Potential of Queer Politics?" GLQ: *A Journal of Lesbian and Gay Studies* 3, no. 4 (1997): 437–65.

Colibrí Center for Human Rights. "About Us." Accessed September 10, 2024. https://colibricenter.org/about/.

Conan, Neal. "'Dr. Queue' Helps You Avoid Rage in Line." *Talk of the Nation*, NPR. Aired November 24, 2009. https://www.npr.org/templates/story/story.php?storyId=120769732.

Congressional Research Service. "Immigration Provisions of the Violence Against Women Act (VAWA)." Updated August 9, 2013. Accessed September 1, 2024. https://crsreports.congress.gov/product/pdf/R/R42477.

Conlon, Deirdre, and Nancy Hiemstra, eds. *Intimate Economies of Immigration Detention: Critical Perspectives*. New York: Routledge, 2016.

Conlon, Deirdre, and Nancy Hiemstra. "Introduction: Intimate Economies of Immigration Detention." In *Intimate Economies of Immigration Detention: Critical Perspectives*, edited by Deirdre Conlon and Nancy Hiemstra, 1–12. New York: Routledge, 2016.

Constable, Nicole. "The Commodification of Intimacy: Marriage, Sex, and Reproductive Labor." *Annual Review of Anthropology* 38 (2009): 49–64.

Corral, César Montenegro. "Latiné Undocuqueer Students Navigating Microaggressions in California's Public Colleges and Universities." PhD diss., California State University, Long Beach, 2023.

Cott, Nancy F. *Public Vows: A History of Marriage and the Nation*. Cambridge, MA: Harvard University Press, 2000.

Cottle, Jennie. "Debate: How Sanctuary Cities in the US Stand Up to Federal Immigration Enforcement." *Conversation*, October 28, 2018. https://theconversation.com/debate-how-sanctuary-cities-in-the-us-stand-up-to-federal-immigration-enforcement-105180.

Coutin, Susan Bibler. "Being En Route." *American Anthropologist* 107, no. 2 (2005): 195–206.

Coutin, Susan Bibler. "Deportation Studies: Origins, Directions and Themes." *Journal of Ethnic and Migration Studies* 41, no. 4 (2015): 671–81.

Critchfield, Hannah. "Migrants Inside ICE's Only Transgender Unit Decry Conditions." *Phoenix New Times*, July 12, 2019. https://www.phoenixnewtimes.com/news/transgender-migrants-decry-conditions-new-mexico-ice-detention-11325981.

Critical Resistance. "Reformist Reforms vs. Abolitionist Steps to End Imprisonment. 2021." Accessed September 4, 2024. https://criticalresistance.org/wp-content/uploads/2021/08/CR_abolitioniststeps_antiexpansion_2021_eng.pdf.

Cullen, Tara Tidwell. "ICE Releases Its Most Comprehensive Immigration Detention Data Yet. It's Alarming." National Immigrant Justice Center, March 13, 2018. https://immigrantjustice.org/staff/blog/ice-released-its-most-comprehensive-immigration-detention-data-yet.

Cummings, William. "John Kelly Defends Separating Families at the Border, Saying 'Name of the Game Is Deterrence.'" *USA Today*, May 11, 2018.

Cunningham, Kasey. "Chaplain Launches 'Operation Save Sergio' to Call for Immigration Reform after Husband Was Detained." WRAL, May 13, 2018. https://www.wral.com/chaplain-launches-operation-save-sergio-to-call-for-immigration-reform-after-husband-was-detained-/17551802/.

Dahms, Betsy. "Queering Citizenship: UndocuQueer and Immigration Reform." *Diálogo* 18, no. 2 (2015): 79–89.

Danisi, Carmelo, Moira Dustin, Nuno Ferreria, and Nina Held. *Queering Asylum in Europe: Legal and Social Experiences of Seeking International Protection on Grounds of Sexual Orientation and Gender Identity*. New York: Springer, 2021.

D'Aoust, Anne-Marie. "Love as a Project of (Im)Mobility: Love, Sovereignty and Governmentality in Marriage Migration Management Practices." *Global Society* 28, no. 3 (2014): 317–35.

D'Aoust, Anne-Marie, ed. *Transnational Marriage and Partner Migration: Constellations of Security, Citizenship, and Rights*. New Brunswick, NJ: Rutgers University Press, 2022.

Darling, Jonathan. "Asylum and the Post-political: Domopolitics, Depoliticisation, and Acts of Citizenship." *Antipode* 46, no. 1 (2014): 72–91.

Das Gupta, Monisha. *All of Us or None: Migrant Organizing in an Era of Deportation and Dispossession*. Durham, NC: Duke University Press, 2024.

Da Silva, Chantal. "ICE Releases U.S. Army Chaplain's Husband in Huge Victory, but Fight Not Over Yet, Couple Says." *Newsweek*, May 15, 2018. https://www.newsweek.com/ice-releases-us-army-chaplains-husband-huge-victory-926425.

Davis, Angela. *An Autobiography*. New York: International Publishers, 1988.

Davis, Angela Y., Gina Dent, Erica R. Meiners, and Beth E. Richie. *Abolition. Feminism. Now*. Chicago: Haymarket Books, 2022.

Define American. "About." Accessed September 10, 2024. https://defineamerican.com/about/.

Defund Hate. *Insights from the Defund Hate Campaign*. 2024. Accessed September 10, 2024. https://defundhatenow.org/wp-content/uploads/2024/05/DH_Report_Eng.pdf.

De Genova, Nicholas. "Afterword: Deportation; The Last Word?" In *After Deportation: Ethnographic Perspectives*, edited by Shahram Khosravi, 253–66. Basingstoke, UK: Palgrave Macmillan, 2018.

De Genova, Nicholas. "Migrant 'Illegality' and Deportability in Everyday Life." *Annual Review of Anthropology* 31 (2002): 419–47.

De Genova, Nicholas. *Working the Boundaries: Race, Space, and "Illegality" in Mexican Chicago*. Durham, NC: Duke University Press, 2005.

de Graauw, Els. "City Government Activists and the Rights of Undocumented Immigrants: Fostering Urban Citizenship within the Confines of U.S. Federalism." *Antipode* 53, no. 2 (2021): 379–98.

De León, Jason. *The Land of Open Graves: Living and Dying on the Migrant Trail.* Oakland: University of California Press, 2015.

de Noronha, Luke. "Hierarchies of Membership and the Management of Global Populations: Reflections on Citizenship and Racial Ordering." *Citizenship Studies* 26, nos. 4-5 (2022): 426–35.

Detention Watch Network. *Ending Immigration Detention: Abolitionist Steps vs. Reformist Reforms.* Accessed February 21, 2024. https://www.detentionwatchnetwork .org/sites/default/files/Abolitionist%20Steps%20vs%20Reformist%20Reforms_DWN _2022.pdf.

Detention Watch Network. "Family Detention." Accessed September 10, 2024. https:// www.detentionwatchnetwork.org/issues/family-detention.

Detention Watch Network. "ICE Death Watch: An Advocacy and Organizing Toolkit." 2016. Accessed September 8, 2024. https://www.detentionwatchnetwork.org/sites /default/files/ICE%20Deaths%20Watch%20Toolkit_DWN%20and%20NIJC_2016.pdf.

Detention Watch Network. "Immigration Detention 101." Accessed July 31, 2022. https://www.detentionwatchnetwork.org/issues/detention-101.

Detention Watch Network. "Mandatory Detention." Accessed March 15, 2024. https:// www.detentionwatchnetwork.org/issues/mandatory-detention.

Detention Watch Network. "Mandatory Detention Fact Sheet." Accessed March 15, 2024. https://www.detentionwatchnetwork.org/sites/default/files/DWN _Mandatory%20Detention_Fact%20Sheet.pdf.

Detention Watch Network and the Center for Constitutional Rights. *Banking on Detention: Local Lockup Quotas and the Immigrant Dragnet.* 2015. https://www .detentionwatchnetwork.org/sites/default/files/reports/DWN%20CCR%20Banking%20on%20Detention%20Report.pdf.

Detention Watch Network and the Center for Constitutional Rights. *Banking on Detention, 2016 Update.* 2016. https://www.detentionwatchnetwork.org/sites/default/files /reports/Banking%20on%20Detention%202016%20Update_DWN%2C%20CCR.pdf.

Detention Watch Network and the National Immigrant Justice Center. "ICE Lies: Public Deception, Private Profit." 2018. https://immigrantjustice.org/sites/default/files /content-type/research-item/documents/2018-02/IceLies_DWN_NIJC_Feb2018.pdf.

Dickerson, Caitlin. "Married to an Undocumented Immigrant? You May Not Get a Stimulus Check." *New York Times*, April 28, 2020.

Dickerson, Caitlin. "The Secret History of the U.S. Government's Family Separation Policy." *Atlantic*, August 7, 2022.

DiNatale, Genevieve. "Worcester-Based Ministry Gives LGBTQ Asylum Seekers a New Lease on Life." *Town Square*, January 3, 2022. https://centralmasstownsquare.com /worcester-based-ministry-gives-lgbtq-asylum-seekers-a-new-lease-on-life/.

Dinzey-Flores, Zaire. "Housing." In *Keywords for Latina/o Studies*, edited by Deborah Vargas and Lawrence La Fountain Stokes, 86–89. New York: New York University Press, 2017.

Doonan, Christina. "A House Divided: Humanitarianism and Anti-immigration within U.S. Anti-trafficking Legislation." *Feminist Legal Studies* 24, no. 3 (2016): 273–93.

Douglass, Frederick. *Narrative of the Life of Frederick Douglass, an American Slave.* New York: Dover, 1995.

Dreby, Joanna. *Everyday Illegal: When Policies Undermine Immigrant Families*. Oakland: University of California Press, 2015.

Drotbohm, Heike, and Ines Hasselberg. "Introduction: Deportation, Anxiety, Justice; New Ethnographic Perspectives." *Journal of Ethnic and Migration Studies* 41, no. 4 (2015): 551–62.

Duggan, Lisa. *The Twilight of Equality? Neoliberalism, Cultural Politics, and the Attack on Democracy*. Boston: Beacon, 2003.

Edelman, Lee. *No Future: Queer Theory and the Death Drive*. Durham, NC: Duke University Press, 2004.

Editorial Board. "Immigration Reform as a Path to Conscience Not Just Citizenship." *Christian Science Monitor*, January 28, 2013.

Elmahrek, Adam. "Santa Ana Backs Away from ICE Contract Expansion." *Voice of OC*, February 3, 2016. https://voiceofoc.org/2016/02/santa-ana-backs-away-from-ice -contract-expansion/.

Emejulu, Akwugo, in conversation with Gail Lewis, Miss Major, Zoé Samudzi, and Hortense Spillers. "The Master's Tools Will Never Dismantle the Master's House: Abolitionist Feminist Futures." Panel discussion, August 3, 2020. Posted to Silver Press blog, August 19, 2020. https://silverpress.org/blogs/news/the-master-s-tools -will-never-dismantle-the-master-s-house-abolitionist-feminist-futures.

Engler, Mark, and Paul Engler. "Making Our Demands Both Practical and Visionary." Waging Non-violence, July 27, 2021. https://wagingnonviolence.org/2021/07/making -our-demands-both-practical-visionary/.

Escalante, Juan. "Ireland Waves 'Hello' to the Undocumented Community in the United States." *Latino Rebels*, March 16, 2015. https://www.latinorebels.com/2015/03/16 /ireland-waves-hello-to-the-undocumented-community-in-the-united-states/.

Escobar, Martha D. *Captivity beyond Prisons: Criminalization Experiences of Latina (Im)migrants*. Austin: University of Texas Press, 2016.

Escudero, Kevin. *Organizing While Undocumented: Immigrant Youths' Political Activism under the Law*. New York: New York University Press, 2020.

Eskridge, William N., Jr. "Beyond Lesbian and Gay 'Families We Choose.'" In *Sex, Preference, and Family: Essays on Law and Nature*, edited by David Estlund and Martha C. Nussbaum, 277–89. New York: Oxford University Press, 1998.

Essig, Laurie. *Love Inc.: Dating Apps, the Big White Wedding, and Chasing the Happily Neverafter*. Oakland: University of California Press, 2019.

Evans, Dominick. "Marriage Equality." Center for Disability Rights. Accessed March 7, 2014. https://cdrnys.org/blog/disability-dialogue/the-disability-dialogue-marriage -equality/.

Ewing, Walter A., and Guillermo Cantor. *Deported with No Possessions: The Mishandling of Migrants' Personal Belongings by CBP and ICE*. Washington, DC: American Immigration Council, 2016. https://www.americanimmigrationcouncil.org/research /deported-no-possessions.

Ewing, Walter A., Daniel E. Martínez, and Rubén G. Rumbaut. *The Criminalization of Immigration in the United States*. Washington, DC: American Immigration Council, 2015.

Fassin, Didier. *Humanitarian Reason: A Moral History of the Present*. Berkeley: University of California Press, 2011.

Ferguson, Roderick A. *Aberrations in Black: Toward a Queer of Color Critique*. Minneapolis: University of Minnesota Press, 2004.

Foley, Elise, and Dana Liebelson. "Dreamer Arrested after Speaking to the Media Will Be Deported without Hearing, Attorney Says." *Huffington Post*, March 2, 2017. https://www.huffpost.com/entry/dreamer-deportation-daniela-vargas_n_58b8920fe4b0d2821b4cc632.

Foucault, Michel. *Discipline and Punish: The Birth of the Prison*. Translated by Alan Sheridan. New York: Vintage, 1977.

Foucault, Michel. *The History of Sexuality*. Vol. 1, *An Introduction*. Translated by Robert Hurley. New York: Vintage, 1990.

Foucault, Michel. *Society Must Be Defended: Lectures at the Collège de France, 1975–1976*. Translated by David Macey. New York: Picador, 2003.

Fowler, Sarah. "Exclusive: Detained Mississippi Immigrant Speaks Out." *Clarion Ledger*, March 13, 2017.

Franz, Margaret. "Will to Love, Will to Fear: The Emotional Politics of Illegality and Citizenship in the Campaign against Birthright Citizenship in the US." *Social Identities* 21, no. 2 (2015): 184–98.

Freedom for Immigrants. "Sponsoring an Asylum Seeker." Accessed March 24, 2024. Available at https://docs.google.com/document/d/1x2vCqgt-WcLxI2pGGaTDIUofyOdy5pElSRZ7_ClWJgk/edit#heading=h.w8i207hiujjw.

Freeman, Elizabeth. "Marriage." In *Keywords for American Cultural Studies*, 2nd ed., edited by Bruce Burgett and Glen Hendler, 162–68. New York: New York University Press, 2014.

Freeman, Elizabeth. "The Queer Temporalities of *Queer Temporalities*." GLQ: *A Journal of Lesbian and Gay Studies* 25, no. 1 (2019): 91–95.

Freeman, Elizabeth. *Time Binds: Queer Temporalities, Queer Histories*. Durham, NC: Duke University Press, 2010.

Friedman, Sara L. *Exceptional States: Chinese Immigrants and Taiwanese Sovereignty*. Oakland: University of California Press, 2015.

Friedman, Sara L. "Regulating Cross-Border Intimacy: Authenticity Paradigms and the Specter of Illegality among Chinese Marital Immigrants to Taiwan." In *Migrant Encounters: Intimate Labor, the State, and Mobility across Asia*, edited by Sara L. Friedman and Pardis Mahdavi, 206–29. Philadelphia: University of Pennsylvania Press, 2015.

Fujiwara, Lynn. *Mothers without Citizenship: Asian Immigrant Families and the Consequences of Welfare Reform*. Minneapolis: University of Minnesota Press, 2008.

Galindo, René. "Undocumented and Unafraid: The Dream Act 5 and the Public Disclosure of Undocumented Status as a Political Act." *Urban Review* 44, no. 5 (2012): 589–611.

Galta, Sandra Y. "Intersectional Subaltern Counterpublics: Undocuqueer Online Activism and *Testimonios*." PhD diss., Kansas State University, 2018.

Gálvez, Alyshia. "Unafraid and Unapologetic, Still." NACLA *Report on the Americas*, June 13, 2017. https://nacla.org/news/2017/06/13/unafraid-and-unapologetic-still.

Gamboa, Susana. "A Traffic Violation Could Mean a Call from ICE for Some in Texas." *NBC News*, June 15, 2018. https://www.nbcnews.com/news/latino/texas-highway-patrol-sharing-lists-people-given-traffic-tickets-immigration-n883696.

Gammage, Jeff. "Seeking Legal Status in America, Immigrant Grabbed in Philly by ICE and Jailed." *Inquirer*, February 19, 2018. http://www2.philly.com/philly/news/immigrant-undocumented-philly-ice-deport-gay-detention-20180219.html.

Gardner, Kurt. "Jesús I. Valles' '(Un)Documents' Opens Tonight." *ArtSceneSA*, November 12, 2020. https://www.artscenesa.com/jesus-i-valles-undocuments-opens-tonight/.

Gardner, Martha. *The Qualities of a Citizen: Women, Immigration, and Citizenship, 1870–1965*. Princeton, NJ: Princeton University Press, 2005.

Gehi, Pooja, and Gabriel Arkles. "The Tacit Targeting of Trans Immigrants as 'Criminal Aliens': Old Tactics and New." In *The Unfinished Queer Agenda: After Marriage Equality*, edited by Angela Jones, Joseph Nicholas DeFilippis, and Michael W. Yarbrough, 53–73. New York: Routledge, 2018.

Gelderloos, Peter. *How Non-violence Protects the State*. Boston: South End, 2007.

Gentry, Blake, Raymond Daukei, Lupe Sotelo, and Samuel N. Chambers. *Out of Sight and Out of Mind: An Interpretive Human Rights Report on US-Mexico Border Violence under MPP and Title 42*. Los Angeles: Indigenous Alliance without Borders and Center for Mexican Studies, Latin American Institute, UCLA, 2023.

Georgevich, Mary. "Rethink Immigration: A Homeless, Undocumented, and Detained LGBT Teen's Struggle for Due Process." *Rethink Immigration* (blog). National Immigrant Justice Center, October 16, 2013. https://immigrantjustice.org/staff/blog/rethink-immigration-homeless-undocumented-detained-lgbt-teens-struggle-due-process.

Ghaziani, Amin, and Matt Brim. "Queer Methods: Four Provocations for an Emerging Field." In *Imagining Queer Methods*, edited by Amin Ghaziani and Matt Brim, 3–27. New York: New York University Press, 2019.

Giametta, Calogero. *The Sexual Politics of Asylum: Sexual Orientation and Gender Identity in the UK Asylum System*. London: Routledge, 2017.

Gill, Nick. "Health and Intimacies in Immigration Detention." In *Intimate Economies of Immigration Detention: Critical Perspectives*, edited by Dierdre Conlon and Nancy Hiemstra, 171–86. New York: Routledge, 2016.

Gill-Peterson, Jules. *Histories of the Transgender Child*. Minneapolis: University of Minnesota Press, 2018.

Gilmore, Ruth Wilson. *Golden Gulag: Prisons, Surplus, Crisis, and Opposition in Globalizing California*. Berkeley: University of California Press, 2007.

Gilroy, Paul. "Driving While Black." In *Car Cultures*, edited by Daniel Miller, 81–104. New York: Routledge, 2001.

GLAAD. "Covering LGBTQ Immigration Issues." Accessed August 5, 2019. https://glaad.org/immigration/.

Global Detention Project. "United States Overview." Accessed September 10, 2024. https://www.globaldetentionproject.org/countries/americas/united-states.

Golash-Boza, Tanya Maria. *Deported: Immigrant Policing, Disposable Labor, and Global Capitalism*. New York: New York University Press, 2015.

Goldberg, Shoshana K., and Keith J. Conron. *LGBT Adult Immigrants in the United States*. Los Angeles: Williams Institute, UCLA School of Law, 2021. https://williamsinstitute.law.ucla.edu/publications/lgbt-immigrants-in-the-us/.

Gómez, Laura. "Migrants Held in ICE's Only Transgender Unit Plead for Help, Investigation in Letter." *Arizona Mirror*, July 9, 2019.

Gonzales, Roberto G., Veronica Terriquez, and Stephan P. Ruszczyk. "Becoming DACAmented: Assessing the Short-Term Benefits of Deferred Action for Childhood Arrivals (DACA)." *American Behavioral Scientist* 58, no. 14 (2014): 1852–72.

Goodman, Adam. *The Deportation Machine: America's Long History of Expelling Immigrants*. Princeton, NJ: Princeton University Press, 2020.

Gopinath, Gayatri. *Impossible Desires: Queer Diasporas and South Asian Public Cultures*. Durham, NC: Duke University Press, 2005.

Griffiths, Melanie. "'My Passport Is Just My Way Out of Here': Mixed Immigration Status Families, Immigration Enforcement, and Citizenship Implications." *Identities* 28, no. 1 (2021): 18–36.

Griffiths, Melanie, Ali Rogers, and Bridget Anderson. "Migration, Time, and Temporalities: Review and Prospects." COMPAS Research Resources Paper. Oxford: Centre on Migration Policy and Society, 2013.

Gruberg, Sharita. *Dignity Denied: LGBT Immigrants in U.S. Immigration Detention*. Washington, DC: Center for American Progress, 2013.

Gruberg, Sharita. "No Way Out: Congress' Bed Quota Traps LGBT Immigrants in Detention." Center for American Progress, May 14, 2015. https://www.americanprogress.org/article/no-way-out-congress-bed-quota-traps-lgbt-immigrants-in-detention/.

Gruberg, Sharita. *Serving LGBTQ Immigrants and Building Welcoming Communities*. Washington, DC: Center for American Progress, 2018.

Gutierrez, Trey. "Theater Review: Jesús Valles Takes (Un)Documents Online." *Sightlines*, November 18, 2020. https://sightlinesmag.org/theater-review-jesus-valles-takes-undocuments-online.

Haddal, Chad C. *Border Security: The Role of the U.S. Border Patrol*. Washington, DC: Congressional Research Service, August 11, 2020.

Haley, Sarah. "Abolition." In *Keywords for African American Studies*, edited by Erica R. Edwards, Roderick R. Ferguson, and Jeffrey O. G. Ogbar, 9–14. New York: New York University Press, 2018.

Haritaworn, Jin, Adi Kuntsman, and Silvia Posocco, eds. *Queer Necropolitics*. London: Routledge, 2014.

Hart, Carrie. "The Artivism of Julio Salgado's *I Am Undocuqueer!* Series." Working Papers on Language and Diversity in Education, August 2015, vol. 1, no. 1. https://core.ac.uk/download/pdf/234820201.pdf.

Hartman, Saidiya. *Scenes of Subjection: Terror, Slavery, and Self-Making in Nineteenth Century America*. New York: Oxford University Press, 1997.

Hartman, Saidiya. *Wayward Lives, Beautiful Experiments: Intimate Histories of Riotous Black Girls, Troublesome Women, and Queer Radicals*. New York: Norton, 2019.

Hasso, Frances S. "Bargaining with the Devil: States and Intimate Life." *Journal of Middle East Women's Studies* 10, no. 2 (2014): 107–34.

Hauser, Christine. "Woman Detained after Speaking about Deportation Fear Is Released." *New York Times*, March 10, 2017.

Hereth, Jane E. "'I Don't Think the Police Think We're Human': Legal Socialization among Young Transgender Women." *Journal of Homosexuality* 71, no. 9 (2024): 2175–99.

Hernández, Kelly Lytle. *City of Inmates: Conquest, Rebellion, and the Rise of Human Caging in Los Angeles, 1771–1965*. Chapel Hill: University of North Carolina Press, 2017.

Hester, Torrie. *Deportation: The Origins of U.S. Policy*. Philadelphia: University of Pennsylvania Press, 2017.

Heyman, Josiah. "Ports of Entry as Nodes in the World System." *Identities: Global Studies in Power and Culture* 11, no. 3 (2004): 303–27.

Hiemstra, Nancy, and Deirdre Conlon. "Captive Consumers and Coerced Labourers: Intimate Economies and the Expanding U.S. Detention Regime." In *Intimate Economies of Immigration Detention: Critical Perspectives*, edited by Deirdre Conlon and Nancy Hiemstra, 123–39. New York: Routledge, 2016.

Hill, Annie. *Trafficking Rhetoric: Race, Rhetoric, and the Making of Modern-Day Slavery*. Columbus: Ohio State University Press, 2024.

Hindess, Barry. "Citizenship in the International Management of Population." *American Behavioral Scientist* 43, no. 9 (2000): 1486–98.

Hoffmann, Nathan I., and Kristopher Velasco. "Sexuality, Migration, and LGB Policy: A Portrait of Immigrants in Same-Sex Couples in the United States." *International Migration Review* (August 2023). https://doi.org/10.1177/01979183231187623.

Hogan, Wesley C. *On the Freedom Side: How Five Decades of Youth Activists Have Remixed American History*. Chapel Hill: University of North Carolina Press, 2019.

hooks, bell. *All about Love: New Visions*. New York: HarperCollins, 2001.

Horton, Sarah B., and Josiah Heyman, eds. *Paper Trails: Migrants, Documents, and Legal Insecurity*. Durham, NC: Duke University Press, 2020.

Huag, Oliver. "Over 100 LGBTQ+ Activists Call on Biden to End Trans Detention in White House Protest." *Them*, June 24, 2021. https://www.them.us/story/lgbtq-activists-white-house-ice-trans-detention-protest.

Human Rights Watch. *Chronic Indifference: HIV/AIDS Services for Immigrants Detained by the United States*. December 2007. https://www.hrw.org/sites/default/files/reports/us1207web.pdf.

Human Rights Watch. *"Do You See How Much I'm Suffering Here?": Abuse against Transgender Women in US Immigration Detention*. March 2016. https://www.hrw.org/sites/default/files/report_pdf/us0316_web.pdf.

Human Rights Watch. *"Every Day I Live in Fear": Violence and Discrimination against LGBT People in El Salvador, Guatemala and Honduras, and Obstacles to Asylum in the United States*. October 7, 2020. https://www.hrw.org/report/2020/10/07/every-day-i-live-fear/violence-and-discrimination-against-lgbt-people-el-salvador.

Human Rights Watch. "LGBT Asylum Seekers in Danger at the Border." May 31, 2022. https://www.hrw.org/news/2022/05/31/us-lgbt-asylum-seekers-danger-border.

Human Rights Watch, the ACLU, National Immigrant Justice Center, and Detention Watch Network. *Code Red: The Fatal Consequences of Dangerously Substandard Medical Care in Immigration Detention*. June 20, 2018. https://www.hrw.org/report/2018/06/20/code-red/fatal-consequences-dangerously-substandard-medical-care-immigration.

Human Rights Watch and Immigration Equality. *Family, Unvalued: Discrimination, Denial, and the Fate of Binational Same-Sex Couples under U.S. Immigration Law*. 2006. https://www.hrw.org/reports/2006/us0506/FamilyUnvalued.pdf.

Immigrant Legal Resource Center. "Introduction to Conditional Permanent Residence and Filing the Petition to Remove the Conditions on Residence (Form I-751)." Practice

Advisory, December 2017. https://www.ilrc.org/sites/default/files/resources/i-751
_advisory_final.pdf.

Immigration Policy Center. "Why Don't They Just Get in Line?" March 14, 2013. http://
www.immigrationpolicy.org/just-facts/why-don't-they-just-get-line.

Inda, Jonathan Xavier. *Targeting Immigrants: Government, Technology, and Ethics.*
Malden, MA: Blackwell, 2006.

Inda, Jonathan Xavier. "The Value of Immigrant Life." In *Women and Migration in the
U.S.-Mexico Borderlands: A Reader,* edited by Denise Segura and Patricia Zavella,
134–57. Durham, NC: Duke University Press, 2007.

Ingold, Tom. *Lines: A Brief History.* New York: Routledge, 2007.

Investigate. "CoreCivic Inc." Accessed March 22, 2024. https://investigate.afsc.org
/company/corecivic.

Irwin, Robert McKee. "The Humanizing Deportation Project: Building a Community
Archive of Migrant Feelings, Migrant Knowledge." In *Migrant Feelings, Migrant
Knowledge: Building Community Archives,* edited by Robert McKee Irwin, 3–32.
Austin: University of Texas Press, 2022.

Ishak, Natasha. "How Congress Killed Immigration Reform." *Documented,* April 15, 2022.
https://documentedny.com/2022/04/15/immigration-reform-congress-citizenship/.

Isin, Engin F. "Citizenship in Flux: The Figure of the Activist Citizen." *Subjectivity* 29
(2009): 367–88.

Isin, Engin F. "Theorizing Acts of Citizenship." In *Acts of Citizenship,* edited by Engin F.
Isin and Greg M. Nielsen, 15–43. London: Zed Books, 2008.

Jacobs, Harriet. *Incidents in the Life of a Slave Girl: Written by Herself.* Edited by L.
Maria Child. 1861. Cambridge, MA: Harvard University Press, 1987.

Jakobsen, Janet. "Perverse Justice." *GLQ: A Journal of Lesbian and Gay Studies* 18, no. 1
(2011): 19–45.

Jallow, Ahmed. "What Would Happen If Cops Didn't Make Certain Traffic Stops?"
USA Today, April 15, 2021. https://www.usatoday.com/story/news/nation/2021/04/15
/police-reform-fayetteville-burlington-nc-traffic-stops-policing/7225318002/.

James, Kayla, and Elena Vanko. "The Impacts of Solitary Confinement." Vera Institute
of Justice, April 2021. https://www.vera.org/publications/the-impacts-of-solitary
-confinement.

James, Sandy E., Jody L. Herman, Susan Rankin, Mara Keisling, Lisa Mottet, and
Ma'ayan Anafi. *The Report of the 2015 U.S. Transgender Survey.* Washington, DC:
National Center for Transgender Equality, 2016.

Jawetz, Tom. "Bait and Switch: How the Trump Administration Is Trying to Deport
Spouses of U.S. Citizens." Center for American Progress, February 18, 2020. https://
www.americanprogress.org/issues/immigration/news/2020/02/18/480571/bait
-switch-trump-administration-trying-deport-spouses-u-s-citizens/.

Jeffries, Fiona, and Jennifer Ridgley. "Building the Sanctuary City from the Ground Up:
Abolitionist Solidarity and Transformative Reform." *Citizenship Studies* 24, no. 4
(2020): 548–67.

Johnson, Austin H. "Transnormativity: A New Concept and Its Validation through
Documentary Film about Transgender Men." *Sociological Inquiry* 86, no. 4 (2016):
465–91.

Johnson, Tory. "ICE Has Been Granted the Same Level of Secrecy as the FBI." *Immigration Impact*, July 14, 2020. https://immigrationimpact.com/2020/07/14/ice-security-designation/.

Johnson, Walter. "The Economics of Ferguson: Emerson Electric, Municipal Fines, Discrimination." *Atlantic*, April 26, 2015.

Jordan, Bryant. "Policy Ends Deportation of Troops' Families." *Military.com*, November 20, 2013. https://www.military.com/daily-news/2013/11/20/policy-ends-deportation-of-troops-families.html.

Josephson, Tristan. *On Transits and Transitions: Trans Migrants and U.S. Immigration Law*. New Brunswick, NJ: Rutgers University Press, 2022.

Just Futures Law and Mijente. *The Data Broker to Deportation Pipeline Report: How Thompson Reuters and LexisNexis Share Utility and Commercial Data with ICE*. Accessed January 7, 2023. https://static1.squarespace.com/static/62c3198c117dd661bd99eb3a/t/62df020189b0681d1b9398a8/1658782211567/Commercial+and+Utility+Data+Report.pdf.

Just Futures Law and Mijente. *ICE Digital Prisons: The Expansion of Mass Surveillance as ICE's Alternative to Detention*. May 2021. https://www.flipsnack.com/justfutures/ice-digital-prisons-1u8w3fnd1j/full-view.html.

Kaba, Mariame. "Toward the Horizon of Abolition: Interview by John Duda." In *We Do This 'Til We Free Us: Abolitionist Organizing and Transformative Justice*, 93–101. Chicago: Haymarket Books, 2021.

Kaba, Mariame. *We Do This 'Til We Free Us: Abolitionist Organizing and Transformative Justice*. Chicago: Haymarket Books, 2021.

Kaminer, Michael. "20 Minutes With: Author, Activist, and Businessman Edafe Okporo." *Penta*, March 7, 2022. https://www.barrons.com/articles/20-minutes-with-author-activist-and-businessman-edafe-okporo-01646671511.

Kandaswamy, Priya. "State Austerity and the Racial Politics of Same-Sex Marriage in the US." *Sexualities* 11, no. 6 (2008): 706–25.

Kanstroom, Daniel. *Deportation Nation: Outsiders in American History*. Cambridge, MA: Harvard University Press, 2010.

Keogh Serrano, Ximena. "Dreaming a Radical Citizenship: How Undocumented Queers in the United States Configure Sites of Belonging and Being through Art and Media Technologies." *European Journal of American Studies* 11, no. 3 (2017). https://journals.openedition.org/ejas/11863.

Kessler, Matt. "Dreamer in Process of DACA Renewal to Be Deported without Court Hearing." *Guardian*, March 3, 2017.

Khosravi, Shahram. "Introduction." In *After Deportation: Ethnographic Perspectives*, edited by Shahram Khosravi, 1–14. Basingstoke, UK: Palgrave Macmillan, 2018.

Kight, Stef W. "The For-Profit Detention Circle." *Axios*, February 14, 2022. https://www.axios.com/2022/02/15/biden-for-profit-detention-alternative.

Kilgore, James. "'E-Carceration' Is the Newest Surveillance Trend Spreading across the Globe." *Truthout*, September 11, 2023. https://truthout.org/articles/e-carceration-is-the-newest-surveillance-trend-spreading-across-the-globe/.

Knefel, John. "No Papers, No Fear: Undocumented Immigrant Activists Arrested Outside DNC." *Truthout*, September 12, 2019.

Kocher, Austin, and Angela Stuesse. "Undocumented Activism and Minor Politics: Inside the Cramped Political Spaces of Deportation Defense Campaigns." *Antipode* 53, no. 2 (2021): 331–54.

Kopan, Tal. "ICE Director: Undocumented Immigrants 'Should Be Afraid.'" *CNN*, June 16, 2017. https://www.cnn.com/2017/06/16/politics/ice-immigrants-should-be -afraid-homan/index.html.

Krajeski, Jenna. "The Hypocrisy of Trump's Anti-trafficking Argument for a Border Wall." *New Yorker*, February 5, 2019.

Krikorian, Mark. "Downsizing Illegal Immigration: A Strategy of Attrition through Enforcement." Center for Immigration Studies, May 2005. https://www.cis.org/sites /cis.org/files/articles/2005/back605.pdf.

Kumpf, Kristin, and Lewis Webb Jr. "Why We Support the Call to #FreeThemAll." American Friends Service Committee, April 23, 2020. https://afsc.org/news/why-we -support-call-freethemall.

Kwong, Jessica. "Santa Ana Distances Itself from Immigration Agency in Rare Rejection of Jail Contract Expansion." *Orange County Register*, February 4, 2016. https://www .ocregister.com/2016/02/04/santa-ana-distances-itself-from-immigration-agency-in -rare-rejection-of-jail-contract-expansion/.

La Coalicion de Derechos Humanos and No More Deaths. *Disappeared: How the US Border Enforcement Agencies Are Fueling a Missing Persons Crisis.* Accessed July 1, 2020. http://www.thedisappearedreport.org/uploads/8/3/5/1/83515082/disappeared —introduction.pdf.

Lal, Prerna. "About." Accessed September 10, 2024. https://prernalal.com/about/.

Lal, Prerna. "How Queer Undocumented Youth Built the Immigrant Rights Move- ment." *Huffington Post*, March 28, 2013. https://www.huffpost.com/entry/how-queer -undocumented_b_2973670.

Lamble, Sarah. "Queer Investments in Punitiveness." In *Queer Necropolitics*, edited by Jin Haritaworn, Adi Kuntsman, and Silvia Posocco, 151–71. New York: Routledge, 2014.

Landolt, Patricia, and Luin Goldring. "Assembling Noncitizenship through the Work of Conditionality." *Citizenship Studies* 19, no. 8 (2015): 853–69.

Larkin, Brian. "The Politics and Poetics of Infrastructure." *Annual Review of Anthropol- ogy* 42 (2013): 327–43.

Lawler, Ophelia Garcia. "What Happened to Roxana Hernández, the Trans Woman Who Died in ICE Custody?" *The Cut*, December 5, 2018. https://www.thecut.com /2018/12/roxana-hernndez-a-transgender-woman-died-in-ice-custody.html.

Lee, Catherine. *Fictive Kinship: Family Reunification and the Meaning of Race and Na- tion in American Immigration.* New York: Russell Sage, 2013.

Levitz, Eric. "White House Opens New Office Devoted to Encouraging Fear of Immi- grants." *New York Magazine*, April 26, 2017.

Lewis, Rachel, and Nancy Naples, eds. "Queer Migration, Asylum, and Displacement." Special issue, *Sexualities* 17, no. 8 (2014).

Li, Esther Yu Hsi. "Speeding Tickets, Minor Infractions, Account for at Least Half of Deportations, Report Finds." *Think Progress*, April 9, 2014. https://trac.syr.edu /tracatwork/detail/A1326.html.

Licona, Adela C. "The Non/Image of the Regime of Distortion." In *Precarious Rhetorics*, edited by Wendy S. Hesford, Adela C. Licona, and Christina Teston, 168–88. Columbus: Ohio State University Press, 2018.

Licona, Adela C., and Eithne Luibhéid. "The Regime of Destruction: Separating Families and Caging Children." *Feminist Formations* 33, no. 3 (2018): 45–62.

Lin, Weiqiang, Johan Lindquist, Biao Xiang, and Brenda S. A. Yeoh. "Migration Infrastructures and the Production of Migrant Mobilities." *Mobilities* 12, no. 2 (2017): 167–74.

Longo, Gina Marie. "Keeping It in 'the Family': How Gender Norms Shape U.S. Marriage Migration Politics." *Gender and Society* 32, no. 4 (2018): 469–92.

Longoria, Anthony. "Beyond Butterflies: The UndocuQueer Movement, Intersectionality, and Implications of Education." PhD diss., University of Washington, 2018.

Lorde, Audre. "The Master's Tools Will Never Dismantle the Master's House." In *Sister Outsider: Essays and Speeches by Audre Lorde*, 110–13. New York: Crossing, 1984.

Los Angeles Times. "California Would Bar Immigration Arrests." *KTLA 5*, August 31, 2018. https://ktla.com/2018/08/31/california-would-bar-immigration-arrests-inside-courthouses-under-bill-sent-to-gov-brown/.

Lowe, Lisa. *The Intimacies of Four Continents.* Durham, NC: Duke University Press, 2015.

Loyd, Jenna M., Matt Mitchelson, and Andrew Burridge. "Introduction: Borders, Prisons, and Abolitionist Visions." In *Beyond Walls and Cages: Prisons, Borders, and Global Crisis*, edited by Jenna M. Loyd, Matt Mitchelson, and Andrew Burridge, 1–15. Athens: University of Georgia Press, 2012.

Loyd, Jenna M., and Alison Mountz. *Boats, Borders, and Bases: Race, the Cold War, and the Rise of Migration Detention in the United States.* Oakland: University of California Press, 2018.

Luan, Livia. "Profiting from Enforcement: The Role of Private Prisons in US Immigration Detention." *Migration Information Source*, May 2, 2018. https://www.migrationpolicy.org/article/profiting-enforcement-role-private-prisons-us-immigration-detention.

Lubet, Steven. "Trump's New Citizenship Test Is Full of Conservative Bias—and Dotted with Mistakes." *Politico*, December 3, 2020. https://www.politico.com/news/magazine/2020/12/03/trumps-new-citizenship-test-is-full-of-conservative-biasand-dotted-with-mistakes-442777.

Lugones, Maria. "Playfulness, World-Travelling, and Loving Perception." In *Making Face, Making Soul / Haciendo Caras: Creative and Critical Perspectives of Feminists of Color*, edited by Gloria Anzaldúa, 390–402. San Francisco: Aunt Lute, 1990.

Luhur, Winston, Ilan H. Meyer, and Bianca D. M. Wilson. *Policing LGBTQ People.* Los Angeles: Williams Institute, UCLA School of Law, 2021.

Luibhéid, Eithne. *Entry Denied: Controlling Sexuality at the Border.* Minneapolis: University of Minnesota Press, 2002.

Luibhéid, Eithne. "Introduction: Queering Migration and Citizenship." In *Queer Migrations: Sexuality, Citizenship, and Border Crossings*, edited by Eithne Luibhéid and Lionel Cantú Jr., ix–xlvi. Minneapolis: University of Minnesota Press, 2005.

Luibhéid, Eithne. "National Citizenship, Migrant Deportation, and the Gender/Sexual Logics of Home." *Citizenship Studies* 26, nos. 4–5 (2022): 556–64.

Luibhéid, Eithne. *Pregnant on Arrival: Making the "Illegal" Immigrant*. Minneapolis: University of Minnesota Press, 2013.

Luibhéid, Eithne. "Queer/Migration: An Unruly Body of Scholarship." *GLQ: A Journal of Lesbian and Gay Studies* 14, nos. 2–3 (2008): 169–90.

Luibhéid, Eithne. "Sexualities, Intimacies, and the Citizen/Migrant Distinction." In *Citizenship and Its Others*, edited by Bridget Anderson and Vanessa Hughes, 126–44. London: Palgrave Macmillan, 2015.

Luibhéid, Eithne, and Karma R. Chávez, eds. *Queer and Trans Migrations: Dynamics of Illegalization, Detention, and Deportation*. Champaign: University of Illinois Press, 2020.

Macías-Rojas, Patrisia. *From Deportation to Prison: The Politics of Immigration Enforcement in Post–Civil Rights America*. New York: New York University Press, 2016.

Mackey, Robert. "The Deep Comic Roots of 'Self-Deportation.'" *Lede* (blog), *New York Times*, February 1, 2012. https://archive.nytimes.com/thelede.blogs.nytimes.com /2012/02/01/the-deep-comic-roots-of-self-deportation/.

Mackie, Vera. "Rethinking Sexual Citizenship: Asia-Pacific Perspectives." *Sexualities* 20, nos. 1–2 (2017): 143–58.

Macklin, Audrey, Kathryn Barber, Luin Goldring, Jennifer Hyndman, Anna Korteweg, and Jona Zyfi. "Kindred Spirits? Links between Refugee Sponsorship and Family Sponsorship." In *Strangers to Neighbours: Refugee Sponsorship in Context*, edited by Shauna Labman and Geoffrey Cameron, 177–97. Montreal: McGill-Queen's University Press, 2020.

Malkki, Liisa. "Refugees and Exile: From 'Refugee Studies' to the National Order of Things." *Annual Review of Anthropology* 24 (1995): 495–523.

Maloney, Deirdre. *National Insecurities: Immigrants and U.S. Deportation Policy since 1882*. Chapel Hill: University of North Carolina Press, 2012.

Manalansan, Martin F., IV. *Global Divas: Filipino Gay Men in the Diaspora*. Durham, NC: Duke University Press, 2003.

Mao, Julie, Paromita Shah, Hannah Lucas, Aly Panjwani, and Jacinta Gonzalez. *Automating Deportation: The Artificial Intelligence behind the Department of Homeland Security's Immigration Enforcement Regime*. Just Futures Law and Mijente, June 2024. https://mijente.net/wp-content/uploads/2024/06/Automating-Deportation.pdf.

Marquez-Benitez, Gabriela, and Amalia Pallares. "Not One More: Linking Civil Disobedience and Public Anti-deportation Campaigns." *North American Dialogue* 19, no. 1 (2016): 13–22.

Martínez, Daniel, Guillermo Cantor, and Walter Ewing. *No Action Taken: Lack of CBP Accountability in Responding to Complaints of Abuse*. Washington, DC: American Immigration Council, 2014.

Massey, Douglas J., Jorge Durand, and Nolan J. Malone. *Beyond Smoke and Mirrors: Mexican Immigration in an Era of Economic Integration*. New York: Russell Sage Foundation, 2003.

Masters, Troy. "United States Government Says L.A. Gay Couple's 1975 Marriage Is Valid." *The Pride L.A.*, June 7, 2016. http://thepridela.com/2016/06/united-states -government-says-gay-couples-1975-marriage-is-valid/.

Mata, Irene. "Invoking History: A Queer Roadmap to Liberation." *NACCS Annual Conference Proceedings* 11 (2018). https://scholarworks.sjsu.edu/cgi/viewcontent.cgi ?article=1202&context=naccs.

Mbembe, Achille. "Necropolitics." *Public Culture* 15, no. 1 (2003): 11–40.

McClintock, Anne. "Family Feuds: Gender, Nationalism, and the Family." *Feminist Review* 44 (Summer 1993): 61–80.

McElwee, Sean. "It's Time to Abolish ICE." *Nation*, March 9, 2018. https://www.thenation.com/article/archive/its-time-to-abolish-ice/.

McKeithen, Will. "Queer Ecologies of Home: Heteronormativity, Speciesism, and the Strange Intimacies of Crazy Cat Ladies." *Gender, Place and Culture* 24, no. 1 (2017): 122–34.

Menjívar, Cecelia. "Document Overseers, Enhanced Enforcement, and Racialized Local Contexts." In *Paper Trails: Migrants, Documents, and Legal Insecurity*, edited by Sarah B. Horton and Josiah Heyman, 153–78. Durham, NC: Duke University Press, 2020.

Menjívar, Cecilia, and Daniel Kanstroom, eds. *Constructing Immigrant "Illegality": Critiques, Experiences, and Responses*. Cambridge: Cambridge University Press, 2013.

Migrant Rights Centre Ireland. "A Statement from the Leaders of the Justice for the Undocumented Campaign." March 13, 2016. https://www.mrci.ie/2016/03/13/a-statement-from-the-leaders-of-the-justice-for-the-undocumented-campaign/.

Mijente. "Deportation Defense Toolkit—¡El Pueblo Se Defiende!—Mijente." Accessed March 24, 2024. https://development.mijente.net/defend/.

Mijente. "Deportation Defense under the Biden Administration." November 18, 2021. https://mijente.net/2021/11/deportation-defense-under-the-biden-administration/.

Mijente. "'Movement Spaces Must Be Sanctuaries': Marisa Franco's Award Acceptance Speech at #CC16." January 21, 2016. YouTube video, 7:24. https://www.youtube.com/watch?v=OLuOohA5rOY.

Mijente, Just Futures Law, and No Border Wall Coalition. *The Deadly Digital Border Wall*. 2021. https://notechforice.com/wp-content/uploads/2021/10/Deadly.Digital.Border.Wall_.pdf.

Miller, Thomas G., dir. *Limited Partnership*. United States, 2014. 74 min.

Miller, Todd. *Border Patrol Nation: Dispatches from the Front Lines of Homeland Security*. San Francisco: City Lights Books, 2014.

Miller, Todd. *Empire of Borders: The Expansion of the U.S. Border around the World*. London: Verso, 2019.

Minero, Laura P., Sergio Domínguez Jr., Stephanie L. Budge, and Bamby Salcedo. "Latinx Trans Immigrants' Survival of Torture in U.S. Detention: A Qualitative Investigation of the Psychological Impact of Abuse and Mistreatment." *International Journal of Transgender Health* 23, nos. 1–2 (2022): 36–59.

Morrison, Sara. "Obama Wants to Make Deportations More Humane." *Atlantic*, March 13, 2014.

Mudambi, Veer. "Last Call with Al Green." *Worcester Magazine*, August 25, 2021. https://www.worcestermag.com/story/lifestyle/2021/08/25/last-call-al-green/8183121002/.

Muñoz, Susana. *Identity, Social Activism, and the Pursuit of Higher Education: The Journey Stories of Undocumented and Unafraid Community Activists*. New York: Peter Lang, 2015.

Muñoz, Susana. "Unpacking Legality through La Facultad and Cultural Citizenship: Critical and Legal Consciousness Formation for Politicized Latinx Undocumented Youth Activists." *Equity and Excellence in Education* 51, no. 1 (2018): 78–91.

Murdza, Katy, and Walter Ewing. *The Legacy of Racism within the U.S. Border Patrol.* Washington, DC: American Immigration Council, 2021.

Murphy, Michelle. *The Economization of Life.* Durham, NC: Duke University Press, 2017.

Murray, David A. B. *Real Queer? Sexual Orientation and Gender Identity Refugees in the Canadian Refugee Apparatus.* Lanham, MD: Rowman and Littlefield, 2015.

NACLA. "Civil Disobedience against Deportation." NACLA blog, February 28, 2013. http://nacla.org/blog/2013/2/28/civil-disobedience-against-deportation.

National Commission on Terrorist Attacks upon the United States. *The 9/11 Commission Report.* 2004. https://www.9-11commission.gov/report/911Report.pdf.

National Immigrant Justice Center. "Cut the Contracts: It's Time to End ICE's Corrupt Detention Management System." March 16, 2021. https://immigrantjustice.org/sites/default/files/content-type/research-item/documents/2021-03/Policy-Brief_Cut-the-Contracts_March-2021_Final.pdf.

National Immigrant Justice Center. "Defund Hate." Accessed September 13, 2024. https://immigrantjustice.org/issues/defundhate.

National Immigrant Justice Center. *Lives in Peril: How Ineffective Inspections Make ICE Complicit in Detention Center Abuse.* October 22, 2015. https://immigrantjustice.org/lives-peril-how-ineffective-inspections-make-ice-complicit-detention-center-abuse.

National Immigrant Justice Center. "Mass Civil Rights Complaint Details Systemic Abuse of Sexual Minorities in U.S. Immigration Detention." April 12, 2011. https://www.immigrantjustice.org/press-releases/mass-civil-rights-complaint-details-systemic-abuse-sexual-minorities-us-immigration.

National Immigrant Justice Center. *NIJC Freedom of Information Act Litigation Reveals Systemic Lack of Accountability in Immigration Detention Contracting.* August 2015. https://immigrantjustice.org/immigration-detention-transparency-and-human-rights-project-august-2015-report.

National Immigration Law Center. "DACA." Accessed March 8, 2021. https://www.nilc.org/issues/daca/.

National Immigration Law Center. "Driver's Licenses." Accessed September 10, 2024. https://www.nilc.org/issues/drivers-licenses/.

NDLONvideos. "Blue Ribbon Commission Presents Recommendations for the President." April 11, 2014. YouTube video, 54:29. https://www.youtube.com/watch?v=T1sWyvx56H4.

Negrón-Gonzales, Genevieve. "Undocumented, Unafraid, and Unapologetic: Rearticulatory Practices and Migrant Youth 'Illegality.'" *Latino Studies* 12, no. 2 (2014): 259–78.

Nevins, Joseph. *Dying to Live: A Story of U.S. Immigration in an Age of Global Apartheid.* San Francisco: City Lights Open Media, 2008.

Newton, Lina. "Immigration Politics by Proxy: State Agency in an Era of National Reluctance." *Journal of Ethnic and Migration Studies* 44, no. 12 (2018): 2086–105.

Ngai, Mae M. *Impossible Subjects: Illegal Aliens and the Making of Modern America.* Princeton, NJ: Princeton University Press, 2004.

Nicholls, Walter. "Between Punishment and Discipline: Comparing Strategies to Control Unauthorized Immigration in the United States." *Citizenship Studies* 18, nos. 6–7 (2014): 579–99.

Nicholls, Walter. *The DREAMers: How the Undocumented Youth Movement Trans-formed the Immigrant Rights Debate*. Stanford, CA: Stanford University Press, 2013.

Nolasco, Luis. "What Tom and Guillermo's Detention Center Wedding Reveals." ACLU Southern California, April 1, 2016. https://www.aclusocal.org/en/news/what-tom-and-guillermos-detention-center-wedding-reveals.

Noronha, Luke de. "Hierarchies of Membership and the Management of Global Populations: Reflections on Citizenship and Racial Ordering." *Citizenship Studies* 26, nos. 4–5 (2022): 426–35.

#Not1More. "Tell Santa Ana, End Its ICE Contract. Free Trans Detainees Now." Archived March 31, 2023, at the Wayback Machine. https://web.archive.org/web/20230331152519/http://www.notonemoredeportation.com/santa-ana-90-days/.

#NoTechForICE. "About." Accessed September 10, 2024. https://notechforice.com/about/.

#NotOneMoreDeportation. *Blue Ribbon Commission Report on Deportation Review*. April 10, 2014. Accessed February 29, 2024. http://www.notonemoredeportation.com/2014/04/10/not1morebrc/ [link no longer active]. Summary available at Latino Rebels, "NDLON Publishes Blue Ribbon Immigration Recommendations for President," April 10, 2014, https://www.latinorebels.com/2014/04/10/ndlon-publishes-blue-ribbon-immigration-recommendations-for-president/.

Noyola, Isa. "The Movement for LGBTQ Rights and Immigrant Rights." National Domestic Workers Alliance, Pride in Our Work. Accessed March 24, 2024. https://www.domesticworkers.org/reports-and-publications/pride-in-our-work/.

Nunez-Neto, Blas. *Border Security: The Role of the U.S. Border Patrol*. Washington, DC: Congressional Research Service, 2005.

Office of Inspector General. *ICE's Inspections and Monitoring of Detention Facilities Do Not Lead to Sustained Compliance or Systemic Improvements*. June 26, 2018. https://www.oig.dhs.gov/sites/default/files/assets/2018-06/OIG-18-67-Jun18.pdf.

Okporo, Edafe. *Asylum: A Memoir*. New York: Simon and Schuster, 2022.

Okporo, Edafe. *Bed 26: A Memoir of an African Man's Asylum in the United States*. Bloomington, IN: Xlibris, 2018.

Olayo-Méndez, Alejandro. "La 72: An Oasis along the Migration Routes in Mexico." *Forced Migration Review* 56 (October 2017). https://www.fmreview.org/sites/fmr/files/FMRdownloads/en/latinamerica-caribbean/olayomendez.pdf.

Oliver, Kelly. *Carceral Humanism: Logics of Refugee Detention*. Minneapolis: University of Minnesota Press, 2017.

Oliviero, Katie. "Challenging 'Americans Are Dreamers, Too': Undocumented Youths' Queer and Feminist Coalitional Politics." *Frontiers: A Journal of Women Studies* 42, no. 2 (2021): 49–84.

Ong, Aihwa. *Buddha Is Hiding: Refugees, Citizenship, the New America*. Berkeley: University of California Press, 2003.

Ong, Aihwa. "Cultural Citizenship as Subject-Making: Immigrants Negotiate Racial and Cultural Boundaries in the United States." In *Race, Identity, and Citizenship: A Reader*, edited by Rodolfo D. Torres, Louis F. Mirón, and Jonathan Xavier Inda, 262–93. Malden, MA: Blackwell, 1999.

Orange County Immigrant Youth United. "Immigrant and LGBTQ Leaders to Launch Hunger Strike, Demand End to Immigrant Detention Contract between Santa

Ana and ICE." *Voice of OC*, May 16, 2016. https://voiceofoc.org/2016/05/immigrant
-and-lgbtq-leaders-to-launch-hunger-strike-demand-end-to-immigrant-detention
-contract-between-santa-ana-and-ice/#!.

Orange County Immigrant Youth United, RAIZ, and Familia: Trans Queer Liberation
Movement. "Press Conference: Santa Ana Residents Say No to Detaining More Trans
and Other Immigrants at City Jail City Should Be Cutting Ties with ICE Not Offering
It More Room." *Voice of OC*, February 2, 2016. https://voiceofoc.org/2016/02/press
-conference-santa-ana-residents-say-no-to-detaining-more-trans-other-immigrants-at
-city-jail-city-should-be-cutting-ties-with-ice-not-offering-it-more-room/.

Ortega, Araceli Martínez. "ICE libera a inmigrante que se casó en detención con su
pareja del mismo sexo." *La Opinion*, December 26, 2018.

Oswin, Natalie. "The Modern Model Family Home in Singapore: A Queer Geography."
Transactions of the British Institute of Geographers 35, no. 2 (2010): 256–68.

Oswin, Natalie, and Eric Olund. "Guest Editorial: Governing Intimacy." *Environment
and Planning D: Society and Space* 28 no. 1 (2010): 60–67.

Padilla, Laura T. "Queering Diasporic Activism: Undocumented Latinx Youth Social
Movements in the U.S. Southwest (2006–2016)." PhD diss., San Diego State University, 2017.

Padrón, Karla, and Bamby Salcedo. *TransVisible: Transgender Latina Immigrants in
U.S. Society*. Los Angeles: TransLatin@ Coalition, 2013. Available at https://static1
.squarespace.com/static/55b6e526e4b02f9283ae1969/t/56feaa3eb6aa60ebb6037d03
/1459530307297/transvisible_en.pdf.

Paik, A. Naomi. "Abolishing Police Includes Abolishing ICE and Border Protection."
Truthout, July 13, 2020. https://truthout.org/articles/abolishing-police-includes
-abolishing-ice-and-border-protection/.

Palacios, Lena. "The Prison Rape Elimination Act and the Limits of Liberal Reform."
Gender Policy Report, February 17, 2017. https://genderpolicyreport.umn.edu/the
-prison-rape-elimination-act-and-the-limits-of-liberal-reform/.

Pallares, Amalia, and Ruth Gomberg-Muñoz. "Politics of Motion: Ethnography with
Undocumented Activists and of Undocumented Activism." *North American Dialogue* 19, no. 1 (2016): 4–12.

Panjwani, Aly, and Hannah Lucal. *Tracked and Trapped: Experiences from ICE Digital
Prisons*. May 2022. https://notechforice.com/digitalprisons/.

Park, K-Sue. "Self-Deportation Nation." *Harvard Law Review* 132, no. 7 (2019): 1879–941.

Peña, Susana. *Oye Loca! From the Mariel Boatlift to Gay Cuban Miami*. Minneapolis:
University of Minnesota Press, 2013.

Peutz, Natalie, and Nicholas De Genova. "Introduction." In *The Deportation Regime:
Sovereignty, Space, and the Freedom of Movement*, edited by Nicholas De Genova
and Natalie Peutz, 1–29. Durham, NC: Duke University Press, 2010.

Pixley, Tara. "Where LGBGTQ Migrants Find the True Meaning of Shelter." *New York
Times*, September 8, 2021.

Porotsky, Sophia. "Rotten to the Core: Racism, Xenophobia, and the Border and Immigration Agencies." *Georgetown Immigration Law Journal* 36 (2021): 349–98.

Povinelli, Elizabeth A. *The Empire of Love: Toward a Theory of Intimacy, Genealogy, and
Carnality*. Durham, NC: Duke University Press, 2006.

Povinelli, Elizabeth A. *Geontologies: A Requiem to Late Liberalism.* Durham, NC: Duke University Press, 2016.

Power, Emma R., and Kathleen J. Mee. "Housing: An Infrastructure of Care." *Housing Studies* 35, no. 3 (2020): 484–505.

Puar, Jasbir K. "Homonationalism as Assemblage: Viral Travels, Affective Sexualities." *Jindal Global Law Review* 4, no. 2 (2013): 23–43.

Puar, Jasbir K. *The Right to Maim: Debility, Capacity, Disability.* Durham, NC: Duke University Press, 2017.

Puhl, Em. "Family-Based Petitions for Same-Sex Couples. Considerations When Documenting a Bona Fide Marriage." Immigrant Legal Resource Center, January 8, 2020. https://www.ilrc.org/sites/default/files/resources/bona_fide_marriage_lgbtq_couples_final.pdf.

Quezada, Janet Arelis. "In Oregon, LGBT Lives Are at a Crossroads." *GLAAD*, October 27, 2014. https://www.glaad.org/blog/oregon-lgbt-lives-are-crossroads.

Raboin, Thibaut. *Discourses on LGBT Asylum in the UK: Constructing a Queer Haven.* Manchester, UK: Manchester University Press, 2017.

Rakia, Raven. "It's Not Just Ferguson: Cities Nationwide Are Criminalizing Black People to Pay the Bills." *Nation*, March 5, 2015.

Ramírez, Catherine S. *Assimilation: An Alternative History.* Oakland: University of California Press, 2020.

Ramirez, Maria Liliana. "Beyond Identity: Coming Out as UndocuQueer." In *We Are Not Dreamers: Undocumented Scholars Theorize Undocumented Life in the United States*, edited by Leisy J. Abrego and Genevieve Negrón-Gonzalez, 146–67. Durham, NC: Duke University Press, 2020.

Riley, Angela, and Kristen Carpenter. "Decolonizing Indigenous Migration." *California Law Review* 109 (2021): 63–139.

Ritchie, Andrea J. *Invisible No More: Police Violence against Black Women and Women of Color.* Boston: Beacon, 2017.

Ritholtz, Sam, and Rebecca Buxton. "Queer Kinship and the Rights of Refugee Families." *Migration Studies* 9, no. 3 (2021): 1075–95.

Rodriguez, Naomi Glenn-Levin. *Fragile Families: Foster Care, Immigration, and Citizenship.* Philadelphia: University of Pennsylvania Press, 2017.

Rose, Nikolas. *Powers of Freedom: Reframing Political Thought.* Cambridge: Cambridge University Press, 1999.

Rosenbloom, Rachel E. "The Citizenship Line: Rethinking Immigration Exceptionalism." *Boston College Law Review* 54 (2013): 1964–2024.

Rosenblum, Marc, Randy Capps, and Serena Yi-Ying Lin. *Earned Legalization: Effects of Proposed Requirements on Unauthorized Men, Women, and Children.* Washington, DC: Migration Policy Institute, 2011.

Rosenfeld, Richard. *The Social Construction of Crime.* Oxford: Oxford University Press, 2010.

Rowe, Amy Carrillo, and Francesca T. Royster, eds. "Loving Transgressions: Queer of Color Bodies, Affective Ties, Transformative Community." Special issue, *Journal of Lesbian Studies* 21, no. 3 (2017).

Rubio, Marco. "Frequently Asked Questions about the Border Security, Economic Opportunity, and Immigration Modernization Act of 2013." April 18, 2013. https://www

.rubio.senate.gov/public/_cache/files/34d11591-19fc-4c3d-8db4-ceacae2fa4cb/318B51
623F3F1070EA03571DB9DD7BCE.4-16-13-faq—immigration.pdf.

Rubio, Marco. "Myth vs. Fact: Incorrect to Say This Bill Is an Amnesty." April 18, 2013.
https://www.rubio.senate.gov/public/index.cfm/2013/4/myth-vs-fact-incorrect-to
-say-this-bill-is-amnesty.

Rubio Goldsmith, Raquel, M. Melissa McCormick, Daniel Martínez, and Inez Mag-
dalena Duarte. "The 'Funnel Effect' and Recovered Bodies Processed by the Pima
County Office of the Medical Examiner, 1990–2005." Tucson: Binational Migration
Institute, 2006. https://bmi.arizona.edu/sites/bmi.arizona.edu/files/BMI-The-Funnel
-Effect-2006.pdf.

Rueb, Emily S. "Is Trump Pushing Immigrants and Same-Sex Couples to Marriage?"
Boston Globe, December 29, 2016.

Ryo, Emily, and Ian Peacock. *The Landscape of Immigration Detention in the United
States*. Washington, DC: American Immigration Council, 2018.

Sacchetti, Maria. "ICE Chief Tells Lawmakers Agency Needs Much More Money for
Immigration Arrests." *Washington Post*, June 13, 2017.

Saleh, Myram. "As Trump Announces Mass Immigration Raid, Documents Show How
ICE Uses Arrest Quota." *Intercept*, July 3, 2019. https://theintercept.com/2019/07/03
/ice-raids-arrest-quotas/.

Sampaio, Anna. *Terrorizing Latina/o Immigrants: Race, Gender, and Immigration Politics in the Age of Security*. Philadelphia: Temple University Press, 2015.

Sanchez, Alex. "Updated: Statement Regarding the Death of Roxsana Hernandez." University of New Mexico Health Sciences Newsroom, April 9, 2019. https://hsc.unm
.edu/news/news/statement-regarding-the-death-of-roxsana-hernandez.html.

Sánchez Cruz, Jorge. "Debility, Negative Affect, Mobility: Undocuqueer Aesthetics and
the Right to Thrive." *Social Text* 40, no. 2 (2022): 69–92.

Sandoval, Chela. *Methodology of the Oppressed*. Minneapolis: University of Minnesota
Press, 2000.

Sandoval, Edgar. "More Than Violence: UndocuQueers' Narratives of Disidentification
and World-Making in Seattle, Washington, USA." *Gender, Place and Culture* 25,
no. 12 (2018): 1759–80.

Sandoval, Edgar. "Undocuqueer Disidentifications: 'Being Undocumented and Gay,
Just Like Death, Means Having to Navigate Two Worlds.'" PhD diss., University of
Washington, 2017.

Sarı, Elif. "Lesbian Refugees in Transit: The Making of Authenticity and Legitimacy in
Turkey." In *Lives That Resist Telling: Migrant and Refugee Lesbians*, edited by Eithne
Luibhéid, 84–102. New York: Routledge, 2021.

Schaeffer-Grabiel, Felicity. *Love and Empire: Cybermarriage and Citizenship across the
Americas*. New York: New York University Press, 2012.

Schey, Peter. "Analysis of Senate Bill 744's Pathway to Legalization and Citizenship."
Center for Human Rights and Constitutional Law, June 2013. http://mexmigration
.blogspot.com/2013/06/peter-schey-deconstructs-s-744.html.

Schmitz, Sigrid, and Sara Ahmed. "Affect/Emotion: Orientation Matters. A Conversation between Sigrid Schmitz and Sara Ahmed." *Freiburger Zeitschrift für Geschlech-
terStudien* 20, no. 2 (2014): 97–108.

Schreiber, Rebecca. *The Undocumented Everyday: Migrant Lives and the Politics of Visibility*. Minneapolis: University of Minnesota Press, 2018.

Schroeder, Robert D. *Holding the Line in the 21st Century*. US Customs and Border Protection, November 25, 2014. https://www.cbp.gov/document/publications/holding-line-21st-century-0.

Schuller, Kyla. *The Biopolitics of Feeling: Race, Sex, and Science in the Nineteenth Century*. Durham, NC: Duke University Press, 2017.

Schwiertz, Helge. "Transformations of the Undocumented Youth Movement and Radical Egalitarian Citizenship." *Citizenship Studies* 20, no. 5 (2016): 610–28.

Seeley, Samantha. *Race, Removal, and Right to Remain*. Chapel Hill: University of North Carolina Press, 2021.

Seif, Hinda. "'Layers of Humanity': Interview with Undocuqueer Artivist Julio Salgado." *Latino Studies* 12, no. 2 (2014): 300–309.

Seif, Hinda. "Unapologetic and Unafraid: Immigrant Youth Come Out of the Shadows." *New Directions for Child and Adolescent Development* 134 (2011): 59–75.

Seif, Hinda. "'We Define Ourselves': 1.5-Generation Undocumented Immigrant Activist Identities and Insurgent Discourse." *North American Dialogue* 19, no. 1 (2016): 23–35.

Sen, Kendra. "Driver's Licenses and Undocumented Immigrants." Government Law Center, Albany Law School, July 15, 2019. https://www.albanylaw.edu/government-law-center/drivers-licenses-and-undocumented-immigrants#_edn2.

Seo, Sarah A. *Policing the Open Road: How Cars Transformed American Freedom*. Cambridge, MA: Harvard University Press, 2019.

Shachar, Aylet. *The Birthright Lottery: Citizenship and Global Inequality*. Cambridge, MA: Harvard University Press, 2009.

Shadel, JD. "Inside America's Mass Detention of Queer Asylum Seekers." *Them*, June 22, 2018. https://www.them.us/story/queer-asylum-seekers-detention.

Shah, Nayan. *Contagious Divides: Epidemics and Race in San Francisco's Chinatown*. Berkeley: University of California Press, 2001.

Shah, Nayan. *Stranger Intimacy: Contesting Race, Sexuality, and the Law in the North American West*. Berkeley: University of California Press, 2011.

Shah, Silky. *Unbuild Walls: Why Immigrant Justice Needs Abolition*. Chicago: Haymarket Books, 2024.

Shahksari, Sima. "The Queer Time of Death: Temporality, Geopolitics, and Refugee Rights." *Sexualities* 17, no. 4 (2014): 998–1015.

Shakur, Prince. "Roxsana Hernández, a 33-Year-Old Honduran Trans Woman, Died in ICE Custody amid Concerns She Was Abused." *Teen Vogue*, December 4, 2018. https://www.teenvogue.com/story/roxsana-hernandez-honduran-trans-woman-died-ice-custody-abuse-concerns-autopsy.

Shapiro, Sarah, and Catherine Brown. *The State of Civics Education*. Washington, DC: Center for American Progress, 2018.

Sharma, Nandita. "Global Apartheid and Nation Statehood: Instituting Border Regimes." In *Nationalism and Global Solidarities*, edited by James Goodman and Paul James, 71–90. New York: Routledge, 2007.

Sharpe, Christina. *Monstrous Intimacies: Making Post-slavery Subjects*. Durham, NC: Duke University Press, 2010.

Shaw, Ari, and Namrata Verghese. *LGBTQI Refugees and Asylum Seekers: A Review of Research and Data Needs*. Los Angeles: Williams Institute, UCLA School of Law, 2022. https://williamsinstitute.law.ucla.edu/wp-content/uploads/LGBTQI-Refugee-Review-Jul-2022.pdf.

Shoichet, Catherine E. "The Death Toll in ICE Custody Is the Highest It's Been in 15 Years." *CNN*, September 30, 2020. https://www.cnn.com/2020/09/30/us/ice-deaths-detention-2020/index.html.

Shull, Tina. "QTGNC Stories from US Immigration Detention and Abolitionist Imaginaries, 1980–Present." In *Abolition Feminisms: Organizing, Survival and Transformative Practices*, edited by Alisa Bierria, Jakeya Caruthers, and Brooke Lober, 159–89. Chicago: Haymarket Books, 2022.

Shut Down Adelanto. "About Us." Accessed January 10, 2024. https://shutdownadelanto.org.

Shut Down Adelanto. "Adelanto Toxic Tour." September 26, 2022. https://shutdownadelanto.org/campaigns/f/adelanto-toxic-tour.

Siegfried, Kate. "Feeling Collective: The Queer Politics of Affect in the Riot Grrrl Movement." *Women's Studies in Communication* 42, no. 1 (2019): 21–38.

Simón, Yara. "The Sustained Efforts of Activists Pay Off as Daniela Vargas Is Released from ICE Custody." *Remezcla*, March 10, 2017. https://remezcla.com/culture/daniela-vargas-freed/.

Simpson, Leanne Betasamosake. *Islands of Decolonial Love*. Winnipeg: Arbeiter Ring, 2013.

Sinha, Shreeya, and Sean Plambeck. "Green Card Marriage Interview: Can You Pass It?" *New York Times*, April 19, 2018. https://www.nytimes.com/2018/04/19/us/green-card-marriage-interview-test.html.

Solis, Gustavo. "Gay Couple Wedding First in a US Immigration Detention Center." *Desert Sun*, March 14, 2016.

Solis, Gustavo. "Immigration Arrest Moves Gay Wedding to Detention Center." *Desert Sun*, March 4, 2016.

Solis, Gustavo. "Rancho Mirage Man Celebrates Gratitude Every Day of the Year." *Desert Sun*, December 8, 2016.

Solis, Gustavo. "Should Feds Close Private Immigration Detention Centers?" *Desert Sun*, September 12, 2016.

Solórzano, Rafael Ramirez, Jr. "The Trail of Dreams: Mobilizing Corazones and Forging New Visions of Migrant Justice." PhD diss., University of California, Los Angeles, 2019.

Somerville, Siobhan B. "Queer." In *Keywords for American Cultural Studies*, 2nd ed., edited by Bruce Burgett and Glenn Hendler, 203–7. New York: New York University Press, 2014.

Somerville, Siobhan B. *Queering the Color Line: Race and the Invention of Homosexuality in American Culture*. Durham, NC: Duke University Press, 2000.

Sorin, Gretchen. *Driving While Black: African American Travel and the Road to Civil Rights*. New York: Liveright, 2020.

Spade, Dean. "Facing the Limits of Law Reform in These Times of Crisis." April 26, 2021. YouTube video, 1:24. https://www.youtube.com/watch?v=t1_htqSV4XE.

Spade, Dean. "Queer Liberation: No Prisons, No Borders (Captioned)." Dean Spade
(website), June 23, 2016. https://www.deanspade.net/2016/06/23/queer-liberation-no
-prisons-no-borders-captioned/.

Speed, Shannon. *Incarcerated Stories: Indigenous Women Migrants and Violence in the
Settler-Capitalist State.* Chapel Hill: University of North Carolina Press, 2019.

Speri, Alice. "Detained, Then Violated." *Intercept,* April 11, 2018. https://theintercept
.com/2018/04/11/immigration-detention-sexual-abuse-ice-dhs/.

Spijkerboer, Thomas. *Fleeing Homophobia: Sexual Orientation, Gender Identity, and
Asylum.* New York: Routledge, 2013.

Spijkerboer, Thomas. "The Global Mobility Infrastructure: Reconceptualizing the
Externalization of Migration Control." *European Journal of Migration and Law* 20,
no. 4 (2018): 452–69.

Spira, Tamara Lea. "Intimate Internationalisms: 1970s 'Third World' Queer Feminist
Solidarity with Chile." *Feminist Theory* 15, no. 2 (2014): 119–40.

Squire, Vicki. "Governing Migration through Death in Europe and the US: Identification, Burial, and the Crisis of Modern Humanism." *European Journal of International
Relations* 23, no. 3 (2017): 513–32.

Stahl, Aviva. "Transgender Prisoners Suffer Abuse at Record Numbers." *Vice,* June 12,
2017. https://www.vice.com/en_us/article/43g5jd/why-is-ice-closing-its-only
-detention-center-for-transgender-detainees-v24n5.

Sterling, Terry Greene, and Jude Joffe-Block. *Driving While Brown: Sheriff Joe Arpaio
versus the Latino Resistance.* Oakland: University of California Press, 2022.

Stoler, Ann Laura. *Carnal Knowledge and Imperial Power: Race and the Intimate in
Colonial Rule.* Berkeley: University of California Press, 2002.

Stuesse, Angela. "Vengeance Drives Trump Immigration Policy." *Progressive,* April 24,
2019. https://progressive.org/op-eds/vengeance-drives-trump-immigration-policy
-stuesse-190424/.

Stumpf, Juliet. "The Crimmigration Crisis: Immigrants, Crime, and Sovereign Power."
American University Law Review 56, no. 2 (2006): 367–419.

Sullivan, Eileen. "Biden to Ask Congress for 9000 Fewer Immigration Detention Beds."
New York Times, March 25, 2022.

Swerts, Thomas, and Walter Nicholls. "Undocumented Immigrant Activism and the
Political: Disrupting the Order or Reproducing the Status Quo?" *Antipode* 53, no. 2
(2021): 319–30.

Tazzioli, Martina. "Choking without Killing: Opacity and the Grey Area of Migration Governmentality." *Political Geography* 89 (2021): 1–9. https://doi.org/10.1016/j
.polgeo.2021.102412.

Templeton, Robin. "Baby-Baiting." *Nation,* August 16–23, 2010. https://www.thenation
.com/article/baby-baiting.

Terriquez, Veronica. "Intersectional Mobilization, Social Movement Spillover, and
Queer Youth Leadership in the Immigrant Rights Movement." *Social Problems* 62,
no. 3 (2015): 343–62.

Thompson, Olivia. "Shackled: The Realities of Home Imprisonment." Equal Justice
under Law, June 14, 2018. https://equaljusticeunderlaw.org/thejusticereport/2018/6
/12/electronic-monitoring.

Tomchin, Olga. "Bodies and Bureaucracy: Legal Sex Classification and Marriage-Based Immigration for Trans* People." *California Law Review* 101, no. 3 (2013): 813–62.

Tormey, Anwen. "'Everyone with Eyes Can See the Problem': Moral Citizens and the Space of Irish Nationhood." *International Migration* 45, no. 3 (2007): 69–100.

Torpey, John. *The Invention of the Passport: Surveillance, Citizenship and the State.* Cambridge: Cambridge University Press, 2000.

Torres, Gerardo. "Fearless and Speaking for Ourselves." *Ride for Justice* (blog), August 18, 2012. http://nopapersnofear.org/blog/post.php?s=2012-08-18-fearless-and-speaking-for-ourselves.

Transactional Records Access Clearinghouse. *Secure Communities and ICE Deportation: A Failed Program?* April 8, 2014. https://trac.syr.edu/immigration/reports/349/.

Transgender Law Center. "Beloved Home." Accessed July 31, 2022. https://transgenderlawcenter.org/belovedhome.

Transgender Law Center. "ICE Raids." Accessed March 24, 2024. http://transgenderlawcenter.org/wp-content/uploads/2017/09/KYR-ICE-Raids.pdf.

Transgender Law Center. "Trans Agenda for Liberation." Accessed June 15, 2021. https://transgenderlawcenter.org/trans-agenda-for-liberation.

TransLatin@ Coalition. "Research." Accessed November 11, 2023. https://www.translatinacoalition.org/research-and-reports.

Turner, Joseph. "Testing the Liberal Subject: (In)Security, Responsibility and 'Self-Improvement' in the UK Citizenship Test." *Citizenship Studies* 18, nos. 3–4 (2014): 332–48.

UnidosUS. "ICE Intimidates Latino Community with Arrest of DACA Recipient Practicing Free Speech." *UnidosUS* (blog), March 3, 2017. https://unidosus.org/blog/2017/03/03/ice-intimidates-latino-community-arrest-daca-recipient-practicing-free-speech/.

United We Dream. "#BreakTheCage: Stop the Detention and Deportation of LGBTQ Immigrants." Action Network. Accessed March 22, 2024. https://actionnetwork.org/petitions/breakthecage-stop-the-detention-deportation-of-lgbtq-immigrants.

United We Dream. "Know Your Rights." Accessed March 22, 2023. https://unitedwedream.org/resources/know-your-rights/.

United We Dream. *No More Closets: Experiences of Discrimination among the LGBTQ Immigrant Community.* January 2016. http://unitedwedream.org/wp-content/uploads/2016/01/Report-No-More-Closets-1.pdf.

Unzueta Carrasco, Tania A., and Hinda Seif. "Disrupting the Dream: Undocumented Youth Reframe Citizenship and Deportability through Anti-deportation Activism." *Latino Studies* 12, no. 2 (2014): 279–99.

US Border Patrol. *Border Patrol Strategic Plan 1994 and Beyond: National Strategy.* July 1994. Available at Homeland Security Digital Library, https://www.hsdl.org/?abstract&did=721845.

US Citizenship and Immigration Services. "Chapter 2: Background and Security Checks." In *Policy Manual.* Accessed June 5, 2020. http://www.uscis.gov/policymanual/HTML/PolicyManual-Volume12-PartB-Chapter2.html.

US Citizenship and Immigration Services. "EB-5: Employment Based Immigration—Immigrant Investor Program." Accessed September 10, 2024. https://www.uscis

.gov/working-in-the-united-states/permanent-workers/eb-5-immigrant-investor
-program.

US Citizenship and Immigration Services. "Fraud Referral Sheet." Published by *New
York Times*, 2010. Accessed September 10, 2024. http://graphics8.nytimes.com
/packages/pdf/nyregion/USCIS_Fraud_Referral_Sheet.pdf.

US Citizenship and Immigration Services. "Marriage Fraud Is a Federal Crime."
June 2016. https://www.ice.gov/sites/default/files/documents/Document/2016
/marriageFraudBrochure.pdf.

US Citizenship and Immigration Services. "Same-Sex Marriages." Accessed July 14,
2014. https://www.uscis.gov/family/same-sex-marriages.

US Citizenship and Immigration Services. "10 Steps to Naturalization." Accessed
June 21, 2021. https://www.uscis.gov/citizenship/learners/apply-citizenship.

US Commission on Civil Rights. *Civil Rights Implications of State Immigration Laws*.
Public Field Briefing, August 17, 2012. https://www.usccr.gov/files/calendar/trnscrpt
/Transcript_08-17-12.pdf.

US Department of Justice. "Justice Department Announces Findings of Two Civil Rights
Investigations in Ferguson, MO." March 4, 2015. https://www.justice.gov/opa/pr/justice
-department-announces-findings-two-civil-rights-investigations-ferguson-missouri.

US Immigration and Customs Enforcement. "Detainee Death Reporting." Accessed
September 10, 2024. https://www.ice.gov/detain/detainee-death-reporting.

US Immigration and Customs Enforcement. "Eloy Detention Center." Accessed September 10, 2024. https://www.ice.gov/detention-facility/eloy-detention-center.

US Immigration and Customs Enforcement. "ICE Issues New Guidance on the Care
of Transgender Individuals in Custody." June 29, 2015. https://www.ice.gov/news
/releases/ice-issues-new-guidance-care-transgender-individuals-custody.

US Immigration and Customs Enforcement. *Performance-Based National Detention
Standards 2011*. Revised December 2016. https://www.ice.gov/doclib/detention
-standards/2011/pbnds2011r2016.pdf.

US Immigration and Customs Enforcement. "Protected Areas Enforcement Actions."
Accessed September 17, 2024. https://www.ice.gov/factsheets/protected-areas
-courthouse-arrests.

Vallejo, Kandace. "Undocubus Connects Immigrants to Civil Rights Legacy at DNC."
Waging Nonviolence, September 6, 2012. https://wagingnonviolence.org/2012/09
/undocubus-connects-immigrants-to-civil-rights-legacy-at-dnc/.

Valles, Jesús I. "(Un)Documents." *New Republic*, August 24, 2018.

Valverde, Miriam. "In Context: John Kelly's Remarks on 'Lazy' Immigrants and DACA."
PolitiFact, February 7, 2018. https://www.politifact.com/article/2018/feb/07/context
-john-kellys-remarks-lazy-immigrants-daca/.

Vargas, Jose Antonio. *Dear America: Notes of an Undocumented Citizen*. New York:
Dey Street Books, 2018.

Vargas, Jose Antonio. "My Life as an Undocumented Immigrant." *New York Times*,
June 22, 2011.

Vargas, Ximena Ospina. "What It Means to Be UndocuTrans." *Teampoint* (blog), Point
Foundation, September 19, 2017. https://pointfoundation.org/community/blog/what
-it-means-to-be-undocutrans.

Vasquez, Tina. "Hunger Strikers to ICE: End Transgender Immigrant Detention." *Rewire*, May 17, 2016. https://rewirenewsgroup.com/2016/05/17/hunger-strikers-ice -transgender-immigrant/.

Villalon, Roberta. *Violence against Latina Immigrants: Citizenship, Inequality and Community*. New York: New York University Press, 2010.

Villa-Nicholas, Melissa. *Data Borders: How Silicon Valley Is Building an Industry around Immigrants*. Oakland: University of California Press, 2023.

Villarreal, Yezmin. "Dreamer Faces Deportation after Speaking to Media." *Advocate*, March 3, 2017. https://www.advocate.com/politics/2017/3/03/dreamer-faces -deportation-after-speaking-media.

Vogt, Wendy A. *Lives in Transit: Violence and Intimacy on the Migrant Journey*. Oakland: University of California Press, 2018.

Vongkiatkajorn, Kanyakrit. "The Trump Administration Just Made It Easier to Deport Survivors of Human Trafficking and Domestic Abuse." *Mother Jones*, November 19, 2018.

Walia, Harsha. *Border and Rule: Global Migration, Capitalism, and the Rise of Racist Nationalism*. Chicago: Haymarket Books, 2021.

Walia, Harsha. "Dismantle and Transform: On Abolition, Decolonization, and Insurgent Politics." Interview by Andrew Dilts. *Abolition Journal*, May 22, 2016. https:// abolitionjournal.org/dismantle-and-transform/.

Walia, Harsha. *Undoing Border Imperialism*. Oakland, CA: AK Press and the Institute for Anarchist Studies, 2013.

Walker, Harron. "Trans Detainees Say They Were Coerced into ICE Propaganda." *Out*, July 16, 2019. https://www.out.com/news/2019/7/16/trans-detainees-say-they-were -coerced-ice-propaganda.

Walsh, James P. "Watchful Citizens: Immigration Control, Surveillance and Societal Participation." *Social and Legal Studies* 23, no. 2 (2014): 237–59.

Walters, William. "Aviation as Deportation Infrastructure: Airports, Planes, and Expulsion." *Journal of Ethnic and Migration Studies* 44, no. 16 (2018): 2796–817.

Walters, William. "Deportation, Expulsion, and the International Police of Aliens." In *The Deportation Regime: Sovereignty, Space, and the Freedom of Movement*, edited by Nicholas De Genova and Natalie Peutz, 69–100. Durham, NC: Duke University Press, 2010.

Walters, William. "Foucault and Frontiers: Notes on the Birth of the Humanitarian Border." In *Governmentality: Current Issues and Future Challenges*, edited by Ulrich Bröckling, Susanne Krasmann, and Thomas Lemke, 138–64. New York: Taylor and Francis, 2010.

Walters, William, Charles Heller, and Lorenzo Pezzani, eds. *Viapolitics: Borders, Migration, and the Power of Locomotion*. Durham, NC: Duke University Press, 2022.

Wang, Nina, Allison McDonald, Daniel Bateyko, and Emily Tucker. *American Dragnet: Data-Driven Deportation in the 21st Century*. Center on Privacy and Technology at Georgetown Law, May 10, 2022. https://americandragnet.org.

Warner, Michael. *Publics and Counterpublics*. New York: Zone Books, 2002.

Washington, John. *The Case for Open Borders*. Chicago, Haymarket Books, 2024.

Washington, John. "The Epidemic of Hunger Strikes in Immigrant Detention Centers." *Nation*, February 13, 2020. https://www.thenation.com/article/society/immigrant -detention-hunger-strike/.

Washington, John. "ICE Wants to Destroy Its Records of In-Custody Deaths, Sexual Assault, and Other Detainee Files." *Nation*, September 13, 2017. https://www.thenation .com/article/archive/ice-wants-to-destroy-its-records-of-in-custody-deaths-sexual -assault-and-other-detainee-files/.

Waslin, Michele. *Discrediting "Self-Deportation" as Immigration Policy: Why an Attrition through Enforcement Strategy Makes Life Difficult for Everyone.* Washington, DC: American Immigration Council, 2012. https://www.americanimmigrationcouncil.org /research/discrediting-self-deportation-immigration-policy.

Wee, Kellynn, Charmian Goh, and Brenda S. A. Yeoh. "Chutes-and-Ladders: The Migration Industry, Conditionality, and the Production of Precarity among Migrant Domestic Workers in Singapore." *Journal of Ethnic and Migration Studies* 45, no. 14 (2019): 2672–88.

Weeks, Linton. "Pumps and Polls: Why Americans Wait in Lines." *NPR*, October 29, 2012. https://www.npr.org/2012/10/29/163859900/pumps-and-polls-why-americans -wait-in-lines.

Weston, Kath. *Families We Choose: Lesbians, Gays, Kinship.* New York: Columbia University Press, 1997.

White, Melissa Autumn. "Ambivalent Homonationalisms: Transnational Queer Intimacies and Territorialized Belongings." *Interventions* 15, no. 1 (2013): 37–54.

White, Melissa Autumn. "Documenting the Undocumented: Toward a Queer Politics of No Borders." *Sexualities* 17, no. 8 (2014): 976–97.

White House. "Fact Sheet: Fixing Our Broken Immigration System So Everyone Plays by the Rules." January 29, 2013. https://obamawhitehouse.archives.gov/the-press-office/2013 /01/29/fact-sheet-fixing-our-broken-immigration-system-so-everyone-plays-rules.

Whitlock, Kay, and Nancy A. Heitzeg. *Carceral Con: The Deceptive Terrain of Criminal Justice Reform.* Oakland: University of California Press, 2021.

Williams, Erika. "Feds Blocked from Using Marriage Interviews for Deportation." *Courthouse News*, February 10, 2020. https://www.courthousenews.com/feds -blocked-from-using-marriage-interviews-for-deportation/.

Williams, Jill. "Protection as Subjection: Discourses of Vulnerability and Protection in Post-9/11 Border Enforcement Efforts." *City* 15, nos. 3–4 (2011): 414–28.

Williams, Jill M., and Vanessa A. Massaro. "Managing Capacity, Shifting Burdens: Social Reproduction and the Intimate Economies of Immigrant Family Detention." In *Intimate Economies of Immigration Detention: Critical Perspectives,* edited by Deirdre Conlon and Nancy Hiemstra, 87–104. New York: Routledge, 2016.

Wilson, Ara. "The Infrastructure of Intimacy." *Signs: Journal of Women in Culture and Society* 41, no. 2 (2016): 247–80.

Wimark, Thomas. "Homemaking and Perpetual Liminality among Queer Refugees." *Social and Cultural Geography* 22, no. 5 (2021): 647–65.

Wimark, Thomas. "Housing Policy with Violent Outcomes: The Domestication of Queer Asylum Seekers in a Heteronormative Society." *Journal of Ethnic and Migration Studies* 47, no. 3 (2021): 703–22.

Winn, Robert C. *Out of the Closets, Out of the Shadows: LGBTQ Leadership in the Struggle against Deportation*. Neo Philanthropy and Four Freedoms Fund, November 2015. https://neophilanthropy.org/out-of-the-closet-out-of-the-shadows-lgbtq-leadership-in-the-struggle-against-deportation-presented-by-neo-philanthropy/.

Winterman, Denise. "Queueing: Is It Really the British Way?" *BBC News*, July 4, 2013. https://www.bbc.com/news/magazine-23087024.

Wong, Kent, Janna Shadduck-Hernández, Fabiola Inzunza, Julie Munroe, Victor Narro, and Abel Valenzuela Jr., eds. *Undocumented and Unafraid: Tam Tran, Cinthya Felix, and the Immigrant Youth Movement*. Los Angeles: UCLA Center for Labor Research and Education, 2012.

Woodhouse, J. "Waging the Fight for Migrant Justice from under a Border Patrol Truck." *Truthout,* March 12, 2013. https://truthout.org/articles/an-ordinary-arrest-an-extraordinary-act-of-civil-disobedience-and-the-fight-for-migrant-justice-worldwide/.

Wright, John. "Longtime Gay Activist Is 1st to Marry at Immigration Detention Center, Can't Afford Attorney for Husband." *Towleroad*, March 15, 2016. https://www.towleroad.com/2016/03/longtime-gay-activist-1st-marry-immigration-detention-center-cant-afford-attorney-husband/.

Xiang, Biao, and Johan Lindquist. "Migration Infrastructure." *International Migration Review* 48 (2014): S122–48

Yee, Vivian. "A Marriage Used to Prevent Deportation. Not Anymore." *New York Times*, April 19, 2018. https://www.nytimes.com/2018/04/19/us/immigration-marriage-green-card.html.

Yoshikawa, Hirokazu. *Immigrants Raising Citizens: Undocumented Parents and Their Children*. New York: Russell Sage Foundation, 2012.

Zamora, Lazaro. "Comparing Trump and Obama's Deportation Priorities." Bipartisan Policy Center, February 27, 2017. https://bipartisanpolicy.org/blog/comparing-trump-and-obamas-deportation-priorities/.

Zavaleta, Lourdes. "Houston Shelter for Undocumented Trans People Fights to Stay Open." *OutSmart Magazine*, April 26, 2018. https://www.outsmartmagazine.com/2018/04/houston-shelter-for-undocumented-trans-people-fights-to-stay-open/.

Zavella, Patricia. *I'm Neither Here nor There: Mexicans' Quotidian Struggles with Migration and Poverty*. Berkeley: University of California Press, 2011.

Zilberg, Elena. *Spaces of Detention: The Making of a Transnational Gang Crisis between Los Angeles and San Salvador*. Durham, NC: Duke University Press, 2011.

Arkles, Gabriel, 77

Asian exclusion, 85; Chinese Exclusion Act of 1882, 12–13; Page Act of 1875, 59

attrition, 5, 16–18, 21, 31, 127, 144n99, 144n101; abolitionist debates and, 144n95; definition, 15; through enforcement, 80, 84–86, 89–94, 97, 99–100, 143n92, 174n90

Balaguera, Martha, 29, 102, 112–13, 120, 131, 138n8, 174n5, 180n79, 183n108

Beam, Myrl, 66, 159n48

Becerra, Cecilia Sáenz, 49

Beltrán, Cristina, 85, 169n38

Benavides, David, 117

Benjamin, Ruja, 18

Berlant, Lauren, 5–6, 76, 140n34

Bey, Marquis, 26

Biden, Joseph, 34–35, 105, 121, 132, 151n29, 155n91, 185n5

Bier, David J., 38–39

BI Incorporated (GEO Group), 106

biopolitics, 7–8, 60, 140n34, 146n134, 169n34. See also necropolitics

Black Alliance for Just Immigration, 113

Black LGBTQIA+ Migrant Project, 30, 113

Black Lives Matter, 3, 119

Black migrants, 15, 30, 69, 82, 113. See also slavery

Blue Ribbon Commission Report on Deportation Review, 31, 34–35, 48–54, 156n92

Boehner, John, 33, 48–49

Bonds, Anne, 129

Border Patrol. See Customs and Border Protection (CBP)

Border Security, Economic Opportunity, and Immigration Modernization Act (s.744) of 2013, 33–36, 43–44, 47, 49, 51–53, 152n45, 155nn90–91

Boulder, Colorado, petition rejection case, 56–57, 157n3

Bracamontes, Damian Vergara, 110, 178n50, 179n61, 179n63

Brady, Mary Pat, 109

Calexico detention center (California), 68, 70–72

California Proposition 187 (Save Our State Initiative of 1994), 16, 18

Camacho, Alicia Schmidt, 17, 103, 175n11

capitalism, 17–18, 63, 103, 145n121, 147n143; automobility in, 99–100; citizenship and, 35–36, 40–41, 48, 146n142, 151n42; criminalization and, 82, 116, 124, 143n92; data, 14; housing policies and, 129–30; marriage and, 55–56; racial, 8–9, 25–27. See also settler colonialism; slavery

Carbado, Devon W., 40

carcerality, 2, 4, 19, 26, 121, 126, 132, 152n54, 177n43; mass incarceration, 14, 103, 106, 114, 122, 123, 129, 134, 137n7, 175n18. See also detention centers; prison-industrial complex

Carens, Joseph H., 47

Casa Anandrea, 131

Casa De Las Muñecas Tiresias AC, 131

Casa De Luz, 131, 189n44

Casa Frida, 131

Castro, Martin R., 97

Causa, 80, 88, 171n54

Center for Immigration Studies, 6, 87, 170n44

Central America, viii, 15, 18–19, 47, 74–75, 101, 112, 119, 189n46; migrants fleeing from, 10–11, 30, 69, 108, 110–11, 131–32, 141n55, 165n102, 181n89

Centro Legal de la Raza, 71

Chácon, Jennifer M., 81

Chauncey, George, 65

children, 45–46, 65, 75, 94, 126, 144n97, 146n134, 189n44; citizenship and, 11, 36–38, 61–62, 162n75, 165nn103–4; family separation and, 1–2, 21–23, 108–9, 127, 163nn91–92, 176n21, 178n51; fear and, 1, 12, 23, 80, 97–98, 108, 168n26; schools and, 16–17, 21, 89, 144n99, 150n26; Special Immigrant Juvenile Status, 52. See also Deferred Action for Childhood Arrivals (DACA); Development, Relief, and Education for Alien Minors (DREAM Act)

Chinese Exclusion Act, 12–13

chokepoints, 31, 127; in everyday life, 15–18, 60, 79, 81–84, 99–100, 102, 109, 111, 140n43; infrastructure of, 5–8, 22, 31, 81, 102–6, 127, 139n22, 155n88; Prevention Through Deterrence (PTD) and, 140n43; terminology notes, 6–8, 139n27; virtual, 139n26. See also Santa Ana, California

Cibola County Correctional Center (New Mexico), 120, 184nn124–25

www.ingramcontent.com/pod-product-compliance
Lightning Source LLC
Chambersburg PA
CBHW020856270326
41928CB00006B/725